To DAD — Xmas 1992

Don't pick up ANY BAD HABITS...

Love John & Cathy

BLAND
AMBITION

BLAND AMBITION

From Adams to Quayle—

the Cranks, Criminals,

Tax Cheats, and Golfers

Who Made It to

Vice President

STEVE TALLY

A HARVEST/HBJ ORIGINAL

HARCOURT BRACE JOVANOVICH, PUBLISHERS

SAN DIEGO NEW YORK LONDON

HBJ

Library of Congress Cataloging-in-Publication Data

Tally, Steve W.
Bland ambition/Steve W. Tally.—1st ed.
p.   cm.
ISBN 0-15-61340-4
1. Vice-presidents—United States.   2. United States—Politics
and government.   I. Title.
E176.49.T35   1992
353.003′18—dc20   92-16198

Designed by Trina Stahl

Printed in the United States of America

First Edition

D E

CONTENTS

ACKNOWLEDGMENTS

Many of my friends and family members assisted with this book in a multitude of ways, but I assure all my coconspirators that I won't name names, even if I am subpoenaed by a camera-giddy Senate committee. But for those who helped—and you know who you are—allow me to say, sincerely, thank you.

However, one person cannot go unmentioned, for without him this book could never have come about. For that, Mr. Dan Quayle, you have my everlasting thanks.

PREFATORY NOTE
FROM THE AUTHOR

MR. DARWIN, IT NOW APPEARS, MAY HAVE BEEN WRONG.

If the HMS *Beagle* were to sail today up the Potomac River, and were Mr. Darwin to pause at the Capitol to examine the United States's second-highest office, he would see a progression of vice presidents from John Adams and Thomas Jefferson to such men as Millard Fillmore and Hannibal Hamlin, passing through recent vice presidents Spiro Agnew and Walter Mondale, and coming to rest with J. Danforth Quayle.

He would then pause and say to himself, "What could I have been thinking?"

The vice presidency, it seems, is not survival of the fittest but elevation of the mediocre.

I mean that, of course, with all disrespect. Fellow Hoosier and Vice President Thomas Marshall once said that "a great man may be vice president, but he can't be a great vice president because the office itself is unimportant." Although I agree with much of what Mr. Marshall had to say about life, especially

PREFATORY NOTE ☆ xii

his line about needing a good five-cent cigar, I think here he was only half right. No truly great leader would ever seek the vice presidency. Instead the office attracts occupants who have in their character a heaping helping of one thing: bland ambition.

Bland ambition is not some moderate form of aspiration. Quite the opposite, bland ambition is the most bald-faced type of yearning. But most vice presidents, although brimming with desire, have lacked that element of constitution that Vice President George Bush dismissed as "the vision thing." It is their lack of conviction that makes their ambition so bland.

When we listen closely, we hear these mountebanks saying nothing more substantive than "Vote for me—I have Kennedy hair." Spouting bunkum like a fountain, they tell us that they have no aspirations beyond their present stepping-stone. To put it bluntly, any man or woman who would want the job should not be trusted with it.

This is not a new idea. In 1906, the popular humorist Finley Peter Dunne wrote, in the guise of his character Mr. Dooley, "It's not a crime exactly. Ye can't be sent to jail f'r it, but it's kind iv a disgrace. It's like writin' anonymous letters." Even earlier, in 1797, the secretary of the treasury, Oliver Wolcott, said that Thomas Jefferson's willingness to accept the vice presidency was "sufficient proof of some defect of character." The history of our vice presidents would seem to support Mr. Wolcott. One vice president, Aaron Burr, committed murder while in office and fled to the Senate to escape prosecution. Two vice presidents, John Breckinridge and Burr, were charged with treason, and two more, John Calhoun and John Tyler, probably could have been. Two other vice presidents, Schuyler Colfax and Spiro

Agnew, were accused of accepting bribes while in public office (both Colfax and Agnew denied the allegation, but both men conveniently left the vice presidency before the truth could be determined in impeachment hearings). Agnew was also convicted of felonious tax evasion.

But these scoundrels, while not to be ignored, were more the exception than the rule. Most vice presidents were simply quintessential nonentities. For example, who today remembers Private Hannibal Hamlin, who served as a cook in the Maine National Guard during the Civil War? Almost no one, but as incredible as it seems, Private Hamlin also happened to be our vice president during this crucial time in our nation's history.

Nearly all the forty-four vice presidents have passed from the nation's collective memory. The names of men such as Elbridge Gerry, Levi Parsons Morton, and Charles Curtis mean little to even the most well-read fan of U.S. history. This isn't something that has gone unnoticed by the politicos who are threatened with a term as vice president. When Franklin Roosevelt was trying to drag Harry Truman kicking and screaming into the vice presidency in 1944, Truman protested, "Look here . . . I bet I can go down the street and stop the first ten men I see and that they can't tell me the names of two of the last ten vice presidents of the United States." Daniel Webster, when offered the job in 1828, indignantly replied, "I do not propose to be buried until I am dead."

The fact that the vice presidents' stories have been forgotten is a shame, because we can learn a lot from these simple people. Charles de Gaulle once said something to the effect that although John Kennedy was America's mask, Vice President Lyndon

Johnson was its true face. By examining the lives of the vice presidents, we get a look at the true face of American politics throughout our history.

So let this book serve as a warning: In America, each girl and boy can grow up to become vice president, and that is just the chance they have to take.

PROLOGUE

IN 1783 THE BRITISH FINALLY GAVE UP
TRYING TO TEACH THE INSOLENT AMERI-
CANS SOME MANNERS, and the people of the
United States won their independence and the freedom to elect foolish men to high public office if they
had a mind to. But George Washington didn't bring
the U.S. Constitution down from one of the Appala-
chian mountains written on a tablet of stone—it was
four years before the system of government as it is
known today was even conceived.

At the beginning the colonies had decided to
abide by the Articles of Confederation, which had as
a basic theory of governance: "every state for itself."
That plan would have worked if the other countries
of the world had left the new government alone, but
the bullies of Europe—Spain, France, and Great
Britain—realized that tiny sovereign states such as
Vermont and Delaware didn't have enough guns
and bullets to stop them if they should decide to steal
from and harass their citizens, which, naturally, they
did. So in 1787, in order to better defend themselves,
the states decided that it was time to get united and
call the new country to order.

Representatives from twelve of the thirteen states met in Philadelphia (Rhode Island did not attend) to put the country together. Throughout the summer the delegates worked, and they came up with some pretty good ideas—such as a system of checks and balances, a two-house Congress, and a president who would be elected by the people. They wrote their ideas down in a document known as the Constitution and got ready to go back home to their farms and wives.

Before they could leave, however, Alexander Hamilton, who is often described in history books as the Machiavelli of American politics, suggested something he called the vice president, who would take over for the president should he not be able to serve. It seemed like a good idea, so the delegates to the Constitutional Convention decided that the vice president would be the runner-up in the presidential election. This would ensure the election of a vice president many people considered worthy to be president and who, it was assumed, would have the necessary ability to fill that office.

There was a concern that the vice president would be "without employment" and would have no way to fill his afternoons (golf had not yet made its way to America), so the delegates decided to make the vice president the presiding officer of the Senate—though not an actual member of that body. He could vote only in case of a tie. It wasn't enough to keep the vice presidents out of trouble, as it would later turn out, but it sounded like a plausible idea at the time.

Not everyone thought that the vice presidency was such a hot concept. Ben Franklin said that the person holding the office should receive the title His Superfluous Excellency, but others weren't quite so amused by the thought of a presidential sidekick.

Two of the loudest critics of the office were Elbridge Gerry and George Clinton. Gerry complained bitterly that the vice president's role in the Senate would blur the distinction between the legislative and executive branches of government and would disrupt the delicate separation of powers. George Clinton complained that the vice presidency was "useless" and "dangerous." (Clinton and Gerry would later show that they had the qualities necessary for the office when they both conveniently forgot their philosophical opposition to the office and became the nation's fourth and fifth vice presidents.)

In hindsight, it is remarkable that the delegates to the Constitutional Convention didn't polish this idea a bit more, because there were a few glaring flaws. For one thing, the Constitution said, "In the case of the removal of the President from office, or of his death, resignation or inability to discharge the powers and duties of the said office, the same shall devolve upon the Vice President." This left a lot of questions unanswered: Who would decide whether the president was able to discharge his duties? And what did "the same shall devolve upon the Vice President" really mean: that the vice president would become president or that he would "discharge the powers and duties of said office" as acting president? And what *about* the separation-of-powers thing? And who's going to want to waste time in such a meaningless position?

Unfortunately, the delegates in Philadelphia didn't adequately address these concerns. Instead, they decided that the Constitution was good enough for government work, and on September 17, 1787, they signed off on it and went home.

The last laugh was on two men who weren't able to attend the convention: John Adams and Thomas Jefferson. Both were in Europe at the time, and although they were major architects of the new country, neither man was able to express an opinion about the newly formed office. That was probably for the best. As the old saying almost goes, There are two things you don't want to see made: sausages and the vice presidency.

BLAND
AMBITION

JOHN ADAMS

Served with George Washington, 1789–97

Federalist from Massachusetts

D R. [BENJAMIN] FRANKLIN'S ELECTRICAL ROD SMOTE THE EARTH AND OUT SPRUNG GENERAL WASHINGTON," SAID JOHN ADAMS. *"That Franklin* electrified him with his rod—and thence forward these two conducted all the Policy, Negotiations, Legislatures, and War."

Thus, according to Adams, "the history of our

1

Revolution will be one continued Lye from one end to the other."

There aren't any cute legends about Adams's key dangling from a kite or about his honesty regarding the felling of fruit trees. Adams wasn't as cuddly as Ben Franklin or as tall and godlike as George Washington. Quite the opposite. He was short, round, peevish, a loudmouth, and frequently a bore. Alexander Hamilton said Adams was petty, mean, erratic, egotistic, eccentric, jealous, and had a mean temper—and they were in the same party.

Adams was often ill, suffered from fits of depression, and, because he refused to wear his dentures, spoke with a lisp. Women didn't swoon and men didn't rise up to follow him when he walked by. One of the members of his cabinet said that in personal relationships Adams was a born loser: "Whether he is spiteful, playful, witty, kind, cold, drunk, sober, angry, easy, stiff, jealous, cautious, close, open, it is always in the wrong place or to the wrong person."

However, John Adams was also possibly the nation's greatest patriot, the linchpin of the American Revolution, and quite probably the ablest man ever to hold the nation's second-highest office. "You stand alone in the history of our public men in never having had your integrity questioned or even suspected," said one of Adams's contemporaries. "Friends and enemies agree in believing you to be an honest man."

Unfortunately, the sad fact is that schoolchildren don't make up stories about vice presidents—something John Adams knew quite well. "My country has in its wisdom contrived for me the most insignificant office that ever the invention of man contrived or his imagination conceived," he said.

☆ ☆ ☆

MANY OF ADAMS'S faults were counterbalanced by his wife, Abigail, who had a steadying effect on the fiery John—although living with the guy couldn't have been all that easy.

When John first became interested in Abigail Smith, he sent her a list, or "catalogue" as he termed it, of her "Faults, Imperfections, Defects, or whatever you may please to call them." He pointed out that she was not the greatest cardplayer and that she even held her cards incorrectly. She was deficient in other social graces as well. According to the note, she couldn't sing, and when others spoke frankly, she was too quick to blush. Moreover, John said, she didn't walk with a stately strut, and she often sat with her "Leggs across." Abigail may have been a bit prudish, but she didn't lack a sense of humor: "You know I think that a gentleman has no business to concern himself about the Leggs of a Lady," she said.

Abigail's father, a well-to-do minister, was against her marrying a lawyer—especially one who came from such a poor background. The Reverend Smith did finally agree to conduct the wedding ceremony, and he used the text "John came neither eating bread nor drinking wine and ye say, he hath a devil." Abigail, whom Adams called saucy, found all of this quite funny.

☆ ☆ ☆

ADAMS BELIEVED IN the cause of independence for the American colonies, and he was willing to make the sacrifices required, even going so far as to give up his favorite beverage. "Tea must be renounced," John wrote Abigail. "I have drank coffee every afternoon and have borne it well." (Coffee and rum soon became the drinks of choice of Americans. Considering that the New World ruffians were stoked by caffeine and Jamaican rum instead of tea, it's no wonder a fight broke out.)

Adams didn't fight any battles of the revolutionary war himself, although once, while on his way to France, the captain of the ship he was on had to tackle him and drag him below deck to prevent Adams from firing a musket at a British warship. What John Adams did do was mold with his own hands the world's first democratic government.

Adams was one of the leaders of both the First and Second Continental Congresses. He served on the committee with Thomas Jefferson and Benjamin Franklin that wrote the Declaration of Independence, and during the war, he served as a minister to France and Holland. In his spare time he wrote the constitution for the state of Massachusetts.

When the U.S. Constitution was ratified, Adams returned to the United States fully expecting to be the new nation's first vice president, and this one time his political foresight was correct. Despite the conniving efforts of Alexander Hamilton to block Adams from the vice presidency, Adams was elected as the nation's first second officer.

He was not happy, though, that Hamilton's machinations had caused him to receive considerably fewer votes than General Washington. "Is not my election to this office in the scurvy manner in which it was done a curse rather than a blessing?" he asked. "Is there any common sense or decency in this business? Is it not an indelible stain on our Country, Countrymen and Constitution?" Adams was so miffed at his poor showing that he considered refusing the office. He finally came to the conclusion, as only John Adams could, that if he didn't accept the vice presidency, the result would be the "final failure of the government from my refusal." And despite considering the duties of the vice president to be "wholly insignificant," Adams finally conceded to take his place as the vice president of the United States.

Before Washington and Adams could be installed in their offices, however, Congress had to come to order, a feat that was as difficult for that august body to perform two hundred years ago as it is today. On March 4, 1789, cannons fired and church bells pealed in New York City as Congress was to meet to officially announce that George Washington and John Adams were to head up the new government. The noisemakers were premature, however, because not enough senators bothered to attend the opening session. It wasn't until April Fools' Day that enough senators were in town so that the election of Washington and Adams could be made official.

On April 21, Adams rode into the city, accompanied by a troop of cavalry, and was escorted to the Senate chambers, where he assumed the duties of vice president. General Washington had not yet made it to New York, though, and so for two glorious days Adams ruled the roost. George Washington did finally arrive, but because the Federal Hall wasn't yet ready, he didn't take the oath until April 29. Therefore, the vice presidency preceded the presidency by eight days.

As vice president, John Adams was not the quiet type of loyal follower people now associate with the second in command. Although he had great respect for George Washington (okay, so he did say that Washington "is too illiterate, unread, unlearned for his station and reputation," but since this was the worst thing that Adams said about him, it is something akin to flattery), he had no such respect for the legislators. "I have reached the conclusion," Adams said of his legislative charges, "that one useless man is called a disgrace; that two are called a law firm and that three or more become a Congress."

Adams had no qualms about meddling in the affairs of the newly elected senators. He frequently reminded them that he was their presiding officer and that he had a few ideas about the way things should be handled. Senator William Maclay of Pennsylvania kept a diary of those first days in the Senate. "Up got the vice president," wrote Maclay, "and for forty minutes did he harangue us from the chair. . . . All of this was merely prefatory. . . . [H]e said fifty more things equally injudicious which I do not think worth mentioning."

Most pressing—at least in Adams's mind—was the issue that Senator Maclay called Adams's favorite topic, the question of titles. In other words, what should the president and vice president be called? Of course, Adams said, the titles chosen by the Constitutional Convention—president and vice president—were too plebeian to be considered. If you called the chief executive officer president, Adams said, people wouldn't know if you were talking about the head of the federal government or the leader of the local cricket club. Adams lectured the Senate on the "efficacy of pageantry" and said that he had come up with a title of his own: "His Highness, or, if you will, His Mighty Benign Highness."

The vice president wasn't alone in seeing the lack of a feathered title as a major obstacle to the future of the young republic. Several senators in the first Congress formed a committee and spent time discussing the same issue, and even George Washington once asked a friend what he thought of High Mightiness as a new moniker for his position.

The Senate committee proposed several alternative titles, which caused all sorts of commotion in Congress. The Speaker of the House said that although High Mightiness would do for the tall and broad-shouldered Washington, it would become a joke if some short, pudgy, round-shouldered man should become president (at this point, one imagines, everyone turned and looked at Adams). Adams finally decided to let the matter drop when a senator from South Carolina proposed that the portly vice president adopt the title His Rotundity, and nobody could listen to Adams raise the issue without bursting out in loud guffaws.

Once these pressing matters of state had been decided (unsatisfactorily in Adams's mind, no doubt), the vice president and his merry band of senators in the first Congress turned to the back-burner issues, such as freedom of speech, freedom of religion, the right to peaceful assembly—in other words, the Bill of Rights. They also created the Departments of State, War, and Treasury and devised a means for the government to pay its bills. Finally, they decided to move the capital to a swamp located on the Maryland-Virginia border.

While Congress was trying to lay the groundwork for the democracy, Vice President Adams continued to poke his nose into every little discussion. Senator Maclay's journal is filled with reports of Adams's interruptions: "The vice president, as usual, made us two or three speeches." "The vice president made a speech, which really was to me unintelligible." "The vice president made a harangue on the subject of order." Finally, Maclay recorded, "God forgive me for the vile thought, but I cannot help thinking of a monkey just put into breeches when I see him betray such evident marks of self-conceit."

The senators pointed out, quite strongly and quite correctly, that the vice president had no real power in the Senate but to serve as a tiebreaker and that they would call him when such a circumstance arose. John Adams, who often acted the part of the petulant child, decided to run away from home, as it were. He thought that he would perform the bare minimum of the duties spelled out in the Constitution and that soon the senators would notice that he was missing and come running to find him, and they would feel so guilty and wish that they had never spoken to him that way and everybody would like him and maybe even give him some real power as vice president. . . .

Of course, that never happened. The senators were quite happy for Adams to attend to the sparse responsibilities of the office. Adams didn't realize what he had done by pouting instead of carving out something for himself to do. He was the first vice president in the first democracy on earth. Every man who held the office in the future of the country would follow his precedent—and they have.

After serving their first term, Washington and Adams ran for reelection to the executive offices in 1792. Washington was again heralded as the unanimous choice of the electoral college. Adams, on the other hand, had a tougher road to travel to reclaim his post. George Clinton, governor of New York and a political opponent of Adams, received 50 of the 127 electoral votes for the second spot. "Damn 'em, damn 'em, damn 'em," Adams said when he learned of the vote. "You see that an elective government will not do."

☆ ☆ ☆

HAD JOHN ADAMS been the first president instead of the first vice president, the country would be much different today. Adams may have been a man of great intellect, but he had a terrible time telling which direction the winds of history were blowing.

For example, in 1776 he predicted that people should celebrate our nation's independence on the second of July (the date independence was actually declared; the Declaration of Independence was approved and independence was made official on the fourth). "The second day of July will be the most memorable epocha in the history of America," he wrote Abigail. "I am apt to believe that it will be celebrated by succeeding generations as the great anniversary festival. It ought to be solemnized with pomp, and parade, with shows, games, sports, bells, bonfires, and illuminations, from one end of this continent to the other, from this time forward forevermore." By 1777 people were already celebrating the Fourth of July.

He was just as off base on other matters. He didn't quite understand the program of the new democracy. He thought that once elected, each president should serve for life and suggested that there be a hereditary senate, with the senator's seat going to the senator's firstborn son.

While serving as Washington's vice president, Adams often suspected that he would not live long enough to have a chance at the presidency. Even when he was elected president at age 62, he thought that he was nearing his end. He was quite mistaken, living on to the cantankerous age of 90.

When Adams did die, his demise became something of a historical curiosity. On the fiftieth anniversary of the signing of the Declaration of Independence—unknown to Adams—Thomas Jefferson had died in his home in Virginia. Near death, Adams had become unconscious that morning, but at about one o'clock in the afternoon, Adams awoke and whispered, "Thomas Jefferson survives!" Those were his last words, and he died later that evening.

THOMAS
JEFFERSON

Served with John Adams, 1797–1801

Democratic-Republican from Virginia

THE NATION'S SECOND VICE PRESIDENT, THOMAS JEFFERSON, HAS ALWAYS RE-CEIVED GREAT PRESS. Even John F. Kennedy served as a flack for Jefferson when he said that a dinner of Nobel Prize winners was the greatest assemblage of intellect at the White House since TJ dined there alone.

Sure the guy wrote the Declaration of Independence, invented everything from a new plow to the lazy Susan, served as the realtor for the United States in orchestrating the Louisiana Purchase, and had his face carved on a big piece of rock in South Dakota. What history always overlooks is that Jefferson was a really awful vice president.

☆ ☆ ☆

JEFFERSON AND ADAMS had worked together at the Continental Congress in 1775 before their rocky administration. Things had gone well then; when the Congress needed someone to write a document to explain to the king why Americans were so outraged, Adams said that Jefferson had to be the man. Jefferson asked Adams why he got the homework assignment. First of all, Adams explained, Jefferson was from Virginia, and a Southerner should write the Declaration so that it wouldn't appear that the whole idea was just something coming from those crazy Harvard political philosophers. "Reason second," said Adams, "I am obnoxious, suspected, and unpopular. Reason third, you can write ten times better than I can."

Finding that he couldn't disagree in the slightest with any of Adams's points, Jefferson agreed to have a go at writing the nation's second-most-important document. "I will do as well as I can," he said, although not everyone thought he did well enough. They liked the preamble, but they cut out the entire section on slavery ("I tremble for my country when I reflect that God is just," Jefferson said on this point), and they softened the section that called King George a tyrant—they wanted to conduct a violent coup, not upset anyone. Benjamin Franklin helped to tighten up the writing, and several others made a few changes here and there, and finally the document was approved.

Jefferson liked to recall that his document survived further editing because of the meeting hall's proximity to a livery stable. The delegates at the July meeting were besieged by flies from the horse barn, and they were forced to swat themselves with their handkerchiefs even when they were speaking to the distinguished group. Finally, many of the delegates decided that declaring war on Britain was preferable to suffering the infernal flies, and they approved the document and quickly left for home.

Thomas Jefferson returned home to take a seat in the state legislature in 1776, and in 1779 he became governor of Virginia. Although Jefferson didn't serve as a soldier in the revolutionary war, he did have something of a war record. In June of 1781, the British managed to push into the Virginia state capital of Charlottesville, and, well, Tom retreated without bothering to make sure that all the papers were cleared off his desk first, a fact that did not sit well with many Virginians. Some members of the legislature accused him of cowardice and even wanted formal charges to be filed against him.

The state legislature debated whether Governor Jefferson had "managed to provide for his personal safety with a precipitate retreat," as one supporter described it, or whether he panicked and left the state government open to seizure. Six months later they decided—because the British had finally vacated the state—to make the call "no harm, no foul" and let Tom off the hook. Still, Jefferson decided not to try for reelection.

Jefferson was serving as the U.S. minister to France while the Constitution was being written, so the new democracy missed out on his counsel when putting together that document, but he did return from his fling in Europe in time to be in George

Washington's administration as the first secretary of state.

In the middle of Washington's second term, however, Jefferson decided that he was fed up with hearing people—such as Hamilton and Adams—complain about how he was handling his job, and he resigned, saying, "Never again will I be enticed into politics." The decision was short-lived, however, for two years later when Washington said that he didn't plan to keep working all his life, there was Tom, suddenly deciding that he wouldn't mind a turn as president of the new country. This was upsetting news to Vice President John Adams, who had assumed he would inherit the president's office by some form of national acclamation.

The supporters of Adams and Jefferson split into the first political parties, although those parties weren't widely acknowledged, and in 1796, for the first time, the citizens of the United States encountered the never-ending back-and-forth, down-and-dirty substitute for a reasoned discussion of the issues.

Adams was the leader of the group called the Federalists. Like most of the Federalist bigwigs (and they were, literally, big wigs), he had been brought up poor but had become rich, and he knew that he liked the life of luxury much better. The Federalists tended to side with the bankers and big business. They believed that the rich should get richer, and the poor should be happy that somebody was doing well. They went around wearing powdered wigs and silk coats and looking as if they were ready to take their places in the aristocracy if a monarchy were to suddenly break out. It would be too simplistic to say that the Federalists were the Republicans of the day, however, because these guys actually thought that having the biggest and most intrusive federal government possible was the way to ensure everyone's happiness.

The Democratic-Republicans, on the other hand, were the liveried liberals of the day. Although many of them were every bit as rich as the Federalists, they avoided the trappings of the nouveau riche Adamsites. They pulled their hair in simple ponytails, wore plain coats and breeches, and in general adopted the "ridiculous affectation of simplicity," as one Federalist congressman sniffed.

There was something of the scent of hypocrisy in Jefferson's constant petting of the working man, since out of the public eye Tom commonly indulged in the luxurious life. People were thrilled when simple Tom Jefferson wore a gray homespun suit at his first inauguration as president, but President Jefferson had only worn his old laundry because bad weather had delayed the delivery of his velvet suit, as well his new six-thousand-dollar carriage.

The two political parties had each picked candidates for president and vice president. The Federalists chose John Adams for president and Thomas Pickney for vice president, and the Democratic-Republicans (as the Jeffersonians called themselves) picked Thomas Jefferson for president and Aaron Burr for vice president.

The campaign became quite bitter, with the Federalists and Democratic-Republicans slinging mud and making up lies about both presidential candidates. Both Adams and Jefferson were thin-skinned and took the campaign hyperbole personally, and the campaign ruined what up to that point had been a long-standing friendship. When the dust settled, Federalist John Adams had won the election, but Democratic-Republican Thomas Jefferson was elected as his vice president. Although having the runner-up for president become vice president was exactly what the writers of the Constitution had had in mind just fifteen years earlier, neither party was pleased at getting half a ticket elected.

For his part, Jefferson was a gracious loser. He claimed that he did "sincerely wish to be second" instead of president because "the second office of this government is honorable and easy." Jefferson wrote that "a more tranquil and unoffending station could not have been found for me nor one so analogous to the dispositions of my mind; it will give me philosophical evenings in the winter and rural days in the summer." Jefferson also had a more pragmatic reason for accepting the vice presidency: He was nearly broke, and he desperately needed the salary.

ALTHOUGH JEFFERSON WAS elevated to the lofty heights of the vice presidency, he didn't forget his rustic Democratic-Republican ideals. Once while traveling, Tom stopped at the finest inn in Baltimore after spending all day in the saddle. He walked into the lobby, whip in hand, no doubt reeking of horse and covered with mud, and asked for lodging for the night. The owner of the establishment looked him up and down and twice refused Jefferson a room. Jefferson spun on his heels and left, and a person in the lobby rushed up to the innkeeper and told him the identity of the unwashed sojourner. "Murder and death, what have I done?" shrieked the innkeeper, who had apparently mistaken Jefferson for just a congressman. The innkeeper told his servants to find Jefferson and offer him the finest room and meals in the hotel. "Tell him . . . if he has no room for a dirty farmer, he shall have none for the vice president," Jefferson instructed the servants.

Jefferson didn't spend all of his evenings being

philosophical and his days being rural. Although he found his duties as presiding officer of the Senate as trying on his patience as Adams had, instead of lecturing the unruly legislators as Adams had done, Jefferson simply wrote *A Manual of Parliamentary Practice*, a guide to decorum that is still used at times today.

Vice President Jefferson may have been willing to offer his advice to Congress, but he made himself of little use to the president. Tom declined to take part in cabinet meetings, thus establishing an unfortunate precedent that continues to this day. And when it began to look as though the United States might go to war with France, Adams hoped to send Jefferson—who had previously served as minister to that country—back to Paris to straighten things out, but Jefferson refused to go, giving the legalistic excuse that such duties were not listed in his job description in the Constitution.

These were sins of omission, but Jefferson took a more active role in opposing his president over the Alien and Sedition Acts. The laws were passed in anticipation of war with France and basically meant, as one pro-Adams newspaper put it, "It is patriotism to write in favor of our government—it is sedition to write against it." If you complained about the government, you could go to jail, and if you were a foreigner from an enemy country, you would be sent back home. Contrary to conventional wisdom, the acts weren't Adams's idea, although he did sign them into law and, considering his wishes for a monarchy separate from but equal to that of England, he no doubt thought them an idea whose time had come.

The newspapers of the day were more fiction and less journalism than the supermarket tabloids of today, and Adams was not usually amused by what he read about himself in the press. After the acts became law, people began going to jail for saying bad things about the diminutive president.

Jefferson began speaking out (albeit quietly) against this obvious abridgment of freedom of speech. He went so far as to say, "Were it left to me to decide whether we should have a government without newspapers, or newspapers without government, I should not hesitate for a moment to prefer the latter."

For this Jefferson has long been hailed as a defender of the Bill of Rights and of the press. But Jefferson was remarkably opportunistic and inconsistent on the issue—when he later became president, he himself urged the states to prosecute for seditious libel Federalist newspapers that were criticizing his administration—and he seems to have had a personal reason for opposing Adams's policies. Jefferson was himself in danger of being imprisoned, because he had been supporting an anti-Adams newspaper while he was vice president.

Jefferson had once contributed fifty dollars to the literary efforts of James Callender, a man who specialized in yellow journalism. When in 1799 Callender wrote that the public had a choice between "Adams, war and beggary, and Jefferson, peace and competency" and that "the people of the United States have a million good reasons for wishing to see . . . a speedy termination of the reign of Mr. Adams," vice president Tom wrote Callender, praising the editorial and saying, "Such papers cannot fail to produce the best efforts." Callender was arrested, and Jefferson defended him, but apparently not strongly enough, because years later Callender published correspondence that showed that Jefferson had supported the paper's attacks on President Adams.

Jefferson set himself to repealing the Alien and Sedition Acts. He wrote a series of nine resolutions that opposed the Alien and Sedition Acts and sent them to friends in the new commonwealth of Kentucky. The legislature there passed the resolutions into law, and shortly thereafter the Virginia legislature passed a similar resolution.

The efforts of Vice President Jefferson helped to turn public opinion against the acts, and three of the four acts were allowed to expire during Adams's term (the fourth was repealed by Jefferson when he became president).

☆ ☆ ☆

IN THE ELECTION of 1800, for the first time, the vice president (Jefferson) ran against the president (Adams), and for the only time in U.S. history, the vice president won—and in a landslide, to boot. Incensed at Jefferson's election to the presidency, Adams refused to attend the inauguration.

Jefferson was such a popular president that four years later he was elected to a second term. This isn't a big deal for most presidents, but of the four men who have been elected to the presidency while vice president—John Adams, Thomas Jefferson, Martin Van Buren, and George Bush—Jefferson is at this writing the only one who has been able to pull it off.

When Jefferson's daughter died, several years after he had retired to Monticello, Abigail Adams wrote Tom a condolence letter, and this act broke the wall of ice between Jefferson and Adams, and in the years before their deaths they resumed their friendship.

When both men died on the fiftieth anniversary of the signing of the Declaration of Independence, many people in the country took it as a sign from above. But at least one old Democratic-Republican couldn't forget the political battles of the past, and he thought he saw the despicable hand of the Federalists in the act, exclaiming, "It's a damn Yankee trick!"

AARON BURR

Served with Thomas Jefferson, 1801–05

Democratic-Republican from New York

AARON BURR IS THE ONLY MAN WHO COM-
MITTED MURDER WHILE VICE PRESIDENT
(THAT WE KNOW OF, ANYWAY); he was also
one of two vice presidents to have been formally
charged with treason—and these were just his extracurricular activities. As vice president he was able to
work the loopholes of the Constitution to his advantage so often that he nearly displaced Thomas Jeffer-

son as the nation's third president, creating such a mess that a Constitutional amendment was needed to prevent its happening again.

Thomas Jefferson said of his vice president, in words that would later be full of irony, that he was "a crooked gun, or other perverted instrument, whose aim of shot you could never be sure of."

AARON BURR WAS a preacher's kid, the grandson of famed Calvinist minister Jonathan Edwards and the son of the Reverend Aaron Burr, founder of Princeton University. Unlike his father and grandfather, little Burr had no interest in preaching the good word. He did have the intelligence of his ancestors—he entered Princeton at age 13 and graduated when he was 16—but Aaron Jr. had a genius for the dark side. Instead of studying theology, Burr decided to become a lawyer.

His judicial studies were interrupted by the revolutionary war, and Burr put his talents for deception to use as a spy against the British. He served well enough that General George Washington made him a member of his staff, but Washington transferred Burr when he found the young lieutenant colonel reading his mail.

Burr served at Valley Forge, where he often had to deal with desertions and threats to his command. He was able to hold his troops together by a show of force: Calling for a roll call in the middle of one freezing night, he walked down the line of his troops. One of the leaders of a planned overthrow of command stepped from the ranks, pointed a pistol at Burr, and shouted, "Now is your time, boys!" The diminutive Burr raised his sword and, in a single stroke, amputated the man's arm. Needless to say, the troops were better behaved from that point on.

Burr wasn't a maniacal ruler, however. He demanded new shoes for his soldiers, and he allowed prostitutes to visit the camps (although he did insist that when the ladies were leaving, they be searched for papers—down to the stays of their bustiers).

Burr was a lifelong hypochondriac, and after suffering heat exhaustion following one battle, he decided that his condition was so grave that he resigned his post. Burr was already on Washington's bad side, but the general must have considered Burr's military skills valuable, because he never forgave Burr for abandoning the army during its time of greatest need.

☆ ☆ ☆

ALTHOUGH BURR WAS not tall, dark, and handsome—shrimpy, wheezy, and hooknosed would have been a better description—he was slick enough to become quite popular with the opposite sex. He met his first wife, Theodosia, while she was married to a British officer. Burr never worried too much about wedding vows of faithfulness, either his own or those of others, and he soon became quite close to Theodosia. When her husband, who was stationed in the tropics, conveniently died, Theodosia and Aaron married and moved into a house on Wall Street.

Burr passed the bar and soon became the most accomplished lawyer in New York. The death of his wife gave him even more time to concentrate on his career; he soon joined the state legislature, where he developed a following of Burrites and where, it has long been rumored, he founded the infamously corrupt Tammany Hall political machine. When he was 35 years old, Burr took his act nationwide by defeating Alexander Hamilton's father-in-law for a seat in the U.S. Senate.

Burr was able to gather enough political support that he hoped to be considered his party's candidate for president in 1800. The nomination went to Thomas Jefferson instead, but that did not mean that Burr would quietly accept his party's wishes.

Burr first worked to disrail the campaign of incumbent president John Adams, who was trying for a second term. Alexander Hamilton, although a Federalist, was opposed to Adams and hoped that his fellow Federalists would vote for the Federalist vice-presidential candidate Charles Pickney instead of Adams. (Hamilton, born an illegitimate child in the West Indies and unable to become president himself because of his foreign birth, was ever active in politics at the national level. Aaron Burr even thought that George Washington was "completely under the influence of Alexander Hamilton.")

This plan hoped to take advantage of a quirk in the Constitution. At that time, the vice president was the person who received the second-highest number of votes for president. The political parties tried to get their vice-presidential candidates elected by placing two men on the ballot and having some of their electoral-college voters withhold their votes from the man appointed as second in command. It was a confusing system that invited the type of political manipulation at which Burr and Hamilton excelled.

To convince his peers to support Pickney, Hamilton wrote an attack on Adams that he planned to distribute to other influential Federalists. Somehow one of the copies found its way from the printer to the hands of Burr, who knew exactly what to do with the Federalists' dirty laundry—hang it out for everyone to see. The attack on Adams by a member of his own party doomed the president's campaign for reelection.

That meant that the only man between Burr and

the presidency was Tom Jefferson. Behind closed doors Burr began promoting himself as a candidate for the top spot. When the votes came in, Burr and Jefferson tied for president with seventy-three votes each, which meant that it was up to the House of Representatives to pick the winner. Jefferson thought he saw Burr's hand in this strange occurrence, and he wrote a sarcastic note to Burr, saying that "it was badly managed to have arranged with certainty what seems to have been left to hazard [by allowing the House to decide the election]."

Burr could have announced that he was content with the vice presidency and allowed Jefferson to take his place as president, but he had no intention of doing such an altruistic thing. In a high-minded remark, he said that if the only way to preserve the government was for him to assume the presidency, then he was willing to do that, adding that Jefferson would naturally be his choice as vice president.

When the House began voting in February 1801, Washington was crowded with people eager to see who would be selected as president. The winner needed a simple majority of the sixteen states to be declared a winner; on the first ballot Jefferson received eight votes and Burr six. Two states abstained because they were themselves evenly split. As with most American political squabbles, some people immediately offered to pick up their rifles and begin shooting, but no one was quite ready for a civil war, and they were shouted down.

There was a second ballot, then a third, with the same result as the first. The deadlock continued through six days and thirty-six ballots when, finally, some of Burr's supporters abstained from voting, which meant that Jefferson had the necessary votes, and he was selected as the country's third president.

As one would deduce, Burr was persona non

grata in the subsequent Jefferson administration, and Jefferson proved so popular and powerful that his isolation of Burr was duplicated by all of Washington. When the Democratic-Republicans met in 1804 to select their candidates, Jefferson had no opposition for president, and Burr didn't receive a single vote for the vice presidential nomination. One observer said at the caucus that "not a word was lisped in [Burr's] favor."

☆ ☆ ☆

BURR DECIDED THAT if he was unloved in Washington, he would return to New York and become his home state's next governor. But Burr had fallen out of favor there as well, thanks in part to his nemesis Alexander Hamilton, and the Democratic-Republicans refused to nominate the vice president for governor. Burr then ran for governor as an independent and went on to lose the election by the largest margin ever in that state.

It was during that campaign that the Burr-Hamilton conflict reached its zenith. At a dinner around that time, Hamilton remarked that Burr was "a dangerous man . . . who ought not to be trusted." The evening's host wrote a letter quoting Mr. Hamilton, and someone leaked the letter to the *Albany Register*, which promptly printed it.

Burr ignored the insult, but when his political opponents reprinted the letter in political fliers and pasted them all over the state, the vice president felt obliged to stand up for his honor. He wrote to Hamilton asking for an explanation. Hamilton said that the words were "admissible between political opponents," and so he refused any sort of apology. After a few more exchanges—the danger escalating with each one—Burr said that he had endured Hamilton's "base slanders" for many years and that it was time to "announce these things to the world . . . these things must end." With that Burr invited Hamilton to an interview, which was the term for dueling in those days.

The insults and constant political opposition were reason enough to resort to flintlocks, but Burr may have had yet another reason for wanting to kill Hamilton. Burr had gone as far as he could go in American political life. It wasn't nearly as far, however, as his ambition wished to take him. He had already hatched a plan of leading a revolution in the Spanish colonies of the American Southwest and establishing himself as the first ruler—only to learn that Hamilton had a similar idea. The Burr-Hamilton duel may have been the first this-territory-isn't-big-enough-for-the-two-of-us western shoot-out.

Neither Hamilton nor Burr was a stranger to dueling. Burr had once interceded and stopped a duel between Alexander Hamilton and James Monroe that was to decide which of the two combatants would continue his adulterous affair with a married woman. Burr himself had once fought a duel with Hamilton's brother-in-law, John Church, on the same spot in Weehawken, New Jersey, that was chosen for his fight with Hamilton and with the same guns that would be used in the Hamilton-Burr battle. In Burr's first duel both men missed their shots, although Church did manage to nick Burr's coat.

Alexander Hamilton had also visited the dueling site in New Jersey before. While Hamilton watched, his son had fought in a duel there. His son had been mortally wounded in the fight, and Hamilton had held the dying young man in his arms.

Given these memories, no doubt both men understood the gravity of what they were about to do when they met at 7:00 A.M. on July 11, 1804. When they arrived at the dueling ground, the seconds marched off ten paces, and the combatants took their places. By prior arrangement, when Burr's second asked if they were ready, they were to respond "present" and then fire. The second gave the command, and although accounts differed as to who fired first, both sides agreed that Hamilton immediately fell to the ground, saying, "I am a dead man."

Some reports say Hamilton was shot in the groin; others simply say he was hit in a "vital part." Regardless, the .54-caliber ball apparently shattered and pierced his diaphragm and liver and lodged in his spinal column, splintering a vertebra. He died the next day.

Burr was remarkably calm after the battle. Although he tried to rush to speak to the dying Hamilton, his second pulled him into an awaiting boat, which returned him to New York. At eight o'clock that morning, just minutes after he had shot Hamilton, a visitor stopped by the vice president's house and found him eating breakfast. Burr asked the man to eat with him, and they chatted casually. It wasn't until the man left and was walking down the street that he learned of Burr's early-morning activities.

For nearly two centuries history saw Hamilton as something of a martyr who insisted that he never meant to harm his good rival, Burr. But Hamilton did not undergo this miraculous change of heart when confronted with the possibility of his own mortality at the hands of his enemy, Aaron Burr. Instead, it now appears that he lost the duel and died because he had tried to use an unfair advantage to kill the vice president.

As a part of the U.S. bicentennial celebration, the Smithsonian Institution decided to have the pistols used in the Burr-Hamilton duel restored. What they found was that the guns—which had been provided for the duel by Hamilton—had several features that

were not allowed on dueling pistols, such as adjusta-
ble front and rear sights, larger-caliber balls than allowed by custom, and most significantly, a special
hair-trigger feature. By surreptitiously setting the
trigger so that only a half pound of pressure—instead of the normal ten to twelve pounds—was
needed to fire the gun, a duelist could gain an incredible advantage, since both men were to fire at
the same time.

Instead of displaying nearly godlike mercy, Hamilton planned to kill Burr before Burr had a chance
to fire. But in his nervousness, Hamilton apparently
held the gun too tightly, firing it too soon, and the
shot struck the leaves over Burr's head.

Burr was soon charged with murder in New
York, where Hamilton had finally died, and later in
New Jersey, where the duel had taken place. He fled
first to Philadelphia, where he visited the British
minister to the United States. There, the vice president asked the minister if he would help pay for a
war to separate the western states from the United
States.

Burr then traveled south, not only to escape arrest but because he thought that if he were to take
control of the Spanish territories in the American
Southwest and Mexico, the first step would be to capture Florida. Burr scouted around for a few months
and decided that Florida was not the best route to
Mexico, and he returned to Washington, where he
was free from extradition.

Burr then resumed his duties as presiding officer
of the Senate. Although a few people squawked—
one senator complained, "We are indeed fallen on
evil times. The high office of president is filled by an
infidel, that of vice president by a murderer"—most
of Washington did not think it strange that a high
government official would be charged with a capital

crime, and Burr continued to execute his duties, which included presiding over the impeachment trial of Supreme Court Justice Samuel Chase.

Burr's final act in the Senate was to give a farewell address that remains one of the most famous speeches given before that body. A day before his term was to end, Burr told the senators that he had a sore throat and wanted to go home early. He spoke for twenty minutes, and then, as the senators remained silent, he walked down the aisle and slammed the door behind him as he left. The speech had been so moving that some senators admitted to weeping for several minutes after he was gone.

DESPITE HIS OATH to always uphold the document, Burr was not a big believer in the Constitution. He often said that he didn't think the covenant between the states would last more than fifty years. Besides, Burr said, law was merely "whatever is boldly asserted and plausibly attained."

Following his term as vice president, Burr immediately set out to commit treason. He traveled to what is now the Midwest, where he tried to raise money for his revolution. He claimed that the U.S. government was weak and that if he wanted to, he could take New York with just five hundred men and push the members of Congress into the Potomac with just two hundred men. He then began traveling toward New Orleans, all the while gathering support for his new army. Somewhere along the line Burr made the claim that once the western states were free, he would kick out Congress and hang President Thomas Jefferson.

Burr's expedition did not pass unnoticed in Washington. Jefferson called an emergency cabinet meeting to discuss how to handle Burr. They sent warnings to the western territorial governors, and Jefferson ordered seven gunboats to set sail for the Mississippi River. Two days later Jefferson decided it would be better to send out the marines, and he directed them to shore up the fort at New Orleans.

Burr was arrested in January, and Jefferson sent a message to Congress, explaining Burr's attempted conspiracy. Jefferson was a bit vague about what had happened—he withheld names and details of what had taken place—but there was no doubt, he said, that the former vice president "was the principal actor, whose guilt is placed beyond question."

Eventually Burr was charged with treason, and one of the country's first public-spectacle trials took place. Burr stunned the court by subpoenaing President Thomas Jefferson, but Jefferson created an even bigger stir when he refused to appear in court, citing, for the first time, executive privilege. The jury must have wondered what Jefferson was hiding, because they voted to acquit Burr.

Burr escaped the scaffold, but there were still people after him. A mob of fifteen hundred people met him in Baltimore, carrying rope, tar, and feathers. Burr quickly found passage to Philadelphia, where he was greeted by creditors, and, deciding that the water was just too warm in the United States, he traveled to Europe, where, it was rumored, he contacted Napoléon about an attack on Boston.

Burr did find time for leisure activities while on the continent. He sent letters to his daughter, Theodosia, in which he rated the many prostitutes he had had the privilege to patronize, noting the price paid and general performance. In one of his entries he mentioned that he was suffering from a bite "by a venemous animal." The letter went on to say that the animal had been two legged and female.

On his eventual return to the United States, Burr

was met by the death of his only daughter and grandson. He still had trouble with creditors, and he was forced to sell many of his personal belongings to pay his bills. At age 77 he met and married a wealthy widow—a former prostitute who was said to be the richest woman in America and who was a mere 57 years old. Even this cozy arrangement was short-lived, because Burr was able to run through much of her fortune in just four months.

Burr was finally coming to the end, and he began trying to put some events of his life in order. He made out a will that included two illegitimate daughters, both of whom were younger than 10 years old. (Burr had once said, "When a lady sees fit to name me as the father of her children, why should I deny her that honor?") But other eternal matters he left to chance: In his final hours a minister asked him if he had made his peace with God and expected to receive salvation after death, but Burr would only say, "On that subject I am coy."

Burr died on his eightieth birthday, on the same day that his divorce from his second wife became final, on grounds of adultery—his.

THE CORONATION OF BLAND AMBITION

The Twelfth Amendment to the

U.S. Constitution

Some men are born mediocre; others have mediocrity thrust upon them. The latter was the case for the nation's first three vice presidents—John Adams, Thomas Jefferson, and Aaron Burr—who each had the intelligence and ability to assume the presidency. This situation would soon change, however, as the Twelfth Amendment to the U.S. Constitution turned the vice presidency into a tinny magnet for those possessing bland ambition.

After witnessing the disastrous vice presidencies of Thomas Jefferson and Aaron Burr, the leaders of the country knew that they had to do something to prevent the United States from being paralyzed by partisan politics revolving around the second office. In 1804 amendments to the Constitution were introduced into both the Senate and the House of Representatives that would have simply eliminated the vice presidency. Neither bill passed.

Instead, the Senate and House passed an amendment that would allow the electoral-college voters to specify one person for president and one person for vice president, thus establishing the system now in effect. The amendment also said that if either candidate failed to get a majority of the electoral-college votes, the House would pick the president and the Senate the vice president (a strange choice since the Senate is supposedly the more august body).

When the amendment was proposed, it didn't find universal support. One senator likened the new vice presidency to "a fifth wheel to a coach." Gouverneur Morris of New York said that the revised vice presidency would only attract inferior men who would degrade the office. A Senator Plumer from New Hampshire said that instead of voting for a person capable of being president, people would "seek a man of moderate talents, whose ambition is bounded by that office, and whose influence will aid them in electing the president."

If the Twelfth Amendment had not passed, however, the results could have been ruinous for the country. It would have meant that in every difficult moment for a president, there would be at least one person in his administration hoping he would fail. In the most extreme example, if in 1860 John Breckinridge—who would be charged with treason after he left the Senate to join the Confederacy—had been elected vice president, he would have been a constant threat to President Abraham Lincoln's life, not just to his policies.

On the other hand, a good argument exists for having left the Constitution the way the founders of the country originally planned: It would have been great entertainment. The thought of homespun and explosive Andrew Jackson serving with the proper and prim John Quincy Adams or of Richard Nixon lurking in the shadows of the Kennedy White House or of a bitter and whining Jimmy Carter tugging at Reagan's pant leg is more entertaining and captivating than a pulp novel.

And that, unfortunately, is why the people with the power to make the change will never go back to the original plan. Political parties have enough problems with credibility without including in every administration a built-in critic.

So just one mortal life away from the most powerful democratic office in the world, U.S. citizens are left with men who were never thought capable of the presidency, men who were not really elected to their lofty post by anyone other than their party's presidential nominee. Every four years when voters hold their noses and elect another one, they want to send the same message to the president that Mark Hanna, chairman of the Republican National Committee in 1900, sent to newly reelected President William McKinley: "Your duty is to *live* for [the next] four years."

GEORGE CLINTON

Served with Thomas Jefferson, 1805–09;

James Madison, 1809–12

Democratic-Republican from New York

WITH THE RATIFICATION OF THE TWELFTH AMENDMENT, THE PRACTICE OF OFFERING THE VICE PRESIDENT'S OFFICE AS A CONSOLATION PRIZE TO THE LOSER OF THE PRESIDENTIAL RACE WAS OVER. The vice presidency became a second-rate office, something to which only second-rate men would aspire.

Hitting leadoff in this new ruling order was George Clinton of New York.

☆ ☆ ☆

FROM THE BEGINNING of his political life, Clinton hated the British and hated the king, and those who didn't—the Tories—he made to suffer: "They were by his orders tarred and feathered, carted, whipped, fined, banished," said one account of a Clintonian political discussion. "In short, every kind of cruelty, death not excepted, was practiced by this emissary of revolution." Apologists for Clinton said that this treatment was reserved for those people still loyal to the British crown, but considering how quickly the poor son of a farmer was able to rise politically, it would not be surprising to find that a few of his political enemies made their way into the pitch bath as well.

During the revolutionary war Clinton had fought against kin, his cousin Sir Henry Clinton. Although the American Clinton held the rank of brigadier general, the only maneuvers he was familiar with had to do with political gamesmanship. The literal battlefield was another fight altogether, and Sir Henry, a more experienced military man, bloodied his cousin's nose at every meeting. "From Fatal experience," George Clinton said of his military command, "I find that I am not able to render my country that Service which they may have Reason to expect of me."

☆ ☆ ☆

CLINTON MAY HAVE been willing to tar and feather anyone who dared to drink English tea, to put himself on the line against the redcoats in the revolutionary war, but no one ever hung the tag *patriot* on him. That was because Clinton opposed the new democratic government with all his might. He hated every word of the Constitution, and he fought it as strenuously as he could. Clinton didn't want elected officials; as the most powerful man in the most powerful state of the original thirteen, he wanted a new monarchy. Clinton hoped that New York would become its own country—and, of course, he would be king.

When it became clear to Clinton that he wasn't about to become King George redux, he tried to validate his power by becoming New York's first governor. Clinton wasn't overly confident of his victory in his first assault on the top-dog office in New York, however, and so to better his chances at postelection employment, he ran for both lieutenant governor and governor. He won both elections, and seeing his double election as some sort of mandate, he decided to keep both offices.

During the next fifteen years Clinton held on to his governorship at each turn, despite the best efforts of the democratic aristocracy to displace him. Finally, in 1792, the Federalists were successful when their candidate won the election by a comfortable margin. Such a small matter as losing the election wouldn't unseat an experienced rapscallion such as George Clinton, however. He simply declared the votes in three Federalist counties invalid, and he remained in the governor's office for another term.

By 1795, the voters had had enough of George. Facing certain defeat if he ran for yet another term as governor, Clinton finally retired for what he said were health reasons. His excuse wasn't far-fetched—his health was failing. Infirmity came early to Clinton for, although he was only 65 years old, physically he was an elderly man. Writing to his nephew DeWitt Clinton, he asked for help in pulling together a few final remarks for the state legislature:

"I found it extremely difficult to draft [a speech] for the last session without committing Plagiarism," the old general said.

To Clinton, however, impending senility and failing health didn't mean that he should quit politics. Instead, he thought he should accelerate his plans to become president if he was ever to attain that office. In 1804, Clinton went to the first publicly acknowledged political caucus, hoping that the delegates would make him their presidential nominee, but they passed him over for Thomas Jefferson.

When the Democratic-Republicans began looking to fill the second spot on the ticket, the last thing they were seeking was an active, politically viable person who would cause headaches for his president as fellow Democratic-Republicans Burr and Jefferson had done during their vice presidencies. Under the new rules of the Twelfth Amendment they were free to pursue mediocrity. They found it in the infirm George Clinton of New York. Jefferson and Clinton made for a winning team, and they won the electoral contest by the convincing margin of 162 to 14.

During his first vice-presidential term of 1805–09, Clinton was an embarrassment as the presiding officer of the Senate. His memory frequently failed him: He sometimes declared a bill passed or defeated before it had been voted on; at other times he forgot to announce the outcome of the votes after they had been tallied. He routinely omitted most of the basic elements of parliamentary procedure (although he may have been ignorant of such rules since he had never served in a legislative body).

One senator wrote that "a worse choice than Mr. Clinton could scarcely [have] been made." Another senator chimed in, writing, "He is old, feeble, and altogether incapable of the duty of presiding in the Senate."

The Democratic-Republicans didn't repudiate that political assessment, but, giddy with the knowledge that they could nominate whomever they wanted for vice president and still win the election—as long as the presidential candidate was strong enough (and James Madison was a pretty good candidate)—the party nominated Clinton for vice president again. George Clinton, of all people, was offended by his renomination. Despite his infirmity, he thought that he deserved his party's nomination for president in 1808, and, after scraping together his own group of supporters, Clinton managed to get himself nominated for the presidency after all.

If failing to get the nomination of his party for president wasn't enough of a slight, Clinton had to suffer the indignity of being ignored. James Madison and the other Democratic-Republicans didn't even notice that their vice-presidential candidate was running against their top nominee, and they kept him on the ticket. Clinton lost and won the election: losing badly to Madison for president but winning a second term as vice president. He was livid at losing the presidential contest and demonstrated his anger by refusing to attend Madison's inauguration and openly opposing Madison's policies.

Clinton was able to get in one last dollop of retribution toward the Democratic-Republicans. When the vote to renew the Bank of the United States came to a tie, Clinton voted against it, despite Madison's strong desire that the legislation be passed. As a result of this final fit of pique, the United States had no means to finance the War of 1812. Clinton didn't hang around to see the results of his vote, however, since he died while in office shortly before the war began.

☆ ☆ ☆

CONSIDERING THE DEBACLE of Clinton's tenure as the second in command, it's a wonder that the Twelfth Amendment wasn't immediately repealed. Unfortunately, no one gave his efforts much notice, and his was a history the country was doomed to see repeated.

ELBRIDGE GERRY

Served with James Madison, 1813–14

Democratic-Republican from Massachusetts

ELBRIDGE GERRY, THE NATION'S FIFTH
VICE PRESIDENT, IS BELOVED BY ALL FANS
OF THE SMASH-JAW WORLD OF AMERICAN
POLITICS AS THE MAN WHO BEGAN THE
QUAINT TRADITION OF GERRYMANDER-
ING. It is most appropriate that Mr. Gerry's
name (which is actually pronounced with a hard *g*)
became associated with such a slimy, slithering

creature because reptilian politics were Gerry's forte.

Gerry began his career with quite a remarkable political pedigree. He was one of the signers of the Declaration of Independence, and he was chosen to be a delegate to the Constitutional Convention. It was there that most people first observed Gerry's slippery ways.

The convention was charged, of course, with creating a new government, one unlike any the world had seen before. The Founding Fathers could not, as in later revolutions, choose governmental features like items from a Chinese menu. Coming at the beginning of the decline of monarchies, the delegates to the American Constitutional Convention didn't have much to go on.

Gerry, his ambition raging like a teenager's hormones, had the dual hopes of leaving his own mark on this new egalitarian government and protecting his substantial interests elsewhere. The result, as one delegate described it, was that Gerry "objected to everything he did not propose." He believed, like John Adams and many of the other optimistic creators of the Constitution, in a strong federal government. Yet he also claimed that he believed in the Jeffersonian idea of republicanism, or a weak federal government, and that is the way he voted. This was a particularly fortunate choice because he was in the clique of Democratic-Republicans (the politicians weren't yet brave enough to admit that they had formed political parties), and an opposing vote on the central point of their existence would have looked bad on his record.

Despite his adherence to party lines, Gerry also managed to mention that he was against political parties, especially "the one devoted to democracy," which, one can only assume, was his own. He asserted that he was against "the friends of the aristocracy," forgetting his own friends and well-to-do background. On the other hand, despite his vote of confidence for republicanism and his stand for the little people, he wasn't about to let the rabble rule in Washington, and he voted against letting the people vote for their own government. He described this new idea of democracy as "the worst of all evils." (If at this point you are confused, imagine how Gerry's contemporaries felt.)

Gerry thought the Constitution was a terrible document, so vile that its adoption would lead to civil war. He said that it should have been drawn up "in a more mediating shape"—meaning, of course, that everyone should have listened more when he was talking. In the end, there was one clause in particular that stuck in his craw, and that had to do with the vice presidency. He complained that the vice president should not serve as president of the Senate, because that blurred the delineation between the executive and legislative branches of government (okay, so he had a good point there). With self-righteous indignation, he announced that he could not "pledge himself to abide by" such a clause, and he refused to sign the Constitution. That, of course, did not stop him from immediately accepting the nomination to very same vice presidency several years later. As fellow Vice President Hubert Humphrey would say many years later, "Where I stand depends on where I sit."

ELBRIDGE GERRY WAS a small man, both in stature and in attitude. Unlike most vice presidents, Gerry was never a lawyer. After graduating from Harvard, he managed the family business of codfish shipping and later added to the family fortune by putting guns on his codfish boats and renting them to the U.S. government as warships.

Although he had grown up in a small, foul-smelling fishing village, Gerry quickly took on the trappings of aristocracy. He built a huge estate, wore the finest and most expensive clothes, and even traveled in a chariot. And because he was one of the richest men in Massachusetts, Gerry had time to dabble in various local offices. Despite such apparent loyalty to the British government du jour, Gerry covered his bases by speaking out frequently on the importance of freedom and republicanism.

President Washington did not put the particular talents of Mr. Gerry to use in his administration, but when John Adams became president, he appointed Gerry to a three-man delegation (along with Charles Pickney and John Marshall) to represent the United States in France.

France showed considerable disrespect toward the young nation. The French navy had been playing the role of a pirate brigade and harassing American ships. When the American trio confronted Maurice Talleyrand, minister of foreign affairs, about this problem, he responded that the French navy's escapades would stop immediately, provided, that is, that the American government transferred some moneys over to the French treasury and into the hands of select French officials.

Pickney and Marshall stalked out on Talleyrand filled with indignation, but Gerry wasn't so naive. He apparently could understand a little political blackmail, and he certainly understood deviousness, because unbeknownst to Marshall and Pickney, Gerry had been conducting secret negotiations with Talleyrand.

It turned out that the French were bluffing; they

had no inclination to go to war in a strange country against an army that had just handed the British their bright red hats. But Gerry took the credit for the nonwar anyway, claiming that if he hadn't stayed behind after Marshall and Pickney left, they'd all be speaking French. "I have never met a man of less candor and as much duplicity as Mr. Gerry," Pickney said.

Proclaiming Gerry a hero, the Democratic-Republicans promptly nominated their new political star for the office of governor of Massachusetts. The people of Massachusetts weren't fooled, however, and they turned him down for the job in three consecutive elections, each time by a larger margin. Finally, on his fourth try, the citizens of the Bay State grew tired of Gerry's pleading and let him in the governor's office.

Governor Gerry immediately entered the pantheon of American dirty political tricksters by allowing the gerrymander to raise its ugly head during his first term. Gerry didn't come up with the idea of creatively redrawing political districts specifically to create an advantage for the incumbent party—that bit of deviousness actually appeared in a bill prepared by his fellow Democrats in the legislature—but when Gerry signed the redistricting bill into law, he gained the political immortality he had so desired.

☆ ☆ ☆

GEORGE CLINTON DIED just a month before the Republicans met to pick their candidates for the presidential election of 1813. They first considered Clinton's nephew, DeWitt Clinton, for the second spot, but he had seen how the office had derailed his uncle's presidential ambitions and had the good sense to decline. The Democratic-Republicans then gave the nomination to John Langdon of New Hampshire. The only problem was that Langdon didn't want the nomination. Finally—since no one else seemed to want the job—the caucus gave the nomination to Gerry.

Gerry's term as vice president was inconsequential. Elbridge Gerry died after suffering a stroke one evening while riding home in his carriage following a day's work in the Senate. He had come close to the presidency in 1813 when James Madison became very ill (the French foreign minister said that this would result in a "veritable national calamity"), but Madison held on and ended up surviving long enough to see both his vice presidents die in office.

DANIEL D. TOMPKINS

Served with James Monroe, 1817–25

Democratic-Republican from New York

IN 1816 IT OCCURRED TO THE DEMOCRAT-
IC-REPUBLICANS THAT IF THEY DIDN'T
ELECT A HOMICIDAL MEGALOMANIAC, as
they had with Aaron Burr, or an infirm old political
hack, such as George Clinton or Elbridge Gerry,
they might actually be able to use the office to groom
some up-and-charging young pol for the presidency.
And lo and behold, there was Dan Tompkins, one of

the brightest political stars in the country. But eight
years later, instead of using his political influence in
Washington as vice president to slingshot himself to
the presidency, Tompkins was drunk in New York,
his political career ended, the victim of an expense
report that wouldn't balance.

☆ ☆ ☆

TOMPKINS WOULD HAVE been the perfect candidate for political office in today's age of sound
bites. He was friendly, good-looking, and a bit of a
chowderhead. A senator who was around at the time
wrote that Tompkins was "reported to be a good
tempered, inoffensive man of moderate talents." He
was a particular favorite of the ladies, but one pragmatic politician said that this was of little use to him
since the women couldn't vote.

Tompkins was born in Scarsdale, New York, and
after graduating from Columbia University at age
20, he passed the bar at age 22. By the time he was
30, he was named to the New York Supreme Court.

He began his elected career as a protégé of Aaron
Burr. This fact alone may have ended the careers of
some men, but as one early biographer noted, "his
[Tompkins's] capacity for friendship depended on
whether the success of his own career was endan-
gered by the association," and by the time Tompkins
was elected governor of New York in 1807, Burr was
nowhere to be seen.

It was during the War of 1812 that Tompkins
made his name known outside the Empire State.
Things weren't looking good for the home team in
the early days of the war, especially after the fall of
the capital city of Washington. When British Admiral Cockburn entered the House of Representatives,
he sat in the chair of the Speaker of the House and
said that as he was in a democracy, he would put the

fate of the capital to a vote. "Gentlemen," he said, "shall this harbor of Yankee democracy be burned? All in favor say aye." The redcoats let out a cheer, and Admiral Cockburn gave the order: "Light up!"

The great experiment in democracy, it appeared, was about to die an early death. Washington had been captured and burned, Massachusetts refused to send either money or men for the fight, several of the New England states were acting as if they wanted to leave the union, and to top it all off, the federal government was too broke to continue fighting.

It was one thing for the gentlemen of Boston to let their country down, but New York, with its long, exposed border to Canada, was in a more precipitous position. Tompkins took up the cause and rallied the citizenry. He personally raised some four million dollars to help pay for an army. When bankers balked at loaning money to the government (the federal government was not a blue-chip investment at the time), Tompkins gave his personal word for the loans. When even that wasn't enough, he mixed his own funds into the pot.

The United States was only able to fight the British to a draw. John Quincy Adams complained, "We have obtained nothing but peace." That, however, was good enough for most people, and the political stock of Governor Tompkins began to soar. Madison offered him the job of secretary of state, but Tompkins refused this difficult job, preferring to remain in his governor's chair and bask in his glory.

Tompkins had ambitions of riding his newfound popularity into the charred, but still desirable, White House, and he tried to gain the nomination in 1816. The Democratic-Republicans worried that Tompkins's fame was limited to his home state, however, and instead offered him the nomination for vice president, with the presidential nomination going to James Monroe of Virginia.

Daniel Tompkins was 42 years old at the time, which, on the stage of national politics, is a child actor. He had time to take a break and wait for the presidency. He accepted the nomination, and Tompkins and Monroe won an easy victory.

As vice president, Tompkins spent most of his time back home in New York. It may have been that he found no thrill in watching the debates of the bellicose senators, but he was beginning to have personal problems as well. Tompkins had always enjoyed the fine things in life, and over the years he had run up some substantial bills. That situation worsened when he spent much of his own money to fund the war effort. His creditors had run out of patience, and Tompkins was forced to stay in New York to make arrangements.

When it rains, it not only pours but lightning bolts abound. In 1817 new financial problems came to light. The well-meaning folks back home hoped to call their prodigal son back to the governor's office, and the vice president was nominated to another term as governor. But the Federalist state party, led by DeWitt Clinton, the nephew of Vice President George Clinton, had found some dirt on Tompkins. They pointed out that wartime accounts from the Tompkins administration were $120,000 short, and the Federalists accused Tompkins of dipping into the treasury while everyone was watching the war.

Tompkins could not easily wiggle out of the charges, because when he was paying the bills of the war, he had neglected to ask for receipts. The state legislature was willing to forgive the oversight, and they proposed paying Tompkins a commission on the money he had raised that was equal to the missing funds. But Tompkins refused the offer, saying that, in fact, the state owed him an additional $130,000. The state assembly, led by Martin Van Buren, believed that the vice president was guilty only of carelessness, and offered an additional settlement of about twelve thousand dollars to forget the matter. Tompkins was adamant, however, that the amount was too low, and the state assembly finally sued the vice president for the missing moneys.

☆ ☆ ☆

BACK IN WASHINGTON, the Monroe administration and the Democratic-Republicans must have considered this a local squabble, because they renominated Tompkins to a second term as vice president. Actually, in 1820 the nomination for vice president had more than its usual insignificance; the Democratic-Republicans could have nominated Monroe and his horse and still have won the election, because Monroe and Tompkins ran unopposed. After the Federalists did nothing to support the war—giving the impression that they were willing to turn the keys back over to the British king—they were quite literally history, and the party folded.

The electorate was as oblivious to the serious standing accusations of embezzlement against Tompkins as his party, and the team of Monroe and Tompkins won 231 of the 232 electoral votes cast.

Even in the moment of greatest national political victory, Tompkins could not bear to let his actions in the War of 1812 be covered with the stain of mudslinging. He was too despondent to return to Washington to take his oath of office and was instead sworn in at his home on Staten Island in a private ceremony. (Actually he was sworn in twice. Because March 4—the day he was to be sworn in—was a Sunday, Tompkins arranged to have the oath administered on Saturday, March 3. He learned after the ceremony that Monroe wasn't being sworn in until March 5, and he had to repeat the ceremony on that Monday.)

Tompkins tried to wash his troubles away with liquor, and he became, in the words of one observer, "a degraded sot." Tompkins was suffering what he admitted were "toilsome days, sleepless nights." The few times that he did return to Washington to take his place at the head of the Senate, he was often drunk in his chair and, at times, even too drunk to call for a vote on a bill after debate had ended. After one of his visits, another observer said, "I don't think he was perfectly sober during his stay here." In 1823 the Senate elected a president pro tempore to serve in Tompkins's absence, and Tompkins never again set foot in the Capitol. A year after Tompkins's term ended, he died broke and drunk at age 51.

IT TURNS OUT that after his political career was shattered, his reputation forever soiled, and after he died a young but worn-out man, Tompkins may have been right all along. The state of New York went back and did some refiguring and found that they owed Tompkins nearly one hundred thousand dollars, which was virtually the amount Tompkins had claimed was due to him. Daniel D. Tompkins, the hero of the War of 1812, paid the ultimate price because of a bureaucratic blunder.

JOHN CALDWELL
CALHOUN

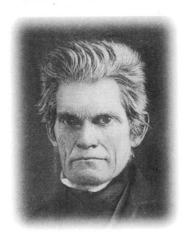

Served with John Quincy Adams, 1825–29;

Andrew Jackson, 1829–32

Democratic-Republican from South Carolina

UNLIKE THE VICE PRESIDENCY'S PLACE IN THE CAREERS OF CLINTON, GERRY, AND TOMPKINS, NO ONE CONSIDERED THE VICE PRESIDENCY TO BE THE APEX OF JOHN C. CALHOUN'S CAREER. The southern orator was only 40 years old when elected to the office, and nearly everyone in the country—especially John

5 3

Calhoun—expected the young vice president to go much farther in his career.

But John Calhoun's ambition was stymied by a widowed tart, a stubborn wife, and a political magician. Before his tenure as vice president was over, Calhoun would become the first vice president to resign, and his president would say with all sincerity that he wished to see Calhoun hanged.

☆ ☆ ☆

IN 1824 THE Federalist party was defunct, and because there was only one political party left, the country entered into what was known as the Era of Good Feelings. Having only one party didn't mean that the voters didn't have a choice for president, though, and it certainly didn't mean that all the politicians were singing in harmony.

John Quincy Adams, providing evidence that arrogance is perhaps an inherited trait, told everyone that he assumed he would follow James Monroe as president. Plenty of people didn't agree with John Q.'s order of succession, and it seemed that most of them were also seeking the job. As the election drew near, the race was down to five men: Adams, Andrew Jackson, Henry Clay, William Crawford, and John C. Calhoun.

Calhoun was a dashing young southern aristocrat, and he was also one of the country's craftiest political thinkers. Seeing that he was unlikely to successfully challenge Adams or Andrew Jackson for the top job, he decided to ensure that the vice presidency would be his.

Calhoun approached John Q. Adams and offered his support in exchange for the vice presidency. Adams had originally wanted Andrew Jackson as his running mate, and his supporters had even worked up a campaign slogan: John Quincy

Adams Who Can Write, Andrew Jackson Who Can Fight. But Jackson was looking more and more like a major contender for the title himself, and Adams accepted Calhoun's offer.

John C. then approached Andrew Jackson and made the same offer: his support in exchange for a place on the ticket. Naturally, this didn't go over well back at Adams's campaign headquarters. John Quincy wrote some of his supporters: "Calhoun's game now is to unite Jackson's supporters and mine on him for vice president. Look out for breakers." But Andy Jackson was amused by Calhoun's chutzpah, and since neither Adams nor Jackson thought the choice of vice president mattered all that much, they both agreed to the deal.

Calhoun had no burning desire to become vice president; his goal was still to become president. Calhoun thought that the support for the four remaining candidates was so evenly split that neither the electoral college nor the House of Representatives would be able to reach a decision on whom to name as president, and that as inauguration day drew near, Vice President-elect Calhoun would be named the president by default. His plan nearly worked.

When the votes were counted, Andrew Jackson had won the most popular votes and the most electoral-college votes, but he didn't have a majority and therefore could not win the election. The decision on whom to name as president was turned over to the House of Representatives, which was to choose among the three top vote getters: Jackson, Adams, and Crawford.

Henry Clay held thirty-seven electoral-college votes, and suddenly Jackson and Adams both remembered how much they had always enjoyed the company of Mr. Clay. When he threw his support to Adams, many cynical political commentators said that there had been a "corrupt bargain," with Adams promising a prominent position in his new administration if he were to be named president. Adams staunchly denied that any such deal had been struck.

Even with Clay's votes, the vote in the House looked as if it would be extremely close. The decision finally came down to the vote of a single man, Stephen Van Rensselaer, who didn't want the responsibility. Fellow congressmen found Van Rensselaer nearly in tears trying to make up his mind. Van Rensselaer wrote out his vote for Crawford, but he didn't have the courage to turn it in. Finally he placed his head on his desk and prayed for a sign. When he lifted his head, he saw a discarded ballot on the floor that had *Adams* written on it. He picked the ballot up off the floor and put it in the ballot box, and John Quincy was declared the winner.

☆ ☆ ☆

AS PRESIDENT OF the Senate, Calhoun was extremely conscientious. He came up with a new term of address for the congressmen, calling them senators (instead of gentlemen) for the first time. During the 1827–28 session he didn't miss a single day, often sitting in his chair for stretches of eight to twelve hours. Calhoun's discipline was especially impressive considering the subtle, and sometimes not so subtle, remarks he was forced to endure about his own ambitions to become president. "Mr. Vice President, and would-be Mr. President," John Randolph of Virginia once addressed the chair, adding, "which God in his infinite mercy prevent."

It was his silence to another outburst by Senator Randolph that drove a wedge between Calhoun and President Adams. Randolph was a frequent critic of the Adams administration and the "corrupt bargain" (okay, it seems Adams did name Henry Clay secretary of state, but that still doesn't mean there was a deal). In one particularly venomous fit, Randolph described Secretary of State Clay and President Adams as "the blackleg and the Puritan."

President Adams instructed his vice president to rule Randolph out of order to stifle Randolph's umbrage, but Calhoun refused, claiming that to do so would be to limit debate. Then a curious thing happened: A letter appeared in the local newspaper condemning Calhoun for allowing the verbal attacks to continue, saying that Calhoun had "permitted John Randolph, day after day, in speeches ten hours long, to drink himself drunk with bottled porter, and in raving balderdash . . . to revile the absent and the present, the living and the dead. This was tolerated by Calhoun because Randolph's ribaldry was all pointed against the administration, especially Mr. Clay and me, and because he was afraid of Randolph." The letter was signed *Patrick Henry*, who had died a quarter of a century before. The author was obviously Mr. J. Q. Adams, who as president could not stoop to argue such a petty senatorial bit of bombast but whose ego could not stand to let such words fly by without appropriate opprobrium.

The letter was rebutted with equally well-stated logic in another letter signed *Onslow* (the great Speaker of the House of Commons). Calhoun left little doubt that he was Onslow, and the fight was on. The public was thrilled to watch a catfight between the nation's top executive officers as letter after letter appeared in the papers.

☆ ☆ ☆

VICE PRESIDENT CALHOUN succeeded in so thoroughly antagonizing President Adams that the Jackson forces decided to follow the misguided political aphorism The Enemy of My Enemy Is My Friend and offered Calhoun the nomination for vice president.

Calhoun was growing tired of holding his tongue in the senatorial debates, however, and was about to turn down the Jacksonians' offer, when the Jackson supporters pointed out that Old Hickory didn't have the same spring in his step as he once did and that the old general could very well be dead within a year. That argument was good enough to convince Calhoun to run for vice president a second time.

The success of the Jackson-Calhoun ticket provided an embarrassing defeat for John Quincy Adams. Not only did he lose to his own vice president's ticket, he joined his father as the only two presidents (up to that point) to be denied second terms. Adding further insult, following the election, the town of Adams, New Hampshire, near Adams's home state of Massachusetts, voted to change its name to Jackson.

WITH THE ELECTION of Andrew Jackson, Washington was treated to a spectacle unlike any it—or John Calhoun—had ever seen. Jackson was a wealthy planter and quite the aristocrat by frontier standards, but Calhoun and the rest of Washington society were horrified by the rough-hewn inauguration celebration. Following his inauguration, Jackson opened up the White House to the common man, and everyone seemed to be having a competition to prove just how common they were. Jackson's supporters stood atop chairs with their boots on, broke the china and crystal, and spat tobacco juice on the carpets—and the men were even worse. The party ended only when White House servants put tubs of hooch out on the front lawn and locked the doors behind the rabble when they ran outside.

Although many in Washington were aghast at the behavior of Andrew Jackson's friends, the new cabinet officers and their wives were almost too busy with another social problem to even notice the etiquette carnage.

Jackson's new secretary of war, John Eaton, had taken a disreputable barmaid as his new wife, and none of the new cabinet officers or their wives were willing to sit down to dinner with either of them.

The woman in question, Peggy O'Neal Eaton, was the daughter of a Washington, D.C., tavern owner and had built her local reputation as a tart while still a teenager. John Eaton conducted an affair with Peggy while her husband, a navy officer, was conveniently at sea—where he soon died. Just before the election Andrew Jackson advised Eaton to marry the widow in order to quell the gossip, but that wasn't good enough for proper Washington society. A delegation of congressmen tried to stop Jackson from appointing Eaton to his cabinet, but Jackson replied, "Do you suppose that I have been sent here by the people to consult the ladies of Washington as to the proper persons to compose my cabinet?" and went on about his business.

Jackson had taken the fight for Peggy's reputation quite personally, because there had been similar rumors about his marriage to his wife, Rachel. Jackson, in fact, had once killed a man in a duel over a slanderous comment about his wife's reputation. Rachel Jackson had died an untimely death between the election and the inauguration, and Jackson publicly blamed her death on the years of slander and innuendo she had been forced to endure. Jackson was not about to back down on the issue.

The commander of the anti-Peggy forces was Floride Calhoun, the nation's second lady, who refused to attend social functions to which Pothouse Peg had been invited. The president decided to reason with the enemy by visiting the vice president's home and talking with Mrs. Calhoun. Floride listened patiently while President Jackson stated his case, then cooly turned to her butler and said, "Show this gentleman to the door." In fact, Floride was so overcome by the thought of an offense to her delicate southern nature that she left Washington for South Carolina because she was afraid that she might see Peggy walking down the street.

Into the fray stepped Secretary of State Martin Van Buren. Van Buren was the ultimate political opportunist, and he saw the brouhaha over Peggy's honor as a way to solidify his position in the Jackson administration. He had already won Jackson's trust by praising Peggy as the perfect young mother and by hosting parties in her honor. When these tactics didn't end the crisis, Van Buren came up with another plan.

At Van Buren's suggestion, and with his help, Jackson asked his entire cabinet to submit their resignations, and the president was able to pick an entirely new cabinet. At one subsequent Washington dinner, a toast was heard: "To the next cabinet. May they all be bachelors—or leave their wives at home."

For his role in this, future vice president Martin Van Buren earned the nickname "the magician" because, it was said, he made Jackson's entire cabinet disappear. With the Eaton affair behind them, Jackson wrote to his new best pal Van Buren that "Calhoun & Co. are politically dead." This turned out to be just a presidential pipe dream.

☆ ☆ ☆

AS IF THESE personal battles weren't enough, Jackson and Calhoun began to have strong philosophical differences as well. Calhoun had begun to play with the explosive concept of nullification, which held that if a state didn't like a federal law (say, on the topic of slavery) it could pass one to override the federal statute. So strong were his feelings that while vice president, Calhoun secretly wrote a treatise on the subject, *The South Carolina Exposition and Protest*, which basically called for the dissolution of the very Constitution he had sworn to uphold. To Jackson and the majority of the American people, the idea of nullification was tantamount to treason, and it was, in fact, the philosophical precursor of the Civil War.

Leave it to Van Buren to hatch a scheme to flush Calhoun out on the issue. At a large banquet commemorating Jefferson Day, Jackson stood and offered a toast that had been written for him by Van Buren. Looking straight at his vice president, Jackson said, "Our Union—It must be preserved." Calhoun glared at the president, and then rose slowly and replied, "To the Union—Next to our liberties, most dear."

Taken at face value the toasts seem to be quite harmless, but everyone in attendance, including Jackson and Calhoun, knew the true meaning behind the words. A reporter at the dinner said that "an order to arrest Calhoun where he sat could not have come with more blinding, staggering force."

Shortly thereafter, Jackson discovered (thanks again to Van Buren) that while Calhoun was secretary of war during the Seminole War of 1818, he had tried to have then General Jackson court-martialed when he pushed the battles into Spanish Florida. President Jackson confronted his vice president, who admitted it was true, adding lamely, "I never questioned your patriotism nor questioned your motives."

Jackson couldn't believe that Calhoun could actively seek his court-martial in 1818 and then run with him as vice president eleven years later. "I never expected to have occasion to say to you, *Et tu, Brute?*" Jackson said.

☆ ☆ ☆

POLITICAL GAMESMANSHIP HAD always been a particular skill of Calhoun's, but in one of his final acts as vice president, Calhoun made what may be the biggest strategic fumble in American history.

President Jackson nominated his trusted friend Martin Van Buren for the cushy post of ambassador to England, but Jackson's opponents in the Senate were able to raise enough questions about Van Buren's fitness to hold the position that the vote on Van Buren's confirmation resulted in a tie. With fiendish delight, the vice president struck a blow against Jackson and Van Buren by voting "No!" and, gleefully springing from the podium, shouting: "That will kill him, Sir, kill him dead! He will never kick, Sir, never kick!"

Senator Thomas Hart Benton, realizing Calhoun's mistake, pointed out that the only office Jackson could then find for Van Buren would be Calhoun's. "You have broken a minister," Benton said, "and elected a vice president."

☆ ☆ ☆

LOCKED OUT OF all political discussion in Washington, and with his chances of reelection at absolute zero, Calhoun began promoting his theories of nullification back home in South Carolina. In 1832 the South Carolina legislature used the principle to de-

clare federal tariffs void in their state. President
Jackson responded by putting two hundred thousand federal troops on alert and telling the troublemakers in South Carolina that there soon wouldn't
be anything left to tax if they continued with their
rebellion. He added that he would hang Calhoun "as
high as Haman" for his part in the revolt.

Calhoun held no political value outside his home
state, and, finding his situation intolerable, he resigned nine weeks before his term as vice president
was to end and returned to the Senate when one of
the South Carolina seats became vacant.

☆ ☆ ☆

IN HIS LAST days Andrew Jackson was asked by
a minister if he had any regrets from his term as
president. "I can tell you, I can tell you," Old Hickory
said, "posterity will condemn me more because I was
persuaded not to hang John C. Calhoun as a traitor
than for any other act in my life!"

MARTIN
VAN BUREN

Served with Andrew Jackson, 1833–37

Democrat from New York

ARTIN VAN BUREN WAS THE "EDDIE HASKELL" OF AMERICAN POLITICS; SMARMY DUPLICITY WAS HIS CALLING CARD.

Some men saw through Van Buren's act. Davy Crockett wrote that when Van Buren was just one year of age he already could "cry out of one side of his face and laugh out of the other," and at every turn Van Buren seemed to pick up nicknames that

referred to his treachery: He was called the American Talleyrand, the Red Fox of Kinderhook, and
Little Magician. But Van Buren managed to fool Andrew Jackson, the most popular—and most powerful—president of the nineteenth century, and Van
Buren knew whence his fortune came.

VAN BUREN MAY have got his genes for political
mischief from the best: Aaron Burr. Although Van
Buren's legal father was a tavern keeper in Kinderhook, New York, there were many rumors that
Aaron Burr, a frequent visitor to the inn, was actually the boy's father. Even John Quincy Adams
wrote in his diary that he thought the story was true.

Some said that Van Buren even looked a bit like
Aaron Burr. Van Buren was short, and his shiny
head was flanked by unruly white hair and muttonchop sideburns. He enjoyed wearing the finest clothes and by several accounts was a bit of a
dandy.

U.S. Congressman Davy Crockett was disgusted
by Van Buren's appearance, saying that if it wasn't
for Van Buren's whiskers, one couldn't tell whether
he was a man or a woman. Several people even
claimed that natty Matty Van Buren wore a woman's
corset, but considering that in that pretelegenic age
a prominent abdomen was considered something of
a badge of distinction for the better class of fellow,
this is likely just mean gossip.

VAN BUREN BEGAN his political career by joining
a fledgling group known as The Tammany Society,
which later began calling itself Tammany Hall. He
later formed his own political machine called the Albany regency, which had many friends. In return for

political support, the machine gave out patronage jobs, many with nonexistent duties.

Through his position as the head of the state regency, Van Buren was able to get appointed to the Senate. Within ten years, Martin had gained enough political clout on Capitol Hill to get himself named as campaign manager for his party's presidential nominee, Andrew Jackson.

It is thanks to Martin Van Buren that the country's quadrennial search for leadership is an exercise in superficiality. As Jackson's campaign manager, Van Buren led a group that was short on political discourse but long on gimmickry. Jackson's followers went around planting hickory trees and waving hickory canes and hickory poles, all to show their support of Old Hickory. The citizenry didn't want a campaign of ideas, they wanted to have fun, and Martin Van Buren saw to it that they got what they wanted.

Van Buren wasn't the type of man to be content with operating behind the scenes—at the same time that he was running Jackson's campaign he was running for governor of New York himself. He won his election and took his place as governor, but when Jackson ousted J. Q. Adams, Van Buren showed the citizens of New York how much their votes had meant to him by leaving the governorship after serving just a few months to take a job in the Jackson administration as secretary of state.

Van Buren wasted no time in purring at the president's feet. When everyone else in Jackson's cabinet shunned the vivacious "Pothouse" Peggy Eaton, Van Buren became Peggy's trusted friend. Van Buren began visiting the Eatons, and on one occasion he casually mentioned that he had been spending a great deal of time reading and thinking about the characteristics of great men. The Little Magician leaned close to Peggy and told her that he had finally decided that President Andrew Jackson was the greatest man who had ever lived. But he quickly told Peggy to never tell the president what he had said. Of course, Peggy couldn't wait to tell Jackson, and when the president heard the news, he was so moved that tears welled up in his eyes.

Van Buren became a trusted adviser to Jackson, while still managing to keep his own opinions and ambitions hidden ("rowing to his object with muffled oars," as John Randolph put it) even when he was placed under intense public scrutiny. Although Van Buren orchestrated Jackson's famous toast at the 1830 Jefferson Day dinner as a way of pushing aside Vice President Calhoun, he refrained from aligning himself too closely with Jackson's pro-Union stance. "Mutual forbearance and reciprocal concessions" was Van Buren's stand.

After Van Buren slayed Calhoun's career he began working to push out the only other member of the Jackson administration who posed a threat to his power: Secretary of War John Eaton.

After several days of drawing up his courage and waiting for the proper moment, Van Buren put his plan in action while out riding horses with the president and Eaton. "General," he said, "there is but one thing that can give you peace."

Jackson fell for the bait and asked, "What is that, sir?"

"My resignation," Van Buren replied.

Jackson was incredulous. "Never, sir!" he said, but Van Buren insisted that they take the matter up with other trusted members of the cabinet the next morning.

The next day, Jackson asked his friend John Eaton to join the discussion. When Van Buren again presented his offer to step aside, Eaton blurted out, "This is all wrong! I am the one who ought to resign," at which point Van Buren coolly asked how Mrs. Eaton would react to her husband's resignation.

With the departures of Van Buren and Eaton, President Jackson felt justified in asking for the resignations of his entire cabinet.

☆ ☆ ☆

ALTHOUGH VAN BUREN had abdicated the position of secretary of state, he had no intention of leaving government. To reward Van Buren for his loyalty, Jackson tried to name him as the new minister to Great Britain, but once Calhoun had foiled that plan Jackson decided that an even better spot for Van Buren would be as his second in command.

No doubt both Jackson and Van Buren took pleasure in the latter's becoming the presiding officer of the body that just a few months earlier had declared him unfit for government duty. This did make for some bitter feelings, however. When Van Buren rushed to the Capitol to take his place as vice president, some newspapers around the country reported that unnamed sources claimed that Van Buren's urgency was necessary to prevent "the chair from the disgrace of being occupied by that bloated mass of corruption—Poindexter." (Had Van Buren been tardy in taking his seat in the Senate, Mississippi Senator George Poindexter would have taken over as the president pro tem.)

When George Poindexter read this, he asked Van Buren to offer his assurances that this was not the case; Van Buren told Poindexter that he shouldn't believe everything he read in the newspaper. President Jackson and a few other senators thought that this answer might not be sufficiently apologetic to appease the hotheaded Poindexter, and they were afraid that George might try to settle things in the time-honored tradition of the Congress by resorting to some violent act. Therefore, in order to protect himself, the newly elected vice president showed up for work on his first day wearing a brace of pistols, locked and loaded.

As vice president, Van Buren continued believing that "opacity is the best policy" and refused to offer his ideas on the topics of the day. Henry Clay, however, one of the wise old men and great orators of the Senate, thought that the vice president might disagree with his president on the issue of whether to renew funds for the Bank of the United States. He decided to confront the vice president on the Senate floor. In an impassioned speech, Clay attacked the president's policy and implored Van Buren to go to President Jackson and offer his advice. When Clay had finished, everyone in attendance turned to hear Van Buren's reply. Instead, the vice president quietly asked someone to take his seat at the head of the Senate, stepped off the podium, and walked down the aisle to the desk of the honorable Mr. Clay.

"Mr. Clay, may I borrow a pinch of your excellent snuff?" he asked calmly. When Clay offered his snuffbox, Van Buren took a pinch, gave a loud sniff of contempt, and strolled out of the Senate chamber.

☆ ☆ ☆

WHEN ANDREW JACKSON completed his second term as president, he was so popular that he was able to virtually appoint his successor. He chose his vice president and good friend, Martin Van Buren. Although Davy Crockett, U.S. congressman from Andrew Jackson's home state of Tennessee, tried to convince the folks back home that Van Buren was "as opposite to General Jackson as dung is to a diamond," enough people voted for Martin that he easily won the election.

On Van Buren's triumphant inaugural day, he still seemed a bit small. Following his inaugural speech, there was polite applause, but the spectators broke into wild cheers when Old Hickory appeared. "For once the rising sun was eclipsed by the setting sun," Senator Thomas Hart Benton commented.

Van Buren's bland ambition had carried him all the way to the presidency, but once there, Van Buren, who had made a career out of vague promises, had no plan, no ideas. He also had few supporters in government, because no one was sure of exactly what he hoped to accomplish. The country was having economic difficulties when Van Buren was elected, and under his uncertain hand, the difficulties turned into a full-scale depression.

Van Buren was turned out of the White House in 1840, losing the electoral-college vote 234 to 60 to Whig (the party formed to oppose the Jacksonian Democrats) William Henry Harrison. Van Buren tried for the presidency again in 1844, but his party refused to renominate the ex-president. Finally, in 1848 Van Buren convinced the Free-Soilers, an upstart political party, to make him their presidential nominee. Van Buren failed to carry a single state, and in fact, he didn't receive a single vote in any state except Virginia, where he gathered a total of nine.

Van Buren and the Free-Soilers were embarrassed by the low vote count in Virginia, and they claimed that the vote had been fraudulent. "Yes, fraud!" agreed one Virginian. "And we're still looking for that son of a bitch who voted nine times!"

RICHARD MENTOR

JOHNSON

Served with Martin Van Buren, 1837–41

Democrat from Kentucky

THE MOST VULGAR MAN OF ALL VULGAR MEN IN THIS WORLD" WAS HOW THE DOOR-KEEPER OF THE SENATE DESCRIBED THE NINTH VICE PRESIDENT of the United States, Richard Mentor Johnson, and considering the poor man's post, he was surely something of an expert on the subject.

Johnson had been handpicked for the vice

presidency by outgoing president Andrew Jackson, and although Old Hickory was known to be a bit rough around the edges—even by the prevailing community standards of the 1830s—Richard Mentor Johnson was not a politically correct kind of guy.

Johnson's biggest claim to fame was that he had killed an Indian, albeit a famous Indian chief named Tecumseh. Congressman Johnson was a war hawk during the War of 1812, and when it appeared that not everyone in the country was doing his part to give another slap to the British, Johnson left his seat in the House of Representatives to lead a regiment of men from Kentucky to Detroit into battle against the British and their mercenary Indian fighters.

Johnson and his horse were both wounded in a skirmish that preceded the actual battle. He told his men to leave him at the site, adding, "Don't return until you bring me tidings of victory." At some point during the ensuing battle, the great Indian chief Tecumseh was shot and killed. With bullets flying in several directions from the British, Indian, and Kentuckian combatants, it might have been virtually impossible to discern exactly who had fired the fatal ball, but Johnson quickly took credit, and as he was the commanding officer, no one contradicted him.

As the years passed, the old Bluegrass soldiers embellished the exploits of themselves and Colonel Johnson so much that, by 1829, an account was published that had Johnson outnumbered three to one, having been shot and wounded twenty-five times but nonetheless riding his horse into the battle to seek out the hated Tecumseh.

Johnson made no effort to discount the most outrageous versions of the battle, and in fact, when a five-act play was produced that celebrated the slaughter of the Indian, Johnson bragged that he had "more friends than ever by the hundreds."

☆ ☆ ☆

BORN IN BEARGRASS, Kentucky, Johnson liked to claim that he had been "born in a cane brake and cradled in a saptrough," which must have brought sympathetic memories to the minds of the Bluegrass electorate, because the citizens of the commonwealth of Kentucky first sent Johnson to Congress when he was just 26 years old.

As a congressman, in addition to killing a famous Indian, Johnson was best known for his favorite issues: He advocated a seven-day workweek for postal employees (he said that receiving letters made him feel good, why not get them every day?), and, because he was just a few dollars from bankruptcy most of his life, he labored to eliminate debtors' prisons and to increase the pay of congressmen.

It was during his tenure in the U.S. House of Representatives that Richard Mentor Johnson managed to offend the mores of polite and not-so-polite society by his choice of bed companions. Johnson had fallen in love with a working woman back home in Kentucky, but his mother had forbidden him to continue his relationship with such a poor choice of a potential mate. Johnson, apparently hoping to send his mother to an early grave, then took as his common-law wife a slave woman named Julia Chinn, whom he had inherited from his recently deceased father.

Johnson lived with this woman for many years and had two daughters with her whom he treated as his own instead of as mere farm property—much to the distress of his Kentucky neighbors. And when his daughters married (both to white men), Johnson gave each of them a large tract of land as a wedding present.

When Julia died in 1833 during a cholera epidemic, Johnson looked no farther than his own plantation and took another of his slaves as his next wife. This woman had the audacity to run off with her common-law husband. Johnson tracked her down, however, and took her to a slave auction where he sold her. Johnson then brought the woman's sister into his house to function as his third slave wife.

At least the third woman might not have gone against her will, because it has been reported that she referred to Johnson as "my dear Colonel." According to some reports, Vice President Johnson wasn't as faithful to wife number three as he apparently had been to the first two women, and he coerced several other of his slave women to become his lovers.

☆ ☆ ☆

HISTORIANS HAVE MADE much of the fact that Andrew Jackson's influence and popularity was such in 1836 that he was able to get his vice president, Martin Van Buren, elected to the presidency. It may say much more about Jackson's power that he was able to get Richard Mentor Johnson elected to the vice presidency.

When the Democrats met in Baltimore, Johnson's nomination as the candidate for vice president was met with boos and hisses, and the Virginia delegation stalked out of the convention. This loss was offset by the unanimous support of the Tennessee delegation. Actually, nobody from Tennessee had bothered to attend the convention, but when a traveling businessman from Nashville heard about the doings, he strolled down to the meeting hall and cast all fifteen Tennessee votes for Van Buren and Johnson.

In the end, the delegates seemed to be thinking, "Good God, if this is Jackson's first choice as vice president, who might be his second?" and gave the nomination to R. M. Johnson. Those lyrical Democrats came up with the campaign slogan Rumpsey Dumpsey, Rumpsey Dumpsey, Colonel Johnson Killed Tecumseh and kept their fingers crossed in hopes that Johnson's marital preferences didn't become a campaign issue.

When the voters cast their ballots that winter, Van Buren won the election hands down, gaining 174 electoral votes. Vice-presidential candidate Johnson, on the other hand, came up with just 147, one vote short of a majority. Even Johnson's home state of Kentucky had refused to vote for him.

For the only time in U.S. history, the election of the vice president was handed over to the Senate to decide. The Little Magician—Vice President and President-elect Martin Van Buren—was still the presiding officer of the upper chamber, and he used his influence to get the senators to agree to give the job to Johnson.

If the women of Washington had objected to "Pothouse" Peggy O'Neal Eaton, it is a wonder they didn't set up bonfires and barricades at the city limits to prevent Johnson from touching the dust of the city streets. Johnson didn't spend much time in Washington, however. He used his newfound celebrity as vice president to his personal profit, opening a hotel, tavern, and spa on his Kentucky farm. A visitor to the resort wrote to a member of Van Buren's cabinet that Johnson was a hands-on manager, personally supervising the purchasing of the chickens and eggs and managing the "watermelon selling department." Other reports from Club Johnson said that the Vice Resident was becoming more slovenly and that he had taken another slave, "a young Delilah of about the complexion of Shakespeare's swarthy Othello," as his third wife.

By the time his term was nearing its end, king-maker Jackson decided that Johnson would be "dead wait" on the ticket and instructed the Democrats to drop him from the ticket in the campaign of 1840. Old Hickory did not, however, say who should take Johnson's place, and the Democrats simply left that spot blank, choosing not to nominate anyone for the vice presidency.

Despite what people were saying about him in Washington, Johnson remained popular in Kentucky. In 1850, shortly before his death, he was elected to the state House of Representatives, but unfortunately he was unable to take his seat, because, as a Louisville newspaper reported, "Col. R. M. Johnson is laboring under an attack of dementia, which renders him totally unfit for business."

JOHN TYLER

Served with William Harrison, 1841

Whig from Virginia

JOHN TYLER WAS THE FIRST VICE PRESI-
DENT TO MOVE UP TO THE PRESIDENCY BY
MEANS OF SUCCESSION. When he first heard
that he was the new president of the United States
of America, Tyler was down on his hands and knees,
about to get his knuckles rapped because he had lost
a game of marbles to a gang of prepubescent boys.
From such inauspicious beginnings are mediocre
presidencies made.

☆ ☆ ☆

WILLIAM HENRY HARRISON had been the hero of the Battle of Tippecanoe Creek in Indiana. Killing Native Americans was his biggest qualification for the presidency; at the time of his nomination his most recent job had been as court clerk of Hamilton County, Ohio. He didn't have a national reputation to overcome as did Whig giants Henry Clay and Daniel Webster, however, so he was the right man for the moment.

The Tyler, Too half of the Tippecanoe and . . . slogan was a rich kid from Virginia. He was an aristocratic snob in fine eastern tradition, and so he provided the Whigs with a good balance to the rough-hewn Harrison.

For most of his career Tyler had been a Jacksonian Democrat, but he didn't trust Old Hickory. When Jackson instructed the Democratic senators to remove from the congressional record a personal censure, Tyler suspected that Jackson was trying to become a virtual dictator by extending his authority into Congress, and Tyler resigned rather than comply.

This, naturally, made him a hero to the Whigs, who didn't care one whit about his political philosophy. They decided that anyone who opposed Jackson in such a public way should be rewarded, but the only thing they could find for Tyler was the vice-presidential nomination. He accepted their offer, despite being a Democrat at heart.

Not all Whigs were happy that Tyler was chosen to help lead their party. One said: "Poor Tippecanoe! It was an evil hour that *Tyler, too* was added to make out the line. There was rhyme but no reason to it." But enough Whigs were willing to go along with the decision of the smoke-filled room and went around chanting:

We'll vote for Tyler, therefore,
Without a why or wherefore

Which pretty much summed up the philosophical discourse of the day.

Tall and gangly, Tyler had a long nose, a thin face, and big ears, which gave him the appearance of a wizened old billy goat. He often had colds and frequently suffered from diarrhea. He was not a big hit on the campaign trail.

Up to one hundred thousand people attended Whig rallies, where they sang dozens of songs about the candidates. One of the favorites came complete with choreography:

Old Tip he wears a homespun suit
He has no ruffled shirt, wirt, wirt;
But Matt he has the golden plate,
And he's a little squirt, wirt, wirt.

The genius of this song was that the boys got to spit everytime somebody said "wirt," which may have been a bit hard on the shoe polish but was a terrific amount of fun.

The Democrats, dainty though they may have been compared to the frontier-spirited Whigs, were able to come up with a few songs of their own, one of which went:

Hush-a-bye baby,
Daddy's a Whig,
Before he comes home,
Hard cider he'll swig;
Then he'll be Tipsy,
And over he'll fall,
And down will come Daddy,
Tip, Tyler and all.

The literary efforts of the Democrats were in vain, however. Van Buren was defeated, ending the Jacksonian stranglehold on the executive offices, and replaced by honest-to-goodness Indian fighter William Harrison and his goat-faced sidekick Tyler, Too. Wirt, wirt.

☆ ☆ ☆

WILLIAM HENRY HARRISON had never had the opportunity to give many speeches, so naturally he saw his chance to make a big score with his inaugural address. With a damn the somnolence and full monotone ahead, on that cold and stormy inaugural day Harrison plunged right into his eighty-five-hundred-word, two-hour speech. For his perseverance, the president immediately came down with a terminal cold. He had promised in his inauguration speech to serve only one term if elected president, and Harrison was one politician who kept his word.

When the news reached Vice President Tyler that Harrison had died, he left for Washington immediately, but it took him fifty-six hours to reach the capital, the longest the country has ever been without a chief executive. When Tyler reached Washington, it was as if everyone looked up from their cider with their good eye and said, "Hey, who's this guy?" No one had thought that the president would actually die; if they had, they certainly wouldn't have put John Tyler in line for the job. As one senator put it, Tyler was "a man never thought of for it by anybody."

The men who had written the Constitution had left one point remarkably ambiguous: What exactly was it that the vice president was supposed to do if the president died? The Constitution said that in the event that the president was unable to carry out "the

Powers and Duties of said Office" that "the Same shall devolve on the Vice President." The debate soon centered on grammatical question of linguistic referents.

The Democrats said that *Same* referred to the powers and duties, which meant that Tyler should just handle the paperwork and leave the title for the next tenant of the Oval Office. Tyler and whoever stood to benefit from his promotion said that *Same* referred to *said Office* and that Tyler was the new chief executive.

While everyone stood around arguing with the officials, Tyler picked up the ball and ran into the end zone. He assumed the presidency without so much as even taking the presidential oath—he thought his oath as vice president about covered it—and he packed up his things and moved into the White House. Insisting that he was the president proper, Tyler stamped any correspondence addressed *Acting President* or *Vice president Acting as President* as *addressee unknown* and returned it to the sender.

Congress tried to pass a motion that would have given Tyler the official title Acting President, but the motion was defeated. When that didn't work, they tried to impeach him. Tyler ignored them. Congress finally did get the legislative version of the last laugh when they refused to pay for the president's heat and other living expenses.

Tyler, Too couldn't even get respect from his own cabinet. At the first meeting of the new administration, Daniel Webster said that he and the other cabinet officers had decided that they should operate as a council, with each member, including the president, having just one vote. Shortly thereafter, his entire cabinet—except Webster, who was broke and needed a job—resigned. Before his term ended, Tyler had run through twenty-three men for just six cabinet posts, a record that still stands.

As if having to constantly put out help-wanted ads for his cabinet wasn't humiliating enough for the president, when Tyler went so far as to vote against his party's major legislative effort, he was stripped of his Whiggery. He thus became the only president in U.S. history without a party affiliation.

☆ ☆ ☆

BY 1844, TYLER'S cabinet had resigned, Congress had tried to impeach him, no party would claim him, and his opponents were calling him the Accident of an Accident and the Executive Ass. But John didn't care. He thought the world was a wonderful place full of wonderful people. Tyler was in love.

After the death of his wife early in his presidency, Tyler had fallen hopelessly in love with a 23-year-old actress, Juliana Gardiner. Tyler was thirty years older than Juliana, but that didn't stop him from pursuing her relentlessly. He began courting her shortly after his wife died, and he even proposed marriage to her at the 1843 Washington Day Ball. The ingenue turned down the offer to be the nation's first lady. She changed her way of thinking, however, when cupid's arrow came flying with the explosion of a cannon.

They were both on board the frigate *Princeton* for a reception when one of the ship's twelve-inch guns blew up. A state senator and a couple of cabinet members were killed, but as Huck Finn might have described it, no people were hurt. Juliana was thrown into Tyler's arms by the blast, and he was there to comfort her over the loss of the state senator—her father.

Soon after, Juliana agreed to marry Tyler. Not

everyone thought it was a good idea. One of Tyler's friends advised him, "You are too far advanced in life to be imprudent in a love-scrape." Tyler protested: "Pooh! Why, dear sir, I am just full in my prime!"

"Yes," said his friend, "you are now in your prime . . . but when she is in her prime, where then will your prime be?"

Juliana Tyler went on to be one of the most flamboyant first ladies. She assumed a regal air and assembled a court of a dozen maids of honor. Whenever someone called on her, she received the visitor sitting on a dais, wearing a crown of flowers, with her ladies surrounding her. Senators Daniel Webster and John Calhoun played right along, addressing her as Mrs. Presidentress.

She even went so far as to have the band wake up and play "Hail to the Chief" whenever the president walked into the room, and she convinced Tyler to waltz with her, an activity he had thought "vulgar."

☆ ☆ ☆

AFTER TYLER LEFT the presidency, he found time to have seven children with Juliana. Combined with the eight from his first marriage, Tyler fathered fifteen children in all, the most of any U.S. president or vice president. Tyler was 70 years old when his youngest child was born—Tyler was born while Washington was president—and that child lived to see the presidency of Harry Truman.

With no political party to claim him, Tyler's career lay fallow for fifteen years. Then when his home state Virginia broke from the Union, Tyler, who had sworn to always uphold the U.S. Constitution, took a seat in the Confederate House of Representatives. He died a short time later, and the U.S. government refused to bury him with honors, the only president who has had this privilege denied. Tyler did receive a Confederate state funeral, however, and he was buried with a Confederate flag draped over his coffin. When Tyler died, his last words may have reflected the sentiments of many: "Perhaps it is best."

"I'M IN CONTROL HERE"

The Twenty-fifth Amendment

to the

U.S. Constitution

Since the death of William Henry Harrison in 1841, people had been wondering what to do when the president died. The writers of the U.S. Constitution were remarkably vague on this point. Harrison's vice president, John Tyler, put the issue on the back burner by his aggressive assumption of the full presidency. But in the middle of the twentieth century the bastard office of "acting president" again became a political possibility, and presidents began reexamining the Tyler precedent.

It may have been Bobby Kennedy, attorney general for his brother John Kennedy, who forced a permanent resolution. Bobby was known to hold extreme animosity toward Lyndon Johnson, and while Johnson was vice president, the younger Kennedy had the Justice

Department staff research Article II of the Constitution. Kennedy said that if his brother were to die in office, only the duties of the presidency, and not the office itself, should go to Lyndon Johnson. This position appeared to throw one hundred years of presidential precedent on the trash heap.

Although no one tried to force a constitutional crisis in the hours following John Kennedy's assassination, some members of Congress realized just how close the country had come to that paralyzing occurrence. Just three weeks after the Kennedy assassination, Democratic senator Birch Bayh of Indiana proposed what would become the Twenty-fifth Amendment to the Constitution.

The amendment said explicitly, "In case of the removal of the president from office or of his death or resignation, the Vice President shall become President." (Before this was spelled out, what did people think the vice president was for?) The amendment also specified that if there were a vacancy in the vice presidency, the president should nominate someone for the office, and that person could assume the office only with the blessing of both the Senate and the House of Representatives. The amendment further stated that the president can designate the vice president as an acting president if he knows he will be unable to carry out his duties for a time; and if the vice president and a majority of the cabinet officers agree that the president is not carrying out the duties of his office, they can recommend his removal without his consent, with Congress having twenty-one days to decide the matter.

The amendment was approved by the required three quarters of the state legislatures in February of 1967 and was signed into law a few days later by President Lyndon Johnson.

Although the Twenty-fifth Amendment worked to perfection in the aftermath of the Watergate scandal, there was a bizarre mix-up during Ronald Reagan's first term as president.

When Reagan was shot in the first weeks of his presidency, White House staff were near panic as Vice President Bush flew back to Washington from Texas, where he had been scheduled to speak. When reporters asked White House spokesman Larry Speakes who was acting as president, Speakes said that he couldn't answer the question. Upon hearing this, Secretary of State Al Haig rushed to the podium and announced, "Constitutionally, gentlemen, you have the president, the vice president, and the secretary of state in that order. . . . As of now, I am in control here, in the White House, pending return of the vice president. . . ."

Leaving the pressroom, Secretary of Defense Casper Weinberger told Haig that he had things a bit facts-backward, and the two men got into a heated argument over who was next in line for the presidency. "Look, you better go home and read your Constitution, *buddy*," Haig told Weinberger. "That's the way it is."

In fact, in discussing the order of succession, the Constitution doesn't even mention the secretary of state or anybody other than the vice president, but in 1947, Congress had passed legislation that set the line of succession as the vice president, the Speaker of the House of Representatives, and then the president pro tempore of the Senate. The line then proceeds through the fourteen cabinet officers, with the secretary of veteran affairs at the bottom of the totem pole.

Bush never did take over as acting president during that crisis, but the Twenty-fifth Amendment was apparently used later when Reagan was under anesthesia during cancer surgery. Even then there was controversy. Although Bush was acting president for the eight hours of Reagan's surgery, Reagan claimed that because the Twenty-fifth Amendment made no allowance for such brief periods of incapacity, the Constitution had not been invoked in the arrangement, leading one to wonder under what authority such an arrangement was made.

Although the Twenty-fifth Amendment settled many questions about the vice presidency, as the world changes and unforeseen situations arise, new questions about the vice president's powers are sure to crop up as well.

GEORGE MIFFLIN

DALLAS

Served with James Polk, 1845–49

Democrat from Pennsylvania

HOW ABOUT MY BROTHER-IN-LAW?" WAS THE RALLYING CRY THAT BROUGHT THE NATION'S ELEVENTH VICE PRESIDENCY TO GEORGE MIFFLIN DALLAS OF PENNSYL-VANIA.

Although the urbane Dallas gained some notoriety by lending his name to the city that would eventually offer the country bad television drama and semipornographic cheerleaders, he was a political unknown until a fortuitous bit of nepotism brought him one pulse away from the presidency.

In 1844, when the Democrats met in Baltimore's Odd Fellows Hall (quite apropos, many in the country thought), they had a terrible time deciding whom they wanted to push on the electorate as their next candidates. President Martin Van Buren would have been the obvious choice, since he was the incumbent president and also happened to be a Democrat, but not all in the party were convinced that he was still the right man for the job. After nine exhausting ballots they chose James Polk of Tennessee as their nominee.

Polk had attended the convention hoping to grab the vice president's job; neither he nor anyone else dreamed that he would end up with the presidential nomination. When a congressman from Polk's home state of Tennessee heard about Polk's nomination, he filed this report: "We are more disposed to laugh at it here than to treat it seriously."

For the second spot the Democrats didn't dally nearly as long. Because Polk was from the South, they needed a Northerner in order to achieve geographic balance, and the Democrats selected Silas Wright of New York to be the next vice president of the United States. There was one catch: They hadn't asked Wright whether he wanted the job.

The Democrats decided to inform Silas of his good fortune by using the latest in electronic technology, a device called the electromagnetic telegraph. Samuel Morse and his associates had just set up a telegraph line from Baltimore to the Capitol, and word of the nomination was flashed at the speed of light to Wright, who was in the Senate chamber.

When he received the message, Wright was not amused. He was solidly for Van Buren and against slavery and had no intention of deviating from either position. Wright announced that he would not ride shotgun "on the black pony [slavery] at the funeral procession of my slaughtered friend" and instructed Morse's helpers to send his refusal back to Baltimore via the same wires.

The delegates to the convention were incredulous that someone would turn down the nomination of their party for vice president. They sent the message again, and again the reply came back "dit-dot-dit-dit-dit—NO!" The conventioneers immediately knew what the problem was: The damn machine didn't work! They assumed that Morse's telegraph was garbling the message, and they sent the nomination committee to Washington to get the answer straight. When the delegates arrived in Washington, Wright wrote out a formal letter of rejection, and because it was too late at night for the trains to run, the letter was sent back to the convention via horse and wagon. By the time Wright's message reached the convention, most of the delegates had got tired of sitting around waiting for a would-be vice president and had gone home. Of the twenty-three delegates sent by Ohio, for example, only one remained to see the thing through to the end.

The party leaders were in a quandary. They had no vice-presidential nominee and almost no delegates. After many shrugged shoulders and looks of dismay, Robert Walker of Mississippi came to the rescue of the caucus by suggesting to the weary delegates that his brother-in-law, George Dallas, might make a good nominee.

Up to that point Dallas had been mayor of Philadelphia, had served part of one term in the U.S. Senate on an interim basis, and had been the minister to Russia for two years (he had become bored in Moscow and had asked to be recalled halfway through his term). The delegates said Good enough! and made Dallas the nominee on the second ballot.

At 5:30 the next morning, George Dallas was awakened by a group of drunken revelers pounding on his door. He opened the door in his nightclothes, holding a shotgun, and was greeted by his brother-in-law and a group of well-lubricated friends. The drunken Democrats rushed into Dallas's front room and began dancing, shouting to Dallas and his startled wife that Dallas was the nominee for vice president of the whole United States.

As the campaign of 1844 got under way, both parties' sloganeers tried to find the literary lightning strike that the Whigs had had with Tippecanoe and Tyler, Too. Because of the prevalent expansionist zeitgeist, the Democrats struck alliterative gold with Fifty-four Forty or Fight! (a rallying cry of Manifest Destiny that insisted the U.S. extend the border of the Oregon territory to the southern boundary of Alaska). The best the Whigs could do with their candidates, Henry Clay and Theodore Frelinghuysen, however, was The Country's Risin' for Clay and Frelinghuysen."

In Polk's home state, the Tennessee Whigs tried to prevent a favorite-son presidency. At a rally in Nashville a Clay supporter, S. S. Prentiss, gave a four-hour speech on his opposition to Polk. Rather than being bored by the political proselytizing, his audience asked him to give the same speech again. That evening Prentiss threw all the fire and brimstone at the Democrats he could muster, until finally, at the end of his proselytizing, he collapsed from exhaustion. The governor of Tennessee, also a Whig, rushed to the stage and whispered: "Die, Prentiss, die! You will never have a more glorious opportunity!"

Prentiss survived, and the Whigs' effort was equally lacking. Clay and Frelinghuysen went down in ignoble defeat to the two unknowns, Polk and Dallas.

☆ ☆ ☆

DALLAS THOUGHT THAT it was the duty of the vice president to bow to the every whim of his chief, and naturally Polk considered Dallas a clear-thinking statesman. Other people thought they could see the strings running to Dallas's hands and feet.

Polk jerked the lines particularly hard over the Tariff Act of 1846. In the years that preceded the Civil War, tariffs were a major political and economic issue. Those in the North wanted them in order to protect their markets for their manufactured goods; those in the South were against them because they reduced the markets for the region's raw materials. Polk, being a Southerner, had a bill introduced into Congress that lowered tariffs. Dallas, of course, wanted high tariffs, as did the people in his home state of Pennsylvania. Dallas would never have had to make his position on the subject known to the president, however, if he hadn't had the misfortune to declare a 27–27 tie in the Senate. It was a lose-lose situation. Dallas remained the loyal vice president and voted for the bill.

The reasonable people of Dallas's home state were willing to accept the vice president's decision, provided, of course, that they got a few things in return. All they wanted was to hang Dallas, burn his house, and kill his family. Editorials were written about "Pennsylvania's recreant son." Mobs formed near his house and burned him in effigy. The outpouring of wrath in Philadelphia toward the vice president and everything and everyone related to him got so bad that Dallas was forced to send the sergeant at arms of the Senate to his house to rescue his wife and offspring.

Not everyone in the country hated the vice president. Early in Polk's term Texas was admitted to the Union, and the citizens of the Lone Star State were so relieved at being in the good graces of the Lord above (after all, the laws of manifest destiny were in full effect) that they named a new burg after the vice president.

Dallas never again held public office, which, considering the debacle of his vice presidency, was probably a mutual decision of both Dallas and the voters.

MILLARD

FILLMORE

Served with Zachary Taylor, 1849–50

Whig from New York

POOR MILLARD. HE MAY HAVE HAD THE GOOD FORTUNE TO LUCK HIS WAY INTO THE PRESIDENCY OF THE UNITED STATES, but because of his strange name he has become the epitome of the obscure historical figure. Considering what he contributed to the Union, obscurity, instead of infamy, may be a blessing.

Millard knew his place in history. A few years

after he left the presidency, Oxford University offered him an honorary degree. Fillmore declined,
saying that the students and faculty would ask:
" 'Who is Fillmore? What's he done? Where did he
come from?' And then my name would, I fear, give
them an excellent opportunity to make jokes at my
expense."

Millard was Fillmore's mother's maiden name, so
it wasn't as though the handle was descriptive of
some character flaw (it wasn't as if everyone called
him Stinky Fillmore). Fillmore tried his best not to
attract attention to his name, which leads one to
question his decision to name his own son Millard.

But Fillmore wasn't just some innocuous dope
with a goofy name. Behind the veneer of banality
was a dangerous dope with a goofy name.

☆   ☆   ☆

FILLMORE CAME FROM the poorest of poor families and spent his fourteenth through nineteenth
years serving as an apprentice wool carder, a job that
is as tedious as its name suggests. He was able to grab
hold of his bootstraps, however, so that by 1847, at
age 47, Fillmore had raised himself to the relatively
prestigious position of state comptroller of New
York. At that point his rocket ride to the presidency
of the United States began.

The Whigs picked Zachary Taylor as their nominee for president in 1848. Ol' Rough-and-Ready
Taylor wasn't much for politics—when a Whig big-
wig first approached him with the idea of running
for the top spot, Zachary told him to "stop your non-
sense and drink your whisky." The former general's
response was in line with his character; his disdain
for pretense was legendary. He was known for wearing plain clothes that gave no indication of his rank.
This genuine aversion to pomp and circumstance

promised to play big with the voters, and the Whigs decided that Taylor was their man.

In order to balance the ticket, the Democrats needed three things in their vice president: They wanted a Northerner, because Taylor was from Louisiana; the person needed to be a political nobody so as to not draw attention to Taylor's lack of political experience; and because Taylor was presumed to be proslavery, they needed someone who was opposed to the slave trade. In nominating Fillmore for the number-two spot, the Democrats satisfied the first two criteria, but they were wrong on the views of both men on their ticket when it came to slavery.

Following the election, Taylor ignored Fillmore. Even worse, he wouldn't permit Fillmore to dispense patronage jobs in his own home state of New York. This left Fillmore with so little political power that when he offered his support to political office seekers in his home state, one of the newspapers laughed that a cow would have a better chance of being elected than someone promoted by Fillmore. But in spite of losing some preliminary political battles to President Taylor, Fillmore was ultimately able to win the most important battle—the one over slavery.

The Democrats and supporting Southerners had been wrong when they assumed that Taylor was completely proslavery. Although he kept about three hundred slaves on his plantation in Louisiana, Taylor wouldn't play ball on the issue. The Democrats wanted to admit California to the Union as a slave state; Taylor said no to that idea and wanted California admitted as a free state without qualification, which provoked one of the country's greatest political brawls.

California's statehood was not the central issue. The battle over the future of slavery was, and it consumed the federal government. Former vice president Calhoun led the proslavery forces in Congress, and his formidable opponent, Daniel Webster, wanted to give slavery no quarter. In the middle was Henry Clay, who went around trying to get everybody to stop fighting and have some team spirit.

Finally Clay came up with a group of bills that he thought would settle the issue. Although known as The Great Compromise, which sounds reasonable, the bills contained among them the most foul piece of legislation ever forced on the citizens (not to mention the slaves) of the United States: the Fugitive Slave Law. This reprehensible bit of congressional pabulum said that slaves escaping to the free North had to be returned to their owners in the South, or those assisting the slaves' flight could be in violation of federal law. The bill would, in effect, make every citizen in the country a coconspirator in slavery.

When The Great Compromise went to the Senate for a vote, it set the stage for one of the most suspicious sets of circumstances involving the vice presidency in American history. President Taylor, a man of strong character, insisted that he would veto the bills if they passed the Senate. In fact, when three congressmen of his own Whig party argued with the president about his position on the Great Compromise and suggested that if he denied its passage, the result could be civil war, Taylor exploded and told the men that if any states tried to secede, as chief executive officer he would lead the troops into battle and have the three congressmen hanged in the same fashion as deserters and spies.

Fillmore, however, wasn't the slavery opponent the Democrats had thought. He was in fact a doughface, a term of the time for a Northerner who sided with the slave owners, and he informed President Taylor that if the vote on the bill went to a tie, he would vote for its passage. But Fillmore never had to worry about breaking a tie in the Senate. Just a few weeks later he was able to sign the bill into law as president, following the strange death of Zachary Taylor.

Taylor had gone to the dedication of the Washington Monument on July 4, 1850, and, after enduring an afternoon of speeches in the suffocating Washington summer heat, he returned to the White House and tried to cool himself with a bowl of iced milk and cold cherries. That night he suffered abdominal cramps, and five days later, the president died.

The symptoms of Taylor's death are similar to those of acute gastroenteritis; they are also quite similar to arsenic poisoning.

Some people have suggested that it might have been his vice president who proved fatal to Taylor. This isn't that extraordinary. Every time a president has died, from Lincoln to Garfield to Kennedy, some member of the public has turned with suspicion to the vice president, who always looks uncomfortably innocent and asks: "You think I did it? Why would you think I had something to do with it?"

The idea of homicide, while improbable, is one that can't easily be dismissed. In a recent exhumation of Taylor's body no arsenic was found, although this doesn't prove that he wasn't poisoned. Because arsenic would have been able to penetrate Taylor's bones only if it had been given to him in small doses over time, acute arsenic poisoning, which would leave no long-term evidence, remains a possible cause of death. Both the proslavery people, who weren't above resorting to violence, and the moderates who supported the bill were glad to see President Taylor out of the picture. Henry Clay's first words on learning of the president's death were: "This will secure the passage of my compromise"—a comment that doesn't seem to express either surprise or grief.

When Millard Fillmore took office as president, the first thing he did was sign The Great Compromise bill. It was the only real mark of Fillmore's presidency.

Two years later, the Whigs thought so little of their president that they nominated another man, Gen. Winfield Scott, to take his place. Fillmore didn't give up his hopes of returning to the presidency, though. Four years later he joined up with a racist, jingoistic, anti-Catholic group officially called the American party (better known as the Know-Nothing party, because whenever members of the party were asked about it in public, they always responded, "I know nothing about it"). As the Know-Nothing candidate, Fillmore was able to carry just one state—Maryland—and soon the Know-Nothings and Millard Fillmore quickly faded from importance.

But Fillmore wasn't to be forgotten. In the past several years there have been several facetious Millard Fillmore associations: One defunct organization called themselves Fillmorons, while the membership of another group consisted of two people and a dog. Today there exists a single Fillmore fan club: The Society for the Preservation and Enhancement of the Recognition of Millard Fillmore, Last of the Whigs, which advertises that it is "dedicated to the celebration of mediocrity in American culture, as epitomized by Millard Fillmore."

WILLIAM RUFUS

DE VANE KING

Served with Franklin Pierce, 1853

Democrat from Alabama

WILLIAM RUFUS DE VANE KING IS JUST
ANOTHER IN A LONG LIST OF FORGOTTEN
VICE PRESIDENTS, ALTHOUGH THERE MAY
BE REASON NOT TO FORGET HIM ENTIRELY.

King was the nation's only bachelor vice president as well as the only vice president to be named
Rufus. Additionally, he is the only executive officer
to have been sworn in outside the country, and he

served his entire term without ever setting foot in Washington. But none of this is reason enough to remember King today.

There is one small historical aside that just might gain King some notice: Although he never admitted such, there is strong evidence that King was homosexual. And what's more, the man who was the object of King's affection went on to become president of the United States.

☆ ☆ ☆

WHEN THE DELEGATES of both parties met to choose their ticket in 1852, they were on a search for mediocrity. Henry Clay's Great Compromise had so stirred up the nation that neither party wanted a candidate who held anything resembling an opinion on the subject of slavery. The Democrats found just what they were looking for in Franklin Pierce. He was a complete stranger to the electorate. He had held no political office; therefore, he had no record to defend. He seemed to have no opinion on any subject. And, if he was not an alcoholic, Pierce at least fit the description thrown at him by one wag, who called him the hero of many a well-fought bottle.

But if the Democrats were successful in their goal of achieving mediocrity in their presidential candidate, when it came to picking the vice-presidential candidate, they did not even strive for this not-so-lofty goal. The only requirement for the vice president was that he be the opposite of the president, which meant that he be from the South, since Franklin Pierce was from New Hampshire. King seemed to fit the bill.

Obviously, the delegates to the convention didn't know much about the man they were nominating. One can't imagine a bellicose delegate standing on a chair and saying: "Mr. Chairman, we need a special man to be vice president this year. We need a man who is a drunk, a man who is dying of a terminal disease, a man with a homosexual past. And, Mr. Chairman, I know just that man."

☆ ☆ ☆

KING DID NOTHING to dispel the stereotype of the effeminate homosexual. He was a flowing dandy who favored silk scarves, brilliant stickpins, and glittery accoutrements. He continued to wear powdered wigs years after they had passed from fashion. King's political peers did not view his esoteric air with quiet tolerance. Andrew Jackson, who had a manly reputation as the winner of numerous duels, referred to King as Miss Nancy. Aaron Brown, a senator from Tennessee and a fellow Democrat, gave King the nickname Aunt Fancy.

King may or may not have preferred alternative sexual relationships; it was sometimes rumored that he had sexual liaisons with some of the male slaves on his plantation, King's Bend. But all of this would have nothing to do with his political biography if it were not for one thing: King is alleged to have had an affair with future president James Buchanan.

King was elected to Congress in 1810, when he was just 24 years old, and to the Senate in 1819. Buchanan first met King upon his own election to the Senate in 1834. King and Buchanan soon became inseparable, and the boys in the cloakrooms began chuckling. Those chuckles turned into roaring rumors when the two men moved in together and shared rooms for many years.

James Buchanan had had one serious heterosexual romance, but even that relationship ended in mystery. Two years before going to Congress, Buchanan was engaged to be married to Anne

Coleman. Shortly before they were to be married, Coleman committed suicide. Coleman's friends blamed Buchanan for her death, and Coleman's father refused to let Buchanan attend the funeral. Why she took her own life has always been a mystery, but many have guessed that it was because of Buchanan's alleged homosexuality.

In 1844 Buchanan and King began talking about running for president and vice president as a team. Buchanan's hopes for the top spot were short-lived, but he urged his *bon ami* to seek the vice presidency. When King realized that Buchanan's failure did not thwart his own ambitions of becoming the nation's superfluous executive, his spirits buoyed. As one observer described the scene: "Mr. Buchanan looks gloomy & dissatisfied & so did his better half until a little private flattery & a certain newspaper puff which you doubtless noticed, excited hopes that by getting a divorce she [King] might set up again in the world to some tolerable advantage. . . . Aunt Fancy may now be seen everyday, triged out in her best clothes and smirking about in hopes of securing better terms than with her former companion."

King lost the bid for the nomination to that unnotable statesman George Dallas, but President Tyler acknowledged King's effort in the election and awarded him an ambassadorship in the fashion capital of the world: Paris. The finery of France did not hold King's interest for long, and soon he began to miss Buchanan. "I am selfish enough," wrote King, "to hope you will not be able to procure an associate who will cause you to feel no regret at our separation. For myself, I shall feel lonely in the midst of Paris. . . ." When Buchanan was tardy in responding to King's letters, King wrote that "this verifies the old adage, out of sight, out of mind." Finally, stinging from the loss of his longtime friend and feeling overwhelmed by his duties, King suggested that he should be replaced as ambassador to France "by someone who has more the spirit of a man."

☆ ☆ ☆

ON THE DAY King was inaugurated in March 1853, Washington, D.C., was cold: A sharp northeast wind was blowing through the streets. But at King's ceremony the observers were enjoying a more idyllic clime. One of those observers described the day, mentioning "the clear sky of the tropics over our heads, the emerald carpet beneath . . . our feet, and the delicious sea breeze of these latitudes sprinkling its coolness all over us." In fact, King's inauguration took place in Cuba.

King had gone to Cuba soon after receiving his nomination to try to regain his health before the election. That the vice-presidential candidate was off dying of tuberculosis in a foreign country was not considered by the electorate as an obstacle to filling the position. His health continued to fade, however, and King was still in Cuba in March of 1853. He was so weak that he had to be propped up by his aides so that he could take the oath. In April the vice president realized that he would soon die and resolved that he should spend his last few days at his home in Alabama.

King had expected to be received back in his home state with a hero's welcome. A large crowd of Alabamans did, in fact, turn out to greet their favorite son. But the crowd stood silent as they saw a man near death being carried from the ship to his carriage by two officers of the ship.

It was a week before King had the strength to travel on to his home, and he died a day after arriving back at his plantation. King had served as vice president for only six weeks. After King's death, no one in Washington thought to fill the vacancy in the office.

☆ ☆ ☆

WHETHER KING AND Buchanan were lovers will never be known. The truth of the relationship appears to have literally gone up in smoke. When Buchanan was in his seventies, he placed on deposit in New York City sealed papers that would explain the true reason for his breakup with Anne Coleman. Buchanan had sent these papers along with others to New York during the Civil War to protect them from Confederate troops. After Buchanan died, the executors of his will met to read the papers but found a note in Buchanan's handwriting that instructed them to burn the package without opening it, which they did.

JOHN CABELL

BRECKINRIDGE

Served with James Buchanan, 1857–61

Democrat from Kentucky

IN THE LATE SUMMER OF 1865, FORMER VICE PRESIDENT JOHN CABELL BRECKIN-RIDGE WAS ADRIFT. He had been elected to the second office when he was only 36 years old—the youngest man ever to hold the office—and it had seemed then that even becoming president would not enable him to reach his potential.

Just five years after leaving the office of the vice

presidency, however, Breckinridge was not simply adrift politically. He was adrift quite literally, bobbing along in a small unnamed, unmasted boat in the Gulf of Mexico, hoping that the currents would land him alive on some friendly and foreign shore where he could live out his days in exile.

Because of his activities during the Civil War, John Cabell Breckinridge had been charged with treason a little more than a year after leaving office. Many, if not most, vice presidents have fallen from favor during their careers. John Cabell Breckinridge is the only one to have been forced to flee for his life.

"Breckinridge," said the staid *New York Times*, "should die the most disgraceful death known to our civilization—death on the Gallows."

☆ ☆ ☆

BRECKINRIDGE HAD ALWAYS been a man in a hurry, his career speeding along at a pace never seen before or since in American politics. He would have been a star in any era. He was tall and exceptionally good-looking. When he spoke, the words came out with such confidence that he might have been considered arrogant if the edge of his words hadn't been softened by the charm of his Kentucky-Bluegrass accent. Breckinridge graduated from college at 17, and he passed the bar at age 20. By age 28 he was a leader in the Kentucky State House of Representatives; he was 31 when elected to the U.S. Congress.

Like any gifted politician, Breckinridge could convince most any audience that he would march with them until the final day—without really stating his exact position. In 1856, a presidential-election year, the zeitgeist was such that a man with eel-slippery opinions, like Breckinridge, was exactly the right man at the right time for public office.

The key issue of 1856 was slavery, and no politician wanted to be too vocal about his stand on the issue and risk alienating half of the electorate and possibly endangering his own life. When the Democrats met in the summer of 1856 to choose their candidates, their nominee for president was James Buchanan, who, conveniently, had spent the four previous years serving as minister to England and, therefore, had missed much of the debate on slavery. Breckinridge was a terrific candidate for the second spot. He was from a border state, had obvious personal appeal, and said whatever his audience wanted said.

During the campaign of 1856, both Buchanan and Breckinridge knew how to play the slavery issue. Buchanan was so quiet on this subject (as well as all others) that Thaddeus Stevens said that Buchanan couldn't be running for president, because "he is dead of lockjaw."

Breckinridge, on the other hand, was never one to keep his mouth shut, but that didn't mean he had to be so conventional as to be consistent with his opinions. A popular political cartoon that fall had Uncle Sam playing a banjo and singing a variation on the popular song "John Anderson, My Joe John":

> *John Breckinridge, my Joe John*
> *When we first acquaint,*
> *You were an abolitionist,*
> *And now you say you ain't.*

Thanks to this political strategy, Buchanan and Breckinridge won the election that year, albeit with just 45 percent of the vote.

☆ ☆ ☆

AS VICE PRESIDENT, Breckinridge cultivated a curious following. Although he had placed his hand on the Holy Bible and sworn to protect the Constitution, for some reason he was extremely popular with the militant, slave-owning factions in the South. As Stephen Douglas said, "Breckinridge may not be for disunion, but all the disunionists are for Breckinridge."

In 1860 Breckinridge tried to become the youngest U.S. president ever. It was a crowded field that year, with each party splitting and nominating both a northern and a southern candidate. Breckinridge ran for president on the ticket of the southern wing of the Democratic party (the northern Democrats had chosen Stephen Douglas). Breckinridge came in third in this horse race with just 18 percent of the vote.

His term as vice president over, Breckinridge began serving as senator for Kentucky. He was then vocal where he had once been coy regarding the status of the Union: Breckinridge wanted out, and he wanted to take Kentucky with him.

When Kentucky didn't resign as a member of the Union, and the northern forces took solid control of his home soil early in the war, Breckinridge left the Senate and joined the Confederate army as a general. Because he was from a state that hadn't left the Union, Breckinridge was immediately charged with treason.

As a Confederate general, Breckinridge played only a minor part in two major battles in the Civil War. In the battle of Stones River, fought in Murfreesboro, Tennessee, Breckinridge was ordered to clear a Union force off a hill, although he knew that to charge up a hill against a Union army was foolish and said so. In the end, however, Breckinridge obeyed the order, and in one hour of fighting, fifteen hundred Confederate soldiers under his command lost their lives. The battle was so fierce that soldiers from both sides plucked cotton from the fields and stuffed it in their ears to keep from going deaf.

Stones River was a terrific Union victory. Explaining the defeat to Jefferson Davis, General Bragg blamed his generals, B. Franklin Cheatham and John Breckinridge, claiming that Cheatham was a drunk and that Breckinridge was simply inept. Breckinridge challenged Bragg to a duel, but the matter was resolved when Confederate president Jefferson Davis fired Bragg.

In 1865 Jefferson Davis named Breckinridge his new secretary of war: The former vice president had become the person in charge of waging war against the United States and the right-hand man of the Confederate president. When the Confederate capital of Richmond fell soon after, Breckinridge and Davis were forced to run for their lives in the middle of the night. Jefferson Davis was soon caught, but John Breckinridge was not and continued his flight through the South.

The trip through Virginia and northern Georgia was relatively easy. Most people in that area were Confederate sympathizers, and to avoid detection by Union forces, Breckinridge had cut off his trademark Kentucky-colonel mustache. In southern Georgia, Breckinridge and the three men who were fleeing with him found a trio of Confederate soldiers who were willing to give them a small boat. It was only seventeen feet long and had a single mast and a sail that had to be held open with a rope, but Breckinridge was grateful, and he offered to give the highest-ranking of the men, a youthful lieutenant, a promotion to major. The young man hesitated before saying thanks, and Breckinridge asked him why he wasn't pleased with his new rank.

"Well, you see, general, there's a feller in our

regiment what ain't done nothin', and he is a major and a quartermaster, and if it's all the same to you, I would like to outrank him for once," the young man said.

With that, Breckinridge took a piece of paper and wrote the young man a commission as a lieutenant colonel. This was the last official act of the Confederate States of America.

Breckinridge and his men floated downstream until they found themselves faced with a twenty-eight-mile portage to the Indian River. They found a man who reluctantly offered his two oxen and wooden cart to carry the boat. The road, however, was rutted and bumpy. The boat and supplies spilled frequently, the oxen were balky, and the cart frequently had to be pushed through the thick mud. Later, one of Breckinridge's companions said that it would have been "less labor to have tied the beasts, put them into the boat, and hauled it across."

The band finally put in to the Atlantic Ocean near present-day Cape Canaveral. Hugging the coast and sleeping on the beach, they found the mosquitoes so abominable that they had to bury themselves in the sand at night to survive. Pretending to be pirates, Breckinridge and his men forced another group to trade boats with them. They were benevolent pirates, however. Besides giving their victims their smaller boat, they also left them with twenty dollars.

The tables were soon turned, however, when Breckinridge and crew were attacked by a real group of pirates. A renegade group of soldiers who had fled from both the Union and Confederate armies had assembled into a huge group of pirates near the Florida Keys. A band of these desperate men began chasing Breckinridge's boat, and Breckinridge fired several shots in response—the only shots he fired during the entire Civil War, which had actually been officially over for several days. To outdistance their pursuers, Breckinridge's group was forced to throw their meager supplies overboard.

After their narrow escape, the men were left in their dinghy (which was so small none of them could lie down to sleep) with no food, little water, and, after a fierce storm tore the mast off their boat, no way to propel themselves. They bobbed on the currents of the Caribbean for nearly two weeks, no doubt thinking that each day could be their last. One can only wonder what the former vice president of the United States thought as he passed those long days and nights in agony—his upper body swollen from tick and mosquito bites, his feet blistered and infected from the salt water on the boat's floor. Floating on the open sea, Breckinridge must have considered whether a quick death by hanging would have been preferable to the slow, humiliating death he was experiencing.

☆ ☆ ☆

FINALLY, TWENTY-EIGHT days after they had begun their escape, the craft sailed into the harbor of Havana, Cuba. There, after some initial troubles over not having the proper papers to enter the country, the group was received as heroes. That night, a group of Cuban Confederates hired a band to serenade their guests. At the reception the band struck up "Dixie" and then, having apparently spent their knowledge of songs of the South, proceeded to play "The Star Spangled Banner" and "Yankee Doodle."

Leaving Cuba, Breckinridge traveled to London and then to Toronto, where he was joined by his family. He returned to Europe and was greeted by many of the heads of state, most of whom had supported the war against the Union.

Breckinridge was not forgotten in this country, however. Although there was talk that he should not have to die for his sins against his country, he refused to return while he still faced charges that would land him in jail. Finally, on Christmas Day 1868, President Johnson declared a general amnesty, and Breckinridge was free to go home. He returned to Kentucky three months later and was met by such enthusiastic crowds that one observer remarked that Kentucky had waited until after the war to secede.

Breckinridge died six years later, in May 1875, when he was just 54 years old. One Minnesota newspaper, which saw Breckinridge as the personification of the rebellion, said that with his passing "there is now no North and no South."

The country, however, was not so quick to forgive and forget. Just because Breckinridge had died didn't mean he was off the hook. It wasn't until 1958 that a federal-court judge in Kentucky dismissed the charges of treason against "John Cabell Breckinridge and other Kentuckians."

HANNIBAL HAMLIN

Served with Abraham Lincoln, 1861–65

Republican from Maine

THE TITLE *MOST ANONYMOUS VICE PRESI-DENT* IS ONE THAT MANY MEN COULD BUILD A CASE FOR, WERE IT NOT SO OB-VIOUSLY REDUNDANT. But of all the vice presidents, Hannibal Hamlin, the man who held the office during the Civil War, was the most insignificant to his administration. It isn't just that people have forgotten about Hamlin over the years—he was forgotten about at the time.

Following the election of 1860, the near apocalypse of civil war raised its bloody head and tore the nation apart. Abraham Lincoln went on to become the Great Emancipator. Hannibal Hamlin went home.

☆ ☆ ☆

MORE HAS BEEN written about the four years when the country endured a civil war than about any other period in American history. Men such as Abraham Lincoln, Ulysses S. Grant, Robert E. Lee, and Stonewall Jackson are known to every schoolchild. Even men whose deeds have passed from history's collective memory, such as Union generals Ambrose Burnside and Joseph Hooker, have become a part of Americans' everyday lives, adding the words *sideburns* and *hooker* to the lexicon. But only the most avid students of the Civil War era remember anything about Hannibal Hamlin.

Most think of Andrew Johnson as Abraham Lincoln's vice president, but Johnson was vice president for only six weeks. Hannibal Hamlin served as vice president for four years. The reason why no one remembers Hamlin is that he chose to sit out the war.

In the summer of 1864 the Civil War was uncomfortably close to Washington. Confederate Gen. Jubal Early had attacked the forts on the outskirts of the capital, and President Lincoln went to the site of the battle to view the men under his command in action. He became more than just a casual spectator, however, when he stood on a parapet and rebel soldiers fired at him. (He is the only president to ever come under enemy fire while in office.)

The vice president, however, was never in danger during the war. Hamlin spent every available moment at his farm in Maine, returning to Washington only to open each new session of Congress. Finally, in the summer of 1864, Hamlin felt he could no longer stand by while the Civil War raged, and at age 55, Hamlin joined Company A of the Maine Coast Guard. While Lincoln was dodging bullets in the Washington suburbs, Hamlin gallantly served guard duty—hundreds of miles from the nearest fighting—and cooked meals for the other men of the Coast Guard, bravely enduring the dangers of splattering grease and clabbered milk. He stayed in the service for only sixty days, never rising above the rank of private. It is the lowest military rank ever held by a high national figure while in office.

☆ ☆ ☆

HANNIBAL HAMLIN WAS born in 1809, the son of a physician who also was a small-town politician. Throughout his career Hamlin was a keen opportunist with a short attention span. He studied law and passed the bar at age 24, but he never spent a minute as a lawyer, deciding instead to become a farmer. He grew tired of the farmer's life, however, and three years later he successfully ran as a Democrat for a seat in the Maine House of Representatives.

Hamlin's job-hopping did not end there. He went from the Maine legislature to the U.S. House of Representatives, moving over to the U.S. Senate a couple of years later. He then resigned from the Senate to run for governor of Maine and won the election. He was governor for only two months, though, before he was called back to his old job in the Senate. This time he also switched parties as well as jobs and was elected to the Senate in 1857 as a Republican.

The power to make law was not what interested Hamlin (he never stayed in one spot long enough to actually form a substantial piece of legislation). He delighted in dispensing patronage and thought that the system of spoils was not just a perk of the American political process but its raison d'être. Hamlin spent more time passing out favors and listening regally to the petitions of job seekers than he did attending to his senatorial duties.

WITH REBELLION IN the wind, the election of 1860 seemed to be one of the most important in the nation's eighty years of existence. The Republicans had two main candidates from which to choose: One was the eloquent William Seward, a man prominent in national affairs who was considered a moderate on the slavery issue, which meant that those who felt strongly either way didn't fully support him; the other was Abraham Lincoln, a tall and awkward rail-splitter from Illinois. Lincoln was less well-known to the majority of the citizens of the land, but he had drawn attention because of his debates and lectures on the issues of the day. Lincoln was nominated on the third ballot.

The leading contender for the vice-presidential nomination had been Cassius Clay of Kentucky. But with Lincoln at the top of the ticket, the party powers needed someone from the East, and the 51-year-old Hamlin was just the person. He had enough political friends, due to his years of doling out patronage jobs, but he had never really enacted any changes, which would have earned him political enemies. Hamlin won the nomination on the second ballot. Before Hamlin's nomination, he and Lincoln had never met.

THE NORTH AND the South couldn't agree even in their disagreements in 1860, and the campaign quickly split into two separate races: Republicans

Lincoln and Hamlin versus Democrats Douglas and Johnson in the North, and Southern Democrats Breckinridge and Lane versus Constitutional Unionists (a party composed of frustrated Whigs) Bell and Everett in the South. The presidential field was so crowded in 1860 that a popular joke had a boy asking his friend, " 'S your father goin' to run for president this year?" "Guess so," replied the other boy, "he says he may as well—everybody else is doin' it."

It was difficult for Hamlin's opponents to object to his record—as he didn't have one. The most virulent attack on Hamlin was by a South Carolina newspaper editor, who chose to take issue with Hamlin's dark complexion. "The Black Republicans," he wrote, "[have put] a renegade Southron on one side for President, for Lincoln is a native Kentuckian, and they put a man of colored blood on the other side for the ticket for Vice President of the United States." Three Southerners took up the false rumor, and, as a bad joke, offered to buy Hamlin from Lincoln.

As was custom, neither Lincoln nor Hamlin spent any time campaigning. The Republicans didn't have any trouble promoting Lincoln's colorful pioneer upbringing—they held rallies of rail-splitters and organized parades of men the same height as Lincoln—but they ran into trouble when it came to promoting their vice president. Their best attempts at sloganizing only produced the weak rallying cry "Abra*Ham Lin*coln."

Bad slogans didn't matter in the election of 1860, however, because the split at the Democratic convention dealt that party a mortal wound. Lincoln and Hamlin drew only 40 percent of the vote, but that was enough to win, as Douglas could sway only 29 percent of the voters, Breckinridge 18 percent, and Bell 13 percent. It was a bittersweet victory, however,

because before Lincoln and Hamlin could be inaugurated, seven states seceded from the Union.

☆ ☆ ☆

HAMLIN HAD HIGH hopes for his new job when
elected. "It will not be hard or unpleasant," he wrote
to his wife, showing that he occasionally had a firm
grasp of the obvious.

One clear connection Hamlin didn't make was
that of congressmen and drink. In his first act as
president of the Senate, Hamlin banned liquor from
the Senate chambers. The Senate has never been
confused with a temperance society, and during a
civil war the members of that august body no doubt
felt they deserved the benefit of an occasional (or not
so occasional) bracing belt.

Hannibal was not popular in Congress, and he
was soon to make an enemy of the president. Lincoln
did not ignore his vice president elect from the beginning. When Lincoln was forming his cabinet, he
gave Hamlin a job that required a delicate political
hand. Lincoln did not want his former party foe Seward to be included in his administration, but he
thought it necessary to offer Seward a post as a gesture of solidarity. Lincoln and Seward had been at
each other's throats for years; he knew that Seward
would turn down any offer to be a part of his administration. Lincoln must have thought that since Seward was going to refuse any proposal, there was no
use making the gesture a small one. He decided to
offer Seward the office of secretary of state, and he
sent Hamlin to receive Seward's refusal. Either Hannibal Hamlin was inept at persuasion or, more likely,
Seward was adept at political gamesmanship, because Seward accepted the offer. Hamlin was embarrassed, and Lincoln was quite angry, because with

Seward in his cabinet, Lincoln was assured of having at least one dissenting voice at every meeting.

The delicate nature of such political maneuverings must have gone over Hamlin's head, because soon afterward he pouted to one of his visitors, "I am not consulted at all, nor do I think there is any disposition to regard any counsel I may give." Hamlin told his wife that he was "the most unimportant man in Washington, ignored by the president, the cabinet, and Congress." With that, Hannibal went back to his farm in Maine.

☆ ☆ ☆

AFTER THE REPUBLICAN nominating convention of 1864, Lincoln was playing up his humble image when he said that the delegates "have concluded that it is not best to swap horses while crossing a river, and have further concluded that I am not so poor a horse that they might not make a botch of it in trying to swap." What Lincoln forgot in making that statement was that he had arranged at least one horse trade—dumping a shocked Hannibal Hamlin from the ticket.

Lincoln was worried about his chances of being reelected. Even his own party had split; some Radical Republicans had formed a new party and nominated John C. Frémont. Looking forward to November and beyond, Lincoln could see that he would easily win New England—what he needed was help in the border states.

The second spot on the ticket was first offered to the proud Union Major General Benjamin of Massachusetts, who bristled at the insult: "Ask him what he thinks I have done to deserve the punishment, at forty-six years of age, of being made to sit as presiding officer over the Senate, to listen to debates, more or less stupid, in which I can take no part nor say a word."

With the war nearing the end, Lincoln knew that a Southerner who had remained loyal to the Union could be invaluable to his administration during the coming reconstruction. Andrew Johnson of Tennessee was just that man, and his name was placed in nomination, along with Hamlin's. When asked which man he favored, Lincoln told the delegates that the party "must judge for itself." His statement was a clear signal to most of the convention to drop Hamlin. The first ballot went to Johnson, although he did not win enough votes to clinch the nomination. Before a second roll-call vote could be organized, there was a stampede of support for Johnson. Even Hamlin's home state of Maine changed its entire vote to Johnson.

☆ ☆ ☆

HAMLIN MAY HAVE got some measure of revenge on Johnson, who was something of a rural innocent. The morning that Johnson and Lincoln were to be inaugurated, Hamlin stopped by Johnson's (formerly his) office. Johnson was ill with typhoid fever and quite nervous about taking the office of the almost great. When he complained to Hamlin that he could stand a shot of whiskey, the teetotaler Hamlin immediately sent an aide for a bottle. Johnson poured himself a few extra-stiff drinks and then went on to deliver a long, rambling, and drunken speech. No doubt Hamlin acted as shocked and embarrassed as the rest of the crowd.

Had Hannibal been successful in his bid for his old Senate seat in 1865, he could have, and most certainly would have, been able to get revenge for losing the vice presidency to Johnson. William Fessenden, who defeated Hamlin for the U.S. Senate, voted not guilty during then president Johnson's impeachment trial. Johnson, who was acquitted by one vote, most certainly would have been kicked out of office had Hamlin been elected.

☆ ☆ ☆

HAMLIN'S DAYS AS the absent vice president came to an end, but he was not ready to forfeit the spoils of government. In 1868 Hamlin was once again elected to the Senate by the citizens of Maine, and he remained in his seat for thirteen more years, retiring at the age of 72. Some might have thought that this was the end of Hamlin's forty-five year political career, but he still had one more prize in sight.

Hamlin had always wanted to go to Europe, but despite his high government salary, he had considered himself too poor to make the voyage. He was able to wrangle an appointment as U.S. minister to Spain and spent most of his eighteen months wandering with his wife from one European country to another, sending the bills to his government.

In 1882 he finally returned to his farm, where he died of heart trouble and dyspepsia on July 4, 1891. He joined Adams and Jefferson as the third vice president to die on Independence Day.

☆ ☆ ☆

THE YEARS OF 1860 to 1864 were an incredibly violent time in the nation's history, due to a war fought, as Scottish writer Thomas Carlyle said, because one side preferred hiring their servants for life and the other by the hour. It is somewhat surprising, given the tenor of the times, that there were only two instances when Hannibal Hamlin nearly became the president of the divided country.

During Hamlin's term there had been two attempts on Lincoln's life, although it was years later before anyone heard about them. The first occurred in 1861, when Lincoln, riding alone at night to the Soldier's Home, was fired on by a man standing less than fifty yards away. In August 1864 he was again shot at, that time the bullet passing through his trademark stovepipe hat.

If fate had taken a slightly different turn, the history of Hamlin's vice presidency could have become even more ludicrous. Had Lincoln died while Private Mr. Vice President was fighting off the coast of Maine, Hannibal Hamlin would have received the greatest promotion in the history of the world: In a single day, he would have gone from private to commander in chief.

There wasn't much chance of that happening, if the editor of the *Cincinnati Commercial* is to be believed. He summed up most of the nation's feelings when he wrote, "I do not speak wantonly when I say that there are persons who feel that it was doing God's service to kill [President Lincoln], if it were not feared that Hamlin is a bigger fool than he is."

AMERICA'S OTHER VICE PRESIDENT

The Vice President of the

Confederate States of America

It is sometimes said that the United States is the only democracy that has a national leader who is solely a spare tire. But this hasn't always been the case; for a time another government had a vice presidency exactly like ours: the rebel government of the Confederate States of America. The vice president was Alexander Hamilton Stephens.

The most noticeable characteristic of Alexander Stephens was that he was frighteningly frail. He was quite short, he never weighed more than one hundred pounds, his skin had an ever-present pallor, and he suffered from constant disease and depression. Although his outward appearance wasn't impressive, Stephens was renowned for his tremendous intellect. One colleague said that

Stephens "carried more brains and more soul for the least flesh than any man God Almighty ever made."

Stephens was born in Georgia in 1812. After he graduated from the University of Georgia in 1832, he tried teaching for a year, but the students weren't kind to the frail man, and he switched to a career in law. Stephens served for a time in the Georgia state legislature, and in 1842 he ran for a seat in the U.S. House of Representatives.

During his run for Congress, his opponent, a Judge Colquitt, hardly took the small man seriously. At one meeting Colquitt contemptuously said, "I could swallow him whole and never know the difference."

"If you did," replied Stephens, "there would be more brains in your belly than there will ever be in your head!"

Stephens won the election, and immediately after taking his seat in Congress he gave a speech saying that his own election was unconstitutional. (Stephens was miffed that Congress had ordered Georgia to divide into congressional districts, because the Constitution said that each state could pick its representatives in any manner it thought appropriate.)

Stephens was a cantankerous member of the House. He challenged representatives from Alabama and Georgia to duels, as he did a fellow Whig, Benjamin Hill, who accused Stephens of being a Judas Iscariot to his party for his continued support of slavery. Hill declined Stephens's invitation to battle, saying, "It might be some satisfaction to you to shoot at me, though I should entertain no great fear of being hit. . . . But I might possibly kill you, and though you may not consider your life valuable, to take it would be a great annoyance to me afterward."

Stephens wouldn't drop the challenge and said that Hill was "not only an impudent braggart but a despicable poltroon besides." Hill still refused, saying, "I have a soul to save and a family to support and you have neither."

In addition to fighting, Stephens was known for his oratory. Following one of the Georgian's well-publicized speeches, newly elected president Abraham Lincoln wrote Stephens asking for a copy (it was rumored that Lincoln was considering the Southerner for a cabinet office). Stephens sent a copy of his speech—along with a letter in which he reminded Lincoln that his opposition to slavery was placing the country in "great peril."

Soon after Lincoln's inauguration, the southern states began leaving the Union. Although Stephens voted against secession in his home state of Georgia, he nonetheless did not hesitate to resign from Congress and join the Confederacy when Georgia voted to leave the Union. On his forty-ninth birthday, Alexander Stephens was inaugurated as the Confederacy's vice president.

As one might expect from a vice president, Stephens contributed significantly to the eventual downfall of the Confederacy. First, in a speech given in Savannah, Stephens said that slavery would become the "cornerstone in our new edifice" of the Confederacy. This undermined the lip service of many Confederates, who were publicly saying that the central issue wasn't slavery but the rights of the individual states to govern as they pleased.

The admission that slavery was the central theme of

the new government had two consequences. Soon after Stephens's speech, thousands of men in the North decided to enlist in the Union army to join the moral battle. More important, Stephens's comments meant that European countries, which were cheering for a breakup of the upstart United States, could not offer support for the new country without angering many of their own citizens. Stephens was also a strict defender of civil liberties for whites, and his pressure on Jefferson Davis prevented Davis from taking steps—such as the draft and the establishment of martial law—that might have aided the southern cause.

By 1865, Stephens was eager to press Lincoln for an end to the fighting. Stephens hoped that the North would recognize the Confederacy and join the Southerners in a war against Maximilian in Mexico. Lincoln agreed to discuss a truce with Stephens, and the men met on board the Union steamer *River Queen* in the harbor near Fort Monroe, Virginia, in what would become known as the Hampton Roads Conference. After Lincoln opened the meeting with a typically homespun quip—telling Stephens that he was the "smallest nubbin to come out of so much husk" as Stephens took off his cloak—the two sides presented their cases. The Confederate delegation had hoped for peace for "two countries," but Lincoln insisted that the Southerners surrender unconditionally. The men parted without any concessions.

A few months later the Confederacy fell, and Stephens was promptly arrested at his home. Stephens was so poor, having spent his fortune in support of his cause, that one of his former slaves lent him money so that he would have funds while in prison, where he stayed for a few months. Shortly after his release he was elected to the U.S. Senate by his home state of Georgia. The senators, understandably, refused to allow Stephens to take his seat. Returning to Georgia, Stephens regained his fortune by writing books defending the Confederacy.

A colleague once remarked that Stephens's ego was such that "he won't be satisfied until he corrects the proofs of his own obituary." Stephens eventually had just that opportunity. The *Atlanta Constitution* prepared an obituary when it appeared that Stephens was near death, but when Stephens recovered, the editor sent the obit to him and asked him to edit the piece, which he cheerfully did.

In 1872 Stephens won election to the U.S. House of Representatives, and that time he was allowed to take his place in Congress, where he served until 1882. Although he had been the picture of ill health all his life, Stephens lived to be 71 years old.

ANDREW JOHNSON

Served with Abraham Lincoln, 1865

National Unionist from Tennessee

OVER ITS HISTORY THE VICE PRESIDENCY HAS SEEN MEN WHO HAVE ABUSED, PE-RUSED, AND GENERALLY MISUSED THE SEC-OND-HIGHEST OFFICE IN THE LAND. But if the office ever misused and abused a man, it was Andrew Johnson of Tennessee.

Andrew Johnson spent his life being an angry man. He was angry at the rich "scrub aristocracy" as he called it; he was incensed at the "hell-born and hell-bound" secessionist movement in his native South; and when he became president via the vice presidency, he was angry at the Congress that tried to lead him around by the nose.

Conciliatory actions and compromise were foreign tactics to Johnson. When he was about to make a speech and he heard that someone in the audience intended to do him harm, Johnson stood at the podium and shouted, "Let the assassin shoot!" When he learned that Congress was about to try him on trumped-up charges, he cried, "Let them impeach and be damned!"

But in the end, the courageous defender of the Constitution found himself silenced and his career demolished because he had the misfortune of being the wrong vice president at the wrong time.

☆ ☆ ☆

ANDREW JOHNSON SUFFERED through a Dickensian childhood. His father died when Johnson was just 3 years old, and Johnson's mother scratched and clawed to support her two sons by taking in laundry and scrubbing tavern floors. When Andrew was 14 years old, his illiterate mother signed her X on the dotted line and gave her two sons over to a North Carolina tailor as indentured servants.

Johnson had never attended a day of school, but while he was serving as a servant to the tailor, he became interested in a book of oration by English statesmen, and he was able to teach himself to read.

After working for the tailor for two years, Andy was old enough to be interested in the opposite sex. One night he visited a house where two "right smart" girls lived, and, throwing a stone at a window, he broke the glass of their mother's bedroom window. Their mother threatened to "persecute," which would cause the indentured servant's life to go from miserable to unbearable. Andrew and his brother, William, ran away, breaking the contract their mother had signed. Johnson was able to avoid capture and to make a living with his needle and thread. When he was 18 he moved to Greeneville, Tennessee, and married a 16-year-old girl named Eliza McCardle.

Eliza had been to school, and she taught Andrew how to write and do arithmetic, as well as reading to him while he worked long hours in his tailor shop. Andrew Johnson became modestly prosperous in his small town, and within a few years he was elected city alderman.

It was a minor political office, but the poor tailor's election shocked the town's leaders. Five years later he was elected to the Tennessee House of Representatives, and from there he steadily made his way up the political ladder, becoming a state senator, then a U.S. congressman, then governor of Tennessee for two terms, and finally, in 1857, a U.S. senator.

It was in the Senate that Johnson attracted the admiration of Abraham Lincoln and others. As the southern states announced that they wanted to secede from the Union, there was a parade of congressmen—some of the most outstanding senators of the day—marching out of the doors of the Capitol to join the Confederacy. But even though his own state of Tennessee voted to join the rebellion, Andrew Johnson refused to budge. He became the only southern Senator who didn't join the rebels. When Jefferson Davis announced that he was leaving the Senate to join the Confederate government, Johnson yelled after him: "If I could not unsheath my sword in vindication of the flag of my country, I would return the sword to its scabbard. I would never sheathe it in the bosom of my mother. Never! Never! Never!"

As one might imagine, there were some in the South who didn't think much of Mr. Johnson's opinions. In 1855, while campaigning for his second term as governor of Tennessee, Johnson learned of an assassination plot. He didn't let this stop him from delivering his speech; instead, setting his pistol on the podium in front of him, he announced: "Fellow citizens, I have been informed that part of the business to be transacted on the present occasion is [my] assassination. . . . I beg respectfully to propose that this be the first business in order. Therefore, if any man has come here tonight for the purpose indicated, I do not say let him speak, but let him shoot."

When the secessionist feelings reached a fever pitch following Lincoln's election as president, the attacks on Johnson became almost routine. In a town ironically named Liberty, Virginia, an armed mob rushed toward Johnson's train as it stopped. When one man rushed toward Johnson yelling that he was going to rip off his nose, Johnson drew his pistol and forced the crowd to back down. As the train pulled from the station, Johnson continued shouting at the mob that he was still for the Union.

In yet another Virginia town, a mob was successful in dragging Johnson off his train and attacking him. The group was about to put a noose around his neck and string him up, when an old man said that the people in Tennessee had already made arrangements to hang Johnson, and that they should have the honor of being able to hang their own senator. Such sage advice won out, and Johnson escaped.

After the Union army gained control of Johnson's home state of Tennessee, Lincoln appointed Senator Johnson as military governor of Tennessee.

He not only was responsible for trying to maintain a government in the midst of a combat zone, but as the acting brigadier of Tennessee soldiers, Johnson was also responsible for raising troops and supplying them with guns and butter. The state and its capital city, Nashville, were under constant attack—in all, nearly five hundred engagements took place on Tennessee soil while Johnson was military governor—but Johnson was not about to see his home be torn once again from the Union; he once threatened to shoot anyone on his staff who mentioned surrender.

President Lincoln said that Johnson conducted himself admirably as he "stood in the furnace of treason." Johnson gained national attention because of his efforts as military governor, and with the 1864 election approaching, Lincoln chose Johnson as his running mate. Not everyone was pleased with the president's selection. In a comment that would foreshadow trouble for Johnson, Senator Thaddeus Stevens asked, "Can't you get a candidate for vice president without going down to a damned rebel province for one?"

But by picking Johnson, Lincoln proved that he had nearly great political vision. As a Southerner, Johnson would be immeasurably valuable in restoring the rift between the North and South. As a former senator, Johnson could help mollify the vengeful New England senators who wanted to see every Southerner suffer for the sins of the Confederacy. As a Democrat in a Republican administration, Johnson could help bring together political foes (the Union Republicans and Democrats joined forces to form the one-term National Union party).

Lincoln may have been the greatest political strategist in the nation's history, but there was one event he couldn't foresee: his own murder. By giving the vice-presidential job to Johnson, Lincoln had picked the most outside of all Washington outsiders. The very things that made Johnson such an ideal person to heal the differences in the country also meant that, in Lincoln's absence, he was a man on the other side of the fence on every point that mattered.

Johnson was, after all, a Southerner and the leader of a state that had tried to rebel against the Union. He was a lifelong Democrat and Jackson supporter who had no intention of changing his political affiliations. Finally, not only was he not a member of polite society, but he tried to spit on it at every opportunity. He was not, in short, likely to win a lot of friends in Washington.

☆ ☆ ☆

ANDY JOHNSON MADE such a splash at his first appearance on the national political stage that a song was written about it:

> *O, was it not a glorious sight,*
> *To see the crowd of black and white,*
> *As well as Andy Johnson tight,*
> *At the inauguration*

To say that Johnson was tight that day would be an incomplete description: He was sick with typhoid fever, drunk, more than a little peeved, and all in all, not in the proper state to address an assemblage of tuxedoed politicians. He had tried to skip the inauguration, but Lincoln had telegraphed a somewhat cryptic message that said: "It is unsafe for you not to be here on the 4th of March. Be sure to reach here by that time."

The morning of the inauguration, Johnson, sick and generally under the weather, helped himself to a jigger or three of spirits and proceeded to the Senate chambers, where he was to give his speech before Lincoln.

Speaking without the benefit of a prepared text or even notes, Johnson began waving his arms and shouting that he was a plebeian and that he was proud of it. He turned to the senators, the Supreme Court justices, and the cabinet officers in attendance and reminded them that they answered to the citizens of the country. He then turned to the ambassadors attending, saying that those "gentlemen of the Diplomatic Corps, in [their] fine feathers and gewgaws" also were to serve the common man. He went on to admit that he would need the help of the senators in administering parliamentary law in the Senate because, he said, "I have only studied how I may best advance the interest of my state and of my country, and not the technical rules of order."

Finally, Johnson announced that his home state of Tennessee was a rightful member of the Union and that its representatives and senators had a right to resume their seats in the Capitol. This was an extremely controversial matter, and even if Lincoln agreed with the full restoration of the states' rights, he had hoped not to make such an announcement until after the proper groundwork had been laid.

Although the foreign diplomats were said to have reacted to the speech with open amusement, the rest of the audience was horrified. Some of the senators literally hid their heads in their desks in embarrassment. Lincoln stared at his shoes through the entire ordeal, and following his own swearing in, he instructed the marshall, "Do not let Johnson speak outside." Most newspapers in the country were too deferential to carry such damning news about the vice president, and even the *New York Times* considered the news unfit to print.

Johnson spent only one day carrying out his duties as vice president presiding over the Senate. The issue that day was whether to bar liquor from the Senate chambers, a direct slap at his inauguration performance. Johnson was humiliated as the senators debated the issue and then voted the Senate dry.

☆ ☆ ☆

THE COUNTRY SOON moved on to happier occurrences. About a month after the inauguration Lee surrendered to Grant, and the great battle between the states was over. It was time for celebration in Washington for everyone except a band of misfits who had a hankering for vengeance.

On the night of April 14, a man by the name of George Atzerodt took a room in the Kirkwood House, the hotel where Vice President Andrew Johnson was staying. Atzerodt, a short Prussian immigrant who sported a goatee, was an incompetent drunk. For once, the vice presidency was blessed to be associated with an inept character, because John Wilkes Booth had assigned Atzerodt the job of murdering Andrew Johnson. At the same time that Booth was assassinating Lincoln, coconspirators were to kill the vice president and leaders of Lincoln's cabinet so as to paralyze the federal government. Atzerodt was to kill Johnson by knocking on his hotel-room door and shooting him point-blank.

On the day that this ambush was to take place, Atzerodt was extremely nervous. After hiding his weapon under his pillow in his room, Atzerodt left the hotel to visit a few local saloons in the hopes of boosting his courage. While he was out, Booth visited the Kirkwood, hoping to give a pep talk to Atzerodt. Finding that Atzerodt wasn't there, Booth did what turned out to be a fiendish thing: He left a calling note for the vice president. When Atzerodt returned to the hotel that afternoon, he headed straight for the bar.

At 10:30 that night, Vice President Johnson was awakened by a furious pounding at his door. Johnson opened the door and found the governor of Wisconsin, who told Johnson that Lincoln had been shot. Atzerodt never was able to screw up the courage to carry out his part in the conspiracy, and he had never left the bar.

Johnson went to the home to which Lincoln had been carried, and finding that the president's wound appeared to be mortal, he went back to his hotel room. Johnson was sworn in as president the next morning.

☆ ☆ ☆

FROM THE BEGINNING of his presidency, Johnson had to endure accusations that he had played a part in the murder of the president. Johnson's family was interrogated, and his bank accounts and speeches were searched for some clue.

There were, in fact, two suspicious bits of evidence: Johnson had turned down an invitation from the president that evening to join him at Ford's Theater—with his typical lack of tact, Johnson had said that it was a "frivolity"—and Booth had left that note at Johnson's hotel the day of the assassination.

In this volatile atmosphere Representative John Ashley stood in Congress and said that he had proof that Andrew Johnson had known about Booth's plot to kill Lincoln and that that was why Johnson had been so nervous on the day of his inauguration. Ashley said that he even had a witness to back up his claim. Johnson's many opponents believed Ashley and thought that the new president had been involved in the conspiracy. But Ashley's witness changed his story when he was refused a pardon, and the congressman's story began to unravel. Ashley said that his proof of Johnson's complicity "is not the kind of evidence which would satisfy the great mass of men" and added that he also believed in his heart that presidents Harrison, Taylor, and Buchanan were all poisoned in order that their vice presidents might take the reins of government.

With that, the congressmen backed away from the thought of charging the president with murder, but they still weren't about to allow Johnson to remain in office. If they couldn't try him for conspiracy, they decided, they could attempt a legislative coup d'état.

Congress passed a law that said Johnson couldn't fire any of his cabinet officers. It was baldly unconstitutional for the Congress to tell the president whom he could and couldn't have on his staff, and Johnson wasn't about to meekly roll over for the congressmen. One of the loudest opposing voices in his own cabinet came from Secretary of War Edwin Stanton. Johnson fired Stanton, but Stanton, who had many friends in Congress, refused to leave and barricaded himself in his office.

Because of this, the House of Representatives immediately impeached President Johnson for what they said were "high crimes and misdemeanors" (an impeachment is similar to an indictment). Senator Thaddeus Stevens gleefully told Johnson, "Unfortunate, unhappy man, meet your doom!" The president pro tem of the Senate, Benjamin Wade, was so sure that he was about to succeed to the presidency that he announced the members of his cabinet.

The vote for Johnson's conviction was close at thirty-five votes for and nineteen votes against, but this count fell one vote short of the two thirds needed to convict a president.

☆ ☆ ☆

WHEN THE REPUBLICANS met to nominate a presidential candidate in 1868, it would be an understatement to say that they decided against renominating the incumbent president. They went so far as to include a clause in their party's platform that said that they "regret the accession to the Presidency of Andrew Johnson, who has acted treacherously to the people who elected him and the cause he was pledged to support."

Johnson's tenure as an executive officer of the country was finished, but he did return to his old seat in the Senate six years later. Shortly after, Johnson suffered a stroke and died. At his request, his body was buried wrapped in an American flag with his head resting on a copy of the Constitution.

SCHUYLER COLFAX

Served with Ulysses Grant, 1869–73

Republican from Indiana

THE COUNTRY HAS LEARNED THE STORY WELL: RICH POLITICIAN FROM INDIANA, KNOWN MORE FOR HIS WINSOME SMILE THAN HIS MENTAL ACUITY, BECOMES THE VICE PRESIDENT. Even a president who is a member of the vice president's own Republican party describes him as "a little intriguer, aspiring beyond his capacity."

The year was 1868, not 1988, and the vice president in question was Schuyler Colfax, not J. Danforth Quayle. Just goes to show that history sometimes repeats itself in the most unwelcome ways.

☆ ☆ ☆

THE JOCKEYING FOR the vice presidency in 1868 was considerable. Unlike previous years—when the vice presidency had been given to whoever had the job of holding the hats of the men with real power—several prominent politicians thought that the vice presidency could position them for the big job when presidential nominee Ulysses Grant retired. In all, ten men tried for the office, but after five ballots, Speaker of the House Schuyler Colfax came out on top.

Colfax stepped down from a powerful position as leader of the Congress to the neutered position of vice president because he assumed that politics was just a passing fancy for the hero of the Civil War. After all, when the Republican leaders had asked General Grant if he was interested in holding a political office, he had said that he wouldn't mind being mayor of his hometown of Galena (he said that he needed a new sidewalk built from his house to the train depot).

Following their election—which had been a virtual lock because of Grant's reputation as the man who had saved the Union—Colfax began building a foundation for his assualt on the presidential pinnacle. After dutifully serving as vice president for several months, Colfax announced that he would not seek a second term as vice president in 1869.

Colfax thought that this deft political maneuver would signal the Republicans that he was ready to begin his campaign for the 1874 election. Grant, however, had grown to like the pomp of the presidency, and when he announced that he would seek a second term, Schuyler "the Smiler" quickly tried to put a spin on his earlier announcement by saying that, of course, if he were nominated at the convention, he would happily serve a second term. Even the inattentive Grant could see that Colfax's ambition was in overdrive and that he would only create havoc in a new administration, and the president instructed the Republicans to pick a new vice-presidential candidate. They selected Henry Wilson of Massachusetts to run with Grant for his second term.

This turned out to be a terrific bit of good fortune for the bumbling Grant. Shortly after the convention in 1872, a headline in the *New York Sun* blared KING OF FRAUDS! with a subhead HOW SOME MEN GET FORTUNES. In this case, some men included Vice President Colfax.

In the 1870s Congress had appropriated a large sum of money to build a railroad system that would stretch across the United States. It was such a large sum, in fact, that a few enterprising people realized that it was much more than the construction costs, and they set about scheming to put the extra money into their pockets. A congressman, Oakes Ames, and his brother Oliver helped form the Crédit Mobilier Corporation to take advantage of the financial surplus. When the last spike was driven in Promontory, Utah, Crédit Mobilier billed the government $173 million for a job that had cost just $83 million. The cut for the Ames brothers was about twenty million dollars.

Some of Ames's colleagues in the Congress began to ask questions about the Crédit Mobilier invoice, and in order to quiet things down a bit, Ames distributed stock in Crédit Mobilier where, as he wrote in a letter, "they will do the most good to us." Stocks went to such notables as future vice presidents Colfax and Wilson and to future president James Garfield.

The congressional stockholders received quite a deal. They were offered the stocks at rock-bottom prices, and if the cost of the initial investment was too high, Ames allowed them to buy the stocks on credit. The stocks paid dividends as high as 340 percent, and in return, Ames was no longer asked embarrassing questions about his ninety-million-dollar overhead.

After the behind-the-scenes dealings were brought into the light by the *New York Sun*, however, Congress finally decided to investigate Crédit Mobilier. When Colfax testified before the investigating committee, he denied ever having anything to do with the company. Ames, however, testified that Speaker Colfax had known about the whole thing and had received twenty shares of the stock in 1867. Furthermore, Ames said, Colfax had received regular dividend and interest payments, including one for twelve hundred dollars. Ames even displayed records of the payments.

When the investigating committee checked Colfax's bank records, they found that he had made a twelve-hundred-dollar deposit on the same day that Ames said he had paid the large dividend. It appeared that in addition to accepting a bribe, the vice president was guilty of perjury.

When he was hauled back before the committee, Colfax said that the bank deposit in question was just a remarkable coincidence. On the very morning of the day of the deposit, he had been having breakfast with his wife and reading his mail when a check for one thousand dollars floated out of an envelope from a supporter who, as luck would have it, had since passed away and would be unable to testify,

God rest his soul. Colfax said he remembered the event so clearly because that type of thing didn't happen to him every day. (Although it did happen more frequently to Colfax than to the common Joe; Colfax had also received a four-thousand-dollar personal "campaign gift" from a contractor while serving as the chairman of the Committee on Post Offices and Post Roads.)

Colfax's explanation didn't really clear his name, but his friends in the Congress weren't in the mood to impeach their old buddy. After all, he only had a few weeks left in his term as vice president, and they had all got a good laugh out of Schuyler's explanation. In a twisted bit of logic, the official reason given for showing mercy to Colfax was that his misconduct had occurred before he became vice president. Colfax's version of this decision was a bit more creative: He claimed that he had been fully exonerated of the charges.

Despite his complete exoneration, Colfax saw fit to retire from politics, and he finished out his years by giving lectures on points of morality and character (in case there is doubt, he was for them). He died at age 61 when he entered a heated train depot after walking three quarters of a mile in subzero weather.

HENRY WILSON

Served with Ulysses Grant, 1873–75

Republican from Massachusetts

IF HENRY WILSON HAD RISEN TO THE PRESI-
DENCY, BEKNICKERED ASPIRING BUSINESS-
MEN WOULD HAVE READ HIS STORY
INSTEAD OF THOSE OF HORATIO ALGER
FOR THEIR INSPIRATION. But by rising only
to the second office, Wilson joined the other vice
presidents on the scrap heap of obscurity. That
doesn't mean that his rise to success was any less

remarkable or his political career any less significant.

Henry Wilson was the personification of the Protestant work ethic. He was the son of a common sawmill laborer and was named Jeremiah Jones Colbath at birth. His father was unable to feed every mouth in his large household, so when Wilson was 10 years old, his father gave him over to a farmer to work as an indentured servant for eleven years.

Wilson did not receive any sort of pay, and the farmer was only obligated to send him to school one month each winter. Nonetheless, Wilson learned to read, and by the time he was granted his freedom at age 21, he had read nearly a thousand books.

When he completed his servanthood, he possessed six sheep and two cattle, which, having had his fill of agriculture, he promptly sold for eighty-three dollars. He then did what few people would have done having just spent eleven years in virtual slavery: He signed on for another type of servanthood, this time as an apprentice shoemaker. Young Mr. Wilson not only completed his brogan apprenticeship, but by the time he was 27 years old, he owned a shoe factory that eventually employed as many as one hundred people.

Even the mass production of shoes was simply a means to an end for Wilson. The books he had read as a young man included many biographies of leaders and politicians (including one obscure Massachusetts politician named Henry Wilson from whom Wilson took his name), and he yearned for the power and prestige of a life as a public figure. At the young age of 28, Wilson entered the U.S. Congress.

☆ ☆ ☆

HE HAD OVERCOME his past, but Wilson didn't forget the working man. He worked to reduce the standard workday from twelve hours to just eight, and he supported collective bargaining to solve disputes in the workplace. His opposition to slavery was even more strident: Wilson said that the denunciation of it should be at the forefront of everyone's mind. "Resolve it, write it over your door-posts, engrave it on the lids of your Bibles," he said. "Proclaim it at the rising of the sun and at the going down of the same, and in the broad light of the moon."

In 1848, when the Whigs nominated soft-on-slavery Zachary Taylor for the presidency, Wilson and another congressman quit the party and formed their own, the Free-Soil party. Six years later, when the Free-Soilers had been unable to enact their platform on a national level, Wilson joined the fledgling Know-Nothing party, because he mistakenly believed that it would work for freedom for slaves. When the party proved to have the opposite philosophy, Wilson vowed to work to "shiver it to atoms." He returned to Congress as a senator in 1855 and said that he would work with any party that opposed slavery.

While in the Senate, Wilson was a spectator to the vicious beating Senator Andrew Butler of South Carolina gave to Massachusetts' Charles Sumner. After Sumner had given a speech attacking slavery, Butler set upon Sumner with his cane and beat him so severely that Sumner suffered permanent neurological damage. Shortly after the episode, fellow Massachusetts senator Henry Wilson spoke out against Butler, saying that his attack of Sumner was a "brutal, murderous, a cowardly assault." Butler challenged Wilson to a duel, but Wilson refused, saying that dueling was the "lingering relic of a barberous civilization." Wilson's antislavery rhetoric clearly did not win favor with everyone, and some of his congressional peers hated his vocal opposition to slavery so much that they unsuccessfully conspired to murder him.

When the Civil War broke out, Wilson returned to Massachusetts and in just more than a month was able to recruit more than two thousand men. Wilson's own son served in the war as a lieutenant colonel in Massachusetts' famed black regiment. Wilson, along with Senators Charles Sumner and Thaddeus Stevens, doggedly pestered a reluctant President Lincoln to emancipate the slaves. "They are constantly coming and urging me," Lincoln said. "Sometimes alone, sometimes in couples, and sometimes all three together, but constantly pressing me."

☆ ☆ ☆

SOME YEARS FOLLOWING the war, when Schuyler Colfax blundered his way out of a second term as Grant's vice president, the Republicans chose Wilson—the Cobbler of Natick, they called him—as their new choice to ride shotgun with Grant.

It is a bit surprising that a man of Wilson's character would take a place in the administration of Ulysses Grant; in fact, Wilson had a low opinion of Grant, except for the general's military prowess. President Grant's first administration had so been so filthy that one senator said, "It is today the most corrupt and debauched political party that has ever existed." Another senator said that it suffered from "nepotism swollen to elephantiasis" because of Grant's propensity to give away high government positions to his pals.

Because of the pervasive corruption and ineptitude of the Grant administration, in the campaign of 1872 a group of Republicans split from the party and formed their own group, called the Liberal Republicans, choosing Horace Greeley as their nominee for president. Greeley would have been perfectly at home at a twentieth-century Democratic political convention. His political philosophy included the promotion of brown bread, spiritualism, socialism, and vegetarianism—which led one political commentator to say that the race between "Useless" Grant and Greeley was a battle between a man of no ideas and a man of too many.

Greeley's running mate was a fellow named B. Gratz Brown. Mr. Brown liked to tipple, and in one memorable address at Yale University, for which Brown apparently gathered his inspiration from a nearby bottle, he lambasted all the citizens of the East Coast. The speech earned the vice-presidential nominee the well-deserved nickname Boozy Brown.

The Grant-led Republicans were having their own problems, however. Just a few weeks before the election the Crédit Mobilier scandal was made public. Like Colfax, Wilson had been involved in the affair, but, unlike Colfax, it did not ruin his political career.

Wilson had received twenty shares of the Crédit Mobilier stock, but he had given them back after thinking it over. Actually, the stock was in his wife's name and had been purchased with thirty-eight hundred dollars in gifts the couple had received from "political admirers" on their twenty-fifth wedding anniversary. Nearly a month after this information became public, Wilson made a statement saying that any blame for the investment had to rest on him, because it was he, not his wife, who had purchased the stock. (As if nobody had seen through his story the first time.)

As it turned out, nobody really cared. After all, Wilson was just a vice president, and compared with the other officials in Grant's administration, his conduct was considered nearly admirable.

☆ ☆ ☆

ALTHOUGH SCANDAL DIDN'T derail Wilson's tenure as vice president, mortality did. He suffered a stroke shortly after taking office, a fact that he tried to conceal, even going so far as to ask the Associated Press to report that he was in terrific health.

Wilson's illness may help explain why he performed so ineptly as the presiding officer of the Senate, where he had frequently to ask clerks how to proceed after a parliamentary action. He suffered a second, more severe stroke two years later (which the physicians attending treated with, among other things, a shot of whiskey injected into his shoulder) and died a few days afterward.

In 1876, as America entered its second century, the vice president's chair was vacant, as it had often been during the first one hundred years.

WILLIAM ALMON

WHEELER

Served with Rutherford Hayes, 1877–81

Republican from New York

EVERYONE THINKS THEY KNOW A BORING REPUBLICAN, BUT WILLIAM WHEELER WAS THE MOST BORING OF ALL THE REPUBLICAN VICE PRESIDENTS, AND FRIENDS, THAT IS SAYING SOMETHING. In selecting Wheeler as their vice president, the Republicans had picked someone entirely out of touch with the tenor of the times. This was the Gilded Age, for goodness' sake, but Wheeler, despite his excellent connections, stayed remarkably clear of scandal and corruption.

Unlike most of the vice presidents in the latter half of the nineteenth century, Wheeler didn't have any conspicuous connections to the railroad robber barons—he had indignantly turned down the offer of Crédit Mobilier stock—and there was no evidence he had ever taken a bribe. He didn't even play ball as a congressman when it came time to vote himself a raise in the infamous Salary Grab of '73. In fact, Wheeler even returned his extra pay to the Treasury when the congressmen made the salary adjustment retroactive for five years.

How did such a plodding, mentally awake, and morally straight Boy Scout of a politican ever reach such a high office? Easy. His nomination was a joke.

Because presidential nominee Rutherford B. Hayes was from Ohio, the delegates to the Republican convention of 1876 needed to pick someone from the important state of New York. They really didn't care who it was; it was just the vice presidency after all, and most of the delegates had to be getting on home. The delegates from New York began joking about which of them would take the nomination. Somebody yelled to future vice president Chester Arthur, "You take it, Chet!" and somebody else said, "You take it, Cornell!" The delegates were nearly beside themselves with merriment when one of the delegates said, "Let's give it to Wheeler!"

They thought this was such a good one that they presented the nomination to the floor. Wheeler's nomination was approved by acclamation, and, according to a newspaper account of the event, "the delegates did not wait to continue the applause, but rushed off in every direction for the hasty dinner . . . and the out-speeding trains." This prompted the presidential-nominee Hayes to write to his wife, "I am ashamed to say, who is Wheeler?"

☆ ☆ ☆

WHEELER HADN'T DONE much, good or bad, to earn any type of reputation. As with many of the vice presidents of the era, Wheeler had been born to a poor family. He attended college, but he didn't have much money—surviving on only bread and water for six weeks at one point in his academic career—and was finally forced to drop out without graduating.

Wheeler began his political career early, and he progressed steadily through the ranks, finally reaching the U.S. House of Representatives when he was 42 years old. In his many years there, he never introduced a single piece of legislation.

There is some indication that Wheeler didn't crave a public life at all but that he was pushed into it by a social-climbing wife. If that is true, she stranded him once he reached his position of highest apathy in the vice presidency, because she had the gall to die three months before he took the oath of office.

Wheeler, however, almost didn't have to suffer through a term as vice president. As it turned out, Hayes and Wheeler lost the election of 1876 by three hundred thousand votes. To the Republicans of the day, however, this was only a small inconvenience in getting their people into the White House.

Despite winning the popular election by a comfortable margin, the Democratic candidates Tilden and Hendricks were a single electoral vote away from victory, having won 184 of the necessary 185. Hayes and Wheeler, on the other hand, had won 165 electoral votes. The remaining twenty electoral votes of three southern states were in dispute.

To win the election, the Democrats needed only to win one of the twenty disputed votes; Republicans Hayes and Wheeler needed to win all twenty. To nearly everyone involved, it looked as if Tilden and Hendricks had the thing sewn up, and some newspapers around the country, including the *New York Tribune*, declared Tilden the winner.

Even Rutherford Hayes, before he went to bed on election night, told a reporter that he had lost the election. But if Hayes and some other Republicans were willing to concede, the editor of the *New York Times* wasn't ready to see a Democrat take over the reins of the democracy. He got together with a few Republican leaders, and they plotted through the night on how to steal the election. They sent telegrams to party officials in the three disputed states, asking: "Can you hold your state? Answer at once."

The election had been dirty on both sides. Democrats had threatened blacks at the polls and prevented them from voting. The Republicans had not only encouraged blacks to vote, but, with the help of federal troops, they often arranged for the blacks to vote more than once. Both sides had tried to spread money around—before and after the returns were counted.

Two months after election day, the outcome was still unknown. Each of the disputed states had sent more than one set of "official" results. This caused a constitutional quandary: Although the Founding Fathers had instructed that the election returns were to be opened and announced in a joint session of the House and Senate, the Constitution does not make allowances for how to handle conflicting "official" vote counts.

The result was that the election was decided by compromise just hours before the inauguration on March 4. Tilden and the Democrats gave up their claim to the executive offices in exchange for the removal of federal troops from the South and other benefits for Southerners, including new roads and railroads.

It was ironic that the Republican-party bosses had struggled so desperately (and successfully) to steal the election for two men who were much closer to being Sunday-school teachers than political henchmen.

Wheeler found the vice presidency dull—quite an insult to the office. He avoided the Washington social life, going out only on Sunday evenings to the White House. There he found people who appreciated a quiet night at home as much as he did.

"Lemonade" Lucy Hayes banned profanity, tobacco, and liquor from 1600 Pennsylvania Avenue, an act that would no doubt bring today's government to a halt. The congressmen and cabinet officers who attended White House functions couldn't have been more uncomfortable if they had been attending a sawdust-floored tent revival. Secretary of State William Evarts complained that at one event "the water flowed like champagne." Vice President Wheeler, on the other hand, found the White House the perfect refuge from the stress of public life. He enjoyed going over to the White House in the evenings for refreshments, and he and the Hayeses would gather around the piano and sing their favorite hymns and folk songs.

The warm feelings Wheeler felt for the president and first lady were reciprocated: The Hayeses found widower Wheeler as snappy as strong lemonade; President Hayes said that "he was one of the few Vice Presidents who were on cordial terms, intimate and friendly, with the President. Our family were heartily fond of him."

What Wheeler really wanted to do, though, was

to return to his small hometown. He was given that opportunity when Hayes declined to pursue a second term. Hayes may have been speaking for himself and Wheeler when he said, "I am heartily tired of this life of bondage, responsibility and toil."

Wheeler died six years later. He did so in such a quiet manner that the local newspaper said, "Life went out so gradually . . . that it was hard to mark the exact moment of its flight."

CHESTER ALAN

ARTHUR

Served with James Garfield, 1881

Republican from New York

ARTHUR WAS A BROADWAY CHARACTER,"
H. L. MENCKEN SAID OF THE TWENTIETH
VICE PRESIDENT OF THE UNITED STATES,
". . . fond of good living, full of humor, but with no
more character than a Prohibition agent." Woodrow
Wilson was a bit more succinct. He said that Arthur
was "a nonentity with side-whiskers."

Both assessments are probably correct. Chester Arthur was such a man that he considered the vice presidency "a greater honor than I have ever dreamed of attaining."

At the time he was offered the second-highest position in the land, Arthur was, professionally speaking, a lackey. He was not just any lackey, however. He was known as a spoilsman's spoilsman, and few people in the country had found political machines to be as profitable as Mr. Arthur.

He was born to a circuit-riding fundamentalist preacher somewhere in or near Vermont. (Arthur may be the only U.S. executive officer to have been born outside the United States—something the U.S. Constitution strictly prohibits. When he became president, some people claimed that Arthur had actually been born in Canada, but Arthur himself really didn't remember, and the matter was dropped.) Arthur must have heard his father preach about the many temptations and ways of the world so often that Chester became sold on sin.

Elegant Chester, as he was called, loved the good life. He ate huge late-night feasts and threw tremendous parties. He loved to put on a new outfit of clothes for each social encounter of the day, and it was said that he owned more then eighty pairs of trousers and had his coats made up twenty-five at a time.

Arthur was a tall man with a soup-strainer mustache and a pair of muttonchop sideburns that would have made Elvis jealous. He was emotional and known to cry easily, but he won many friends.

Arthur had begun his career as a lawyer, but the Civil War changed his plans. Arthur never saw a gun discharged in anger; he served as quartermaster general for the state of New York. For years after he held this post, he liked people to call him, in all seriousness, General Arthur.

During his career, Arthur had become one of U.S. Senator Roscoe Conkling's trusted friends. Conkling was the boss of the New York political machine and had nearly complete control in the state. He was a bully, both in politics and with his fists, as well as a dandy—one fellow senator said that he walked with "a turkey-gobbler strut." When Roscoe Conkling yelled jump, Chester Arthur asked how high on the way up. Arthur was Conkling's front man, and, although Arthur became chairman of the state's Republican committee, nobody had any doubt about who was calling the shots.

When Grant became president, he named Chester Arthur collector of the port of New York. This wasn't some lowly bureaucratic position; as head of the port of New York, Arthur didn't just oversee the longshoremen as they unloaded crates from the ships. In those days the United States didn't have an income tax but made its money largely from the duties and levies placed on imported goods, and the port of New York was the busiest port in the country, bringing in the lion's share of the money.

Arthur (on the advice of Conkling) was responsible for collecting the money (heh, heh), for settling any "disputes" (nudge, nudge), and for making sure that this important source of income for the U.S. government was operated in a forthright manner. His position was a lucrative one: Arthur acknowledged making as much as forty thousand dollars a year, and there's a good chance that he, Conkling, and friends made significantly more. But the gravy train came to an end when reform-minded Rutherford Hayes was elected president.

In 1878 Rutherford Hayes launched an investigation into the workings of the port of New York. He didn't find any evidence of financial wrongdoing that would taint the reputation of Mr. Arthur, but he did notice that the only work Arthur's one thousand employees performed was the occasional job for the Republican party. Hayes fired Arthur, much to the chagrin of Roscoe Conkling, who without irony renamed the president Rutherfraud Hayes.

☆ ☆ ☆

AN UNEMPLOYED CHESTER Arthur then spent his time hanging around boss Roscoe, and that was all he was doing when he attended the 1880 Republican National Convention. Conkling spent most of the convention pouting because his conservative group, the Stalwarts, had been unsuccessful in propping up Ulysses S. Grant for a third term (Conkling knew that he would be able to hide behind Grant's bulk and cigar smoke to carry on all manner of lucrative enterprises). The convention delegates, many of whom hoped to continue to cross the border into the state of New York without persecution by an angry Conkling, had tried to appease Roscoe by offering one of his henchmen the second place on the ticket.

The Republican leaders first offered the vice presidency to Roscoe's friend Levi Parsons Morton. Morton, one of the most powerful men in international finance, went to Conkling like a child begging for a new toy and asked if he could have it. Roscoe considered the vice presidency below the dignity of even his entourage, and he instructed Morton to turn it down, which Morton immediately did.

Arthur, though, didn't have a job (he also had never held elective office before), and when the vice presidency was offered to him, he thought it sounded like the chance of a lifetime. He wanted to accept the nomination but was faced with violating the principal rule of lackeydom: In order to get what he wanted, he would have to stand up to the boss.

Arthur found Conkling sulking in a cloakroom, alone except for a reporter who went unnoticed. Arthur told Conkling that he had been picked for the nomination, but Conkling said, "Well, sir, you should drop it as you would a red-hot [horse]shoe from the forge." Arthur then told Conkling that he had never hoped to rise so high as the vice presidency. Even simply being nominated "would be a great honor," Chester said. "In a calmer moment you will look at this differently. . . . I shall accept the nomination."

Chester and, one presumes, Mrs. Arthur seemed to be the only people who wanted to see Chester in the second spot. Defeated presidential candidate John Sherman thought that Arthur's selection was a dirty trick by Conkling to guarantee that McKinley would lose the election and called the nomination a ridiculous burlesque.

When Hayes had fired Arthur from his position as the head of the port of New York, it had become national news. The only thing most people in the country knew about Chester Arthur was that he was a hack in Roscoe Conkling's political machine, and many people didn't want to vote for him. Some began wondering if it would be legal to vote only for Garfield and not for Arthur, but the publication the *Nation* advised people not to worry, writing, "There is no place in which his powers of mischief will be so small as in the Vice presidency." Besides, wrote the *Nation*, Garfield was a healthy young man only 48 years old. The idea that Garfield would die in office would be "too unlikely a contingency to be worth making extraordinary provision for."

The election was tight, but Garfield and Arthur squeaked through with a bit of "soap," which was the term used in those times for bought votes. Arthur himself admitted the election fraud when, as vice president elect, he spoke at a Republican dinner in New York, adding, "If it were not for the reporters I would tell you the truth, because I know you are intimate friends and devoted adherents to the Republican party."

☆ ☆ ☆

FOLLOWING THE ELECTION, Arthur continued to act as an emissary of the New York political machine. He tried to convince Garfield to name Levi Morton as secretary of the treasury, but Garfield didn't trust the Wall Street financier and refused. Arthur then tried to place one of Conkling's friends in his old job of collector of the port of New York. President Garfield not only refused Arthur again but went so far as to name one of Conkling's most outspoken critics to the post.

This infuriated Conkling so much that he resigned as senator, offering the reason that the president hadn't followed the traditional senatorial courtesy of asking him about the appointment. Conkling also instructed New York's new junior senator, Thomas Platt, to resign, which he did, thereby earning the nickname Me Too Platt.

All this political gamesmanship was reported in the press with the enthusiasm of a pennant race, and emotions on the issue were high. One person who became extremely worked up about the Stalwart's fall from power was Charles Guiteau, a religious fanatic who said his philosophy was "Bible Communism" and who listed his employer as "Jesus Christ & Co."

During the election of 1880, Guiteau had made a nuisance of himself at the New York Republican headquarters. He had copies made of a speech he had written in support of Garfield, and he stood in front of the headquarters handing out the fliers to passersby. During the summer and fall of that year, Arthur ran into Guiteau and chatted with him nearly a dozen times.

When Garfield won the election, Guiteau was sure that Garfield's success was due in part to his efforts. He thought, therefore, that he justly deserved some type of cushy political appointment, and he finally decided that he would like to be the U.S. consul to Paris. Guiteau went to the White House several times, hoping to present his case to Garfield. While there, he snatched some of the official stationery and used it to write to Garfield and ask the president why he hadn't yet sent Guiteau's name to the Senate for confirmation.

Finally, Guiteau realized that Garfield wasn't about to even give him a job washing the presidential horse carriage. Guiteau then knew what he had to do: He had to kill Garfield and give the president's job to his good friend Chester Arthur.

Guiteau might have made a good employee, because he was certainly thorough. The gun he picked to shoot the president with had a pearl handle, because he thought it would look nicer in a museum display than a gun with a standard stock. Guiteau went to the D.C. jail to make sure that it was reasonably comfortable, and then he began practicing his marksmanship (incredibly enough, in a woods near the White House).

Once he had things in order, Guiteau stalked the president several times, hoping to find just the right moment. He once decided against firing because Mrs. Garfield was with the president, and Guiteau didn't want her to see her husband murdered. Finally, on Saturday morning, July 2, 1881, Guiteau shot the president in the back in a Washington rail station and then shouted: "Now Arthur is President of the United States! I am a Stalwart of the Stalwarts!"

☆ ☆ ☆

THE BULLET THAT struck Garfield glanced off one of his vertebrae and lodged in the muscles of his back. The wound was not immediately mortal; Garfield was conscious as he was carried from the train station. Had Garfield's doctors decided to leave the bullet in his back, there is a good chance that the president would have lived. But his physicians constantly probed the wound looking for the bullet—using unsterilized instruments and unwashed fingers—until finally Garfield developed an infection and died nearly three months after being shot.

Arthur was upset to learn of the attempt on the president's life and to hear the assassin's words of support. Garfield was disabled enough during his long medical ordeal that Arthur could have legally assumed the presidency. But Arthur knew that if he made a step in that direction, it might seem that he had had something to do with the assassination, and he kept his distance.

When Arthur was finally sworn in as president, he still didn't have the complete confidence of the public. Even one of his friends was quoted as saying: "Chet Arthur, President of the United States! Good God!" But Arthur turned out to be only a mediocre do-nothing president, much to the relief of many, who were afraid that Arthur would turn the Oval Office into a den of thieves. Instead, Arthur turned the White House into party central. He hosted fabulous dinners and parties and even found time to woo a dancing girl who was younger than his son. About all the fun times Arthur would only say that "I am President of the United States, but my private life is nobody's damned business."

Arthur was playing a dangerous game, though, both for himself and the country. Arthur knew that he had been diagnosed with Bright's disease, an ailment of the kidneys that at the time was considered fatal. The only way for Arthur to prolong his life and ensure good health was to eat a simple diet and avoid alcohol. But Chester loved his parties too much, and he never backed away from the buffet—despite the fact that while he was president he had neglected to name a vice president.

Arthur died shortly after leaving office, and at his direction, his personal and official papers were burned.

THOMAS ANDREWS
HENDRICKS

Served with Grover Cleveland, 1885

Democrat from Indiana

THOMAS HENDRICKS, THE NATION'S TWENTY-FIRST VICE PRESIDENT, WAS A POLITICIAN OF SO LITTLE VALUE that one of the senators from his own state of Indiana said that his thirty years of nonachievement had to be some type of record. He was known as the Professional Candidate, and a Boston newspaper added that he was a "politician of the shilly-shallying order."

167

But do-nothing, vacillating party hacks are well-represented in the hall of vice presidents. What makes Hendricks's election to this high office so galling was his active opposition to human and civil rights. The election of Thomas Hendricks to the nation's second-highest office was a sad day for the republic.

☆ ☆ ☆

HENDRICKS HAD MOVED ploddingly up the political ladder, first as an Indiana state representative, then as a state senator, then on to Congress as a U.S. representative, finally becoming a U.S. senator.

As a senator, Hendricks was known for his vocal opposition to the Thirteenth, Fourteenth, and Fifteenth Amendments to the Constitution, the amendments that freed the slaves, granted them citizenship, and gave them their first civil rights. Hendricks thought that blacks were inferior and that no good would come to the country by granting them such privileges.

Hendricks was more than just a man of words, however; he also backed these racist ideas by his actions. While a U.S. senator, Hendricks served as the defense attorney for a man accused of treason for his actions as a member of the racist Knights of the Golden Circle. In fact, Hendricks's ardent defense of the group led many to believe that he was a member himself. In the bigoted climate of the late nineteenth century, such political rhetoric was popular enough for the Democrats to consider Hendricks as a candidate for president. He failed to gain the presidential nomination, but in 1872 his racist views did help Hendricks get elected governor of Indiana. Hendricks was bitter at not grabbing his party's nomination for president, though, saying spitefully that "any man competent enough to be a notary public could be governor of Indiana."

☆ ☆ ☆

THOMAS HENDRICKS HAD been cheated out of his place as vice president in the corrupt election of 1876 by Rutherfraud Hayes and friends, and by 1884 he thought he was ready for the presidency. He had done nothing in the intervening eight years that would make anyone—not even Hendricks himself—think that he deserved additional recognition, but he was a wily enough politician to know better than to make a frontal assault on the presidency. Instead, Hendricks hoped to get into the Oval Office through the back door.

Although at one time Hendricks had said that he had no intention of playing "second fiddle to Shinplaster Sam" Tilden, by 1884 Hendricks had changed his mind—or so it appeared. There were many sentimental Democrats who wanted Tilden and Hendricks to run again to avenge the loss of 1876, and Hendricks was once more willing to allow himself to be nominated for the vice presidency on a ticket with Tilden.

The reason for this seeming change of heart was that by 1884 Tilden was a frail 70 years old; he had suffered strokes that left him partially paralyzed. He could hardly walk or speak, and he could only see out of one eye. Hendricks knew that if he and Tilden were elected, the articles of the Constitution regarding succession due to presidential disabilities would soon kick in and that he would be the man.

Sam Tilden, though, knew he was too weak to serve. When he heard that Hendricks was to be his running mate redux, Tilden said, "I do not wonder, considering my weakness!"

When Tilden stymied Thomas Hendricks's plan, Hendricks was left with no option but to take dead aim at the presidential nomination. He was one of nine men nominated to be the Democrats' candidate, but when the cigar ashes settled, it was Grover Cleveland of New York who had won the horse race for the presidential nomination.

When the attention turned to choosing Grover's vice-presidential nominee, again Hendricks's name came up. Cleveland was a big strapping healthy fellow, though, and Hendricks didn't want to serve under someone whose medical records were so clean. Hendricks instructed the Indiana delegation to fight against his nomination. But those loyal Democrats couldn't forget the wrong of 1876 as easily as Hendricks, and when one delegate stood and shouted, "He deserves it—Give it to him, for God's sake!" the voices of acclamation in support of Hendricks for vice president drowned out Hendricks's protests.

☆ ☆ ☆

THE DEMOCRATS' PRESIDENTIAL candidate, Grover Cleveland, was an interesting man with some interesting personal habits, and before the election came about, he would not only be attacked by the Republicans but by his running mate.

Before becoming the Democrats' presidential nominee, Grover Cleveland had been the sheriff of Erie County, Ohio. Although he was an authority figure—and, at three hundred pounds, an imposing one—Cleveland didn't let that stop him from having a good time. When at one point he became concerned about his beer-drinking habits, for example, Cleveland vowed to a friend that he would only drink four glasses of beer a day. That ration soon proved to be too small, however, so Cleveland bought a huge tankard to replace the regular-sized mugs he normally used. This allowed him to drink all the suds he wanted and still keep his commitment to moderation.

Cleveland's biggest lapse of personal propriety, however, came when he was sheriff of Buffalo. He had had personal relations with a department-store clerk and part-time prostitute, and when she became pregnant, she said that although she had been with many men, she was sure that Sheriff Cleveland was the father. Cleveland assumed responsibility for the child, in part because all the other men mentioned were married, and he supported the child and looked after him for years. Cleveland didn't try to swear everyone to secrecy about the child—in fact, the boy was named Oscar Cleveland—but in the election of 1884, the Buffalo newspaper printed a story about the presidential candidate under the headline A TERRIBLE TALE: A DARK CHAPTER IN A PUBLIC MAN'S HISTORY. When Cleveland's campaign managers asked him how to proceed, he told them, "Above all, tell the truth."

The Republicans were wild with excitement about the news, which they thought would force Cleveland from the race. They went around chanting: "Ma! Ma! Where's my Pa?" (to which the Democrats added after the election, "Gone to the White House! Ha! Ha! Ha!") And the Republicans weren't the only ones clamoring for Cleveland to withdraw. Thomas Hendricks, Cleveland's running mate, saw this as his final opportunity to claim the presidency.

Hendricks sided with the Republicans and began announcing that he thought Cleveland should withdraw from the race. It was obvious by his own conduct that Hendricks couldn't care less about conventional morality. Instead, Hendricks assumed that at that late date, if Cleveland were forced to withdraw from the race, the Democrats would have no choice but to make him their new presidential nominee.

The *New York Nation* reacted to Hendricks's desperate ploy by saying, "We must take the liberty of warning the Democrats that Mr. Hendricks, already a heavy load to carry, may readily become heavier by making speeches."

Needless to say, Grover Cleveland was not amused by the antics of his running mate. Once the pair was elected, Hendricks complained that Cleveland was making all of the patronage assignments himself, saying: "The Democratic party isn't in power. Grover Cleveland is making a party of his own."

☆   ☆   ☆

THOMAS HENDRICKS HAD made a career out of being a political nuisance, and he managed to be just as irritating as vice president by dying at an inopportune time.

In March 1885, following the inauguration of the new administration, the Senate had called a special session to confirm the nominations of the new president. The senators normally would have also used that time to select a president pro tem to serve in Hendricks's absence. But Hendricks decided to attend the special session each day, so there was no need to name his replacement.

When Hendricks died the following November, the news in Washington wasn't so much about the death of the vice president as that there was nobody in line to replace President Cleveland should he go south as well. There was no president of the Senate, since one had not been named in the special session, and Congress was not going to be in session for another two weeks, so there was no Speaker of the House. As the Constitution then provided, there was nobody backing up Cleveland. It was Grover or bust!

Fortunately, the president did make it through those fourteen days, although because of the concern over his health, he did not travel to Indiana to attend his vice president's funeral. This was a disappointment, because with the lack of loyalty Hendricks had shown Cleveland, it might have been one funeral the president would have enjoyed.

LEVI PARSONS
MORTON

Served with Benjamin Harrison, 1889–93

Republican from New York

IN 1881, THE WEALTHY U.S. AMBASSADOR TO FRANCE, LEVI PARSONS MORTON, REALIZED THE ERROR OF HIS WAYS. He was luxuriating at his summer home, the Château Champ Fleuri (which was much more comfortable than his office, located over a grocer's shop), when he received the news that President James Garfield had been shot. He then knew that if he had accepted the

offer of the Republicans just a year before to be the
vice-presidential nominee, he would be president of
the United States.

Morton had turned down the nomination for the
vice presidency because of money, which made perfect sense, because that's what Levi Parsons Morton
was about—money. He had it, craved it, and knew
how to get his hands on more of it. The son of a
New England minister, Morton had begun his career
early, working as a full-time store clerk for less than
a dollar a week when he was just 14 years old. By the
time he was old enough to vote at age 21, he owned
a dry-goods store that brought in more than one
hundred thousand dollars per year. Eighteen years
later he joined up with Junius Morgan, J. P. Morgan's father, to start an international banking firm,
and soon Morton was one of the world's richest men.

Morton served as the chief fund-raiser for the
Republican party during the 1880 presidential campaign, and instead of accepting the vice presidency,
he had hopes of finding a place in the Garfield administration as the secretary of the treasury. It seems
that seven hundred million dollars in government
bonds were about to come due, and as head of the
Treasury department, Morton would have been able
to supervise the disbursement of the funds. For Morton, who had considerable interest in the bond market because of his international-banking firm, L. P.
Morton & Co., it would have been the most tremendous insider move Wall Street would ever see.

Garfield had been warned to stay away from
Morton and his corrupt cronies on Wall Street, however, and the new president appointed someone else
to the position. Morton was forced to accept a sabbat-
ical ambassadorship in France.

Following his ambassadorship, Morton tried to
restart his political career. Before the Garfield

administration he had served one term in Congress
representing the wealthy citizens of Manhattan.
Back on U.S. soil, Morton decided to try for a Senate
seat in 1885. Morton induced sleep whenever he hit
the campaign trail, however (he tended to speak on
the subject he knew best, international banking,
which isn't a topic that draws a crowd), and he was
defeated. Not discouraged, he ran for the other New
York Senate seat in 1887. Again he lost.

It was this impressive political résumé that Morton brought to the 1888 Republican National Convention. Naturally, the Republicans nominated him
for the vice presidency, to run with Indiana's Benjamin Harrison (a senator and grandson of William
Henry Harrison), and this time Morton accepted.

The Republicans weren't interested in Morton's
dismal record as a campaigner. In order to unseat
the popular president Grover Cleveland, they
needed a bulging war chest, and Morton was their
man. His approach was simple: He sent out a flier
that said, "We want money and we want it quick!"
and the Republican faithful responded. Morton and
the GOP's fund-raiser, John Wanamaker, were able
to raise three million dollars mostly from rich indus-
trialists who were afraid that the Democrats were
about to drop tariffs and allow "foreign free trade."
Some of the money was raised through the selling of
administration posts, and approximately four
hundred thousand dollars went to buy twenty thousand votes in the key swing state of Indiana.

Thanks to Morton's pecuniary efforts, the Harri-
son-led Republicans were able to win enough states
to carry the election, although they lost the popular
election by about one hundred thousand votes. The
Republicans were even able to win New York, Grover
Cleveland's home state.

The Republican faithful had not written the

checks out of a simple belief in the democratic process, however. After the election, Benjamin Harrison
complained: "I could not name my own cabinet.
They had sold out every place to pay the election
expenses." And when a supporter congratulated
Harrison on his victory by saying that it was an act
of Providence, Harrison responded, "Providence
hadn't a damn thing to do with it," adding that he
wondered how many Republicans "were compelled
to approach the gates of the penitentiary" to win the
election.

☆ ☆ ☆

MORTON DID AS fine a job as vice president as he
had as a candidate. In fact, by 1892, the Republicans
began to think that Morton was too effective in his
role as vice president. Morton put his money to work
in Washington. He bought and remodeled a home
to use for entertaining, and he hosted many lavish
affairs. It was said that as many as two thousand people passed through the house in one day.

As the presiding officer of the Senate, Morton
went out of his way to be impartial to the debate.
When the Democrats filibustered to block a piece of
legislation, Morton allowed the filibuster to proceed,
much to the chagrin of his own party. The Republicans tried to convince Morton to allow a president
pro tem to be appointed in order to move him from
the chair, but he wouldn't allow it. They finally became so exasperated with Morton that they told him
that he looked frail and should take to trip to Florida
for his health, but Morton stayed. He even gave up
his lunches so that the Republicans wouldn't try to
rush votes through the chamber in his absence.

Finally, when they could think of no other way to
move Morton aside, the Republicans refused
to renominate him to the vice presidency. The

Democrats responded by hosting a farewell reception in Morton's honor.

Morton returned to New York, where he served one term as governor before retiring to his estate, where he lived to be 96 years old. Morton may have been embarrassed by his party's refusal to renominate him to the nation's second seat, but not everyone considered it a slight. According to one observer at the 1892 Republican convention, the reason Morton was not renominated was that "God was good to him."

VICE-
PRESIDENTIAL
PERQUISITES

Living the Good Life
as Vice President

Milton Friedman may need to recheck his notes, because it does appear that there is a free lunch in America. As you probably already guessed, it's the American vice presidency.

In 1989 *Parade* magazine said that the vice presidency was "one of the softest and most perquisite-laden positions in the federal government." They were being polite. The vice president travels in a chauffeur-driven limousine, lives in a mansion for free, enjoys an extravagant expense budget with virtually no strings attached, is protected by a group of well-armed tough guys, and has a fleet of aircraft at his disposal. The position allows a person to live the luxurious life of a rock star without worrying about all that responsibility.

☆ ☆ ☆

At the time of the nation's beginning in 1789, the vice president's salary was only five thousand dollars—about thirty-five thousand dollars in today's money. Some people at the time thought that was an outrageous sum for someone whose only job was to break ties in the Senate, and they suggested that the vice president be paid only for actual work done. Others were kinder in their assessment when it was pointed out that out of his salary the vice president was expected to entertain foreign dignitaries, many of them royalty who expected lavish treatment—a not-so-insignificant expense. It's no wonder that Alexander Hamilton expressed sympathy to the first vice president, John Adams, and said that he hoped that "the starvation policy will not continue."

Through history, most vice presidents have been wealthy men, selected largely so that they could help pay for the party's campaign expenses. These men were hardly concerned about the vice president's salary, although Teddy Roosevelt once protested that he wasn't rich enough to be vice president. Few vice presidents could claim, as Walter Mondale honestly did, that they took the job because they needed the money.

When Vice President Dan Quayle took office in 1988, his salary was $115,000. Quayle, however, received pay increases in 1991 and 1992 that boosted his salary to $166,200, a raise of $51,200—a healthy 44.5 percent—from 1988. This was an amazing increase considering that at the time it was granted, the nation was suffering from a crippling budget deficit.

In 1789 the president's pay was twenty-five thousand dollars ($173,000 in 1992 dollars), and today it is two hundred thousand dollars. So although over the years the president's salary has increased just 15.6 percent in real dollars, the vice president's salary has increased a whopping 375 percent. But as with any business, good work must be rewarded.

In addition to a salary, the vice president receives allowances of $10,000 for expenses, $75,000 for entertainment, and $180,000 for maintenance of the vice president's mansion. According to public law, these funds are to be spent "solely on the certificate of the Vice President."

Although the nation's third president, Thomas Jefferson, made do with just one secretary and a part-time messenger, and President Woodrow Wilson was able to prosecute World War I with a staff of just fourteen, today the vice president's spouse is entitled to a staff of eight and an office. The vice president himself is allowed to have as many as seventy staffers and three offices. (This number doesn't include, of course, the many navy grounds keepers and stewards who are assigned to the vice president's residence.)

In addition to his office staff, the vice president is entitled to Secret Service protection, as are his spouse and children.

Another vice-presidential benefit: *Air Force Two*, the vice president's airplane. This is a recent perk. When Spiro Agnew held the office, he was assigned a windowless, noisy, rough-riding military-transport airplane that his staff dubbed Air Force Thirteen. Vice President Ford received a hand-me-down aircraft that was said to "creak and groan its way through the skies." But by the time Walter Mondale took the office, the vice president had his own plane, one that a Mondale aide claimed had "windows, engines, wheels, the whole package."

Although an airplane is required equipment for a modern vice president, *Air Force Two* isn't always used for official business. According to Associated Press reports, Vice President Dan Quayle allegedly used *Air Force Two* to fly to golf outings—trips that cost the American taxpayers about twenty-five thousand dollars each, not counting greens fees.

The vice presidency comes with plenty of pomp. According to protocol, vice presidents are to be greeted at official functions by the song "Hail, Columbia" and are to receive a nineteen-gun salute. They also get their own official-looking seal, which they can use on such neat souvenirs as cuff links and golf balls. The eagle on the vice-presidential seal has undergone a bit of a face-lift in recent years: when Nelson Rockefeller was vice president, he thought the eagle on the old seal, with its scrawny torso and down-pointed wings, looked like a "wounded quail." Rocky had a new seal designed, one of an eagle with more arrows in its talons and better pecs, and he paid for it out of his own pocket.

There are also innumerable small privileges. For example, when the Manassas National Battlefield Park was supposedly closed because the lack of a budget had shut down all nonessential federal facilities, Marilyn Quayle and her daughter went horseback riding there. Although the Quayles managed special equestrian privileges that day, Congress later denied their request for fifty thousand dollars to construct special vice-presidential horse stables at the park.

If future vice presidents will have to stable their own horses, there are other athletic facilities right outside their back door. In 1992 Dan Quayle had a putting green built on the grounds of the vice president's estate, which news reports said cost twenty-five thousand dollars (the press didn't say whether the cost included a windmill or a concrete giraffe), more than ten times the price tag of the putting green George Bush had installed at the White House.

The purpose of all this extravagance may be just to soften the blow of being vice president. "I've got all the perks," Vice President Gerald Ford once lamented, "but power? Power is what I left on Capitol Hill."

ADLAI EWING STEVENSON

Served with Grover Cleveland, 1893–97

Democrat from Illinois

THIS IS NOT THE ADLAI STEVENSON EVERYONE HAS HEARD OF—IT'S HIS GRANDFATHER. That said, we must remember that the original Adlai rose to a higher level in politics than his more famous grandson, although in the end, the elder advised his heir that the vice presidency was a job not worth trying for.

☆ ☆ ☆

STEVENSON BEGAN HIS career in Illinois politics by campaigning vigorously against Abraham Lincoln when Abe ran against Stephen Douglas for the state's Senate seat in 1856. Stevenson's anti-Lincoln stance would have been a mortal political wound for a less eloquent and able politician, but Stevenson was twice able to get elected to Congress (in 1872 and 1879) as a Democrat in a state that was considered to be solidly for the GOP.

Stevenson's success as a Democrat in Lincoln's home state is a testament to his easygoing, down-home friendliness. Stevenson played the role of the country lawyer, and he was quick with a homespun story or witty aside. Stevenson was such a friendly rascal, in fact, that although he was basically a party hack who ruthlessly stepped on thousands of people in his rise to the top, nearly everybody, including those with footprints on their backs, thought he was a swell guy.

IN 1885, NEWLY elected Democratic president Grover Cleveland appointed Stevenson as assistant postmaster general, but Stevenson wasted no time in biting the hand that had delivered him his new job. Cleveland was a bit tardy in claiming the spoils of victory for his party, much to the chagrin of the party hacks. The Democrats chastised Cleveland, saying that he should consider "the obligations which an Administration elected by a great historical party owes to that party." Stevenson, devoted Democrat that he was, wrote a letter to the *New York World* saying that although the U.S. Post Office employed tens of thousands of people, most of them were Republicans, and Cleveland should do something about it.

Stevenson's letter seemed to rouse the Democratic senators, who quickly joined the harangue.

One senator said that because Cleveland had allowed so many Republican federal employees to keep their jobs, the president was "a conspicuous and humiliating failure."

The president soon tired of the hounds yapping at his heels, and he told Stevenson, in effect, that if he wanted to fire the entire Post Office, go to it, but let the blood be on Stevenson's hands. Stevenson had none of the distaste for the task that Cleveland exhibited. By the time the firings were over, forty thousand men were out of work. Stevenson liked to brag that he had once "decapitated sixty-five Republican postmasters in two minutes."

Naturally, such ruthless allegiance to the spoils system made Stevenson a primary antagonist of the Republicans, who called him the Axeman and the Headsman. In 1889, at the end of his term, Cleveland tried to reward Stevenson for his efforts with the ultimate patronage job, a seat as a justice on the Supreme Court, but the Republicans in the Senate refused to confirm Adlai's nomination.

The Democrats, on the other hand—many of whom had brand-new jobs as postmasters—loved Stevenson so much that when Grover Cleveland needed a new running mate in 1892, Stevenson got the job.

The election that year featured an incumbent president, Benjamin Harrison, running against past president Grover Cleveland—a rare instance when the voters could choose between two men with experience in the Oval Office. Neither Harrison nor Cleveland did much campaigning, however. Harrison's wife had recently died, and he stayed home in mourning. Cleveland didn't want to appear to be kicking Harrison while he was weak, and so Grover also stayed home.

That left a large portion of the campaigning for

the Democrats to Stevenson, and he was up to the task. When he was campaigning in the Northwest, Stevenson managed to win many votes with an ingenious gimmick. The hottest local issue was whether to name a local landmark Mount Rainier or Mount Tacoma. Stevenson, campaigning from the back of a train, would say, "This controversy must be settled, and settled right now by the national government. . . . I will not rest until this glorious mountain is properly named . . . ," at which point his words were always drowned out by the train's steam whistle. Stevenson had set up the trick by installing a secret cord in his car that he would use to signal the train's engineer that he was ready for the whistle to blow and for the train to move on down the tracks.

☆ ☆ ☆

DESPITE STEVENSON'S OBVIOUS political ingenuity, Cleveland did not put him to use in the new administration. As his four years as vice president were coming to an end, Stevenson remarked that Cleveland had yet to seek his advice, adding optimistically, "but there are still a few weeks of my term remaining."

Stevenson was shut out of the administration's loop to such an extent that he didn't even know that at one time he could have technically, and probably legally, taken over the presidency for a short while. Soon after he became president, Grover Cleveland noticed a fuzzy spot on the roof of his mouth that couldn't be attributed to inaugural-ball hangover. The White House doctors checked out the spot and found it to be a malignant tumor.

This was obviously bad news for Grover, but it was potentially disastrous for the country. At the time, the nation was in the midst of a financial panic. More than six hundred banks had failed, and the

Department of the Treasury was keeping the federal government afloat only by not spending any of the money appropriated by Congress. It was not a good time for the administration to announce to the public that the president had cancer. So they didn't.

Without so much as whispering their plan to the vice president, President Cleveland and Secretary of War Dan Lamont took a train to New York, where, along with a group of physicians, they sneaked on board a private yacht. The main deck of the yacht had been converted into an operating room, with the operating table lashed to the main mast. Using only basic equipment and a new and unproven anesthetic, nitrous oxide (there was concern that the portly Cleveland would suffocate if ether was used), the surgeons removed the president's left upper mandible as the yacht cruised up and down the East River with the Secretary of War and a dentist sunbathing on deck for cover.

The president returned to the White House, where he was fitted with a vulcanized rubber jaw to replace his missing bone. A week later, however, it was discovered that the surgeons had missed part of the cancer, and the entire charade was repeated.

Were it not for the dire financial state of the nation, Cleveland's boat ride would seem to be a foolhardy plan to keep the vice president from assuming power. At the very least, considering the danger involved, Cleveland should have informed the vice president and made arrangements for a transfer of power. Instead, in keeping with presidential precedent, even on this important matter the vice president was ignored.

Following his term as Cleveland's vice president, Stevenson went on to run for the vice presidency once more, sharing the ticket with William Jennings Bryan in 1900. The Democrats lost, however, to the popular duo of William McKinley and Teddy Roosevelt.

Grover Cleveland's ruse finally became public knowledge in 1917, but Adlai Stevenson died in 1914 without ever knowing how close he came to becoming president.

GARRET AUGUSTUS

HOBART

Served with William McKinley, 1897–99

Republican from New Jersey

THERE HAVE BEEN MANY VICE PRESIDENTS IN THE NATION'S HISTORY, AND THE MOST THAT CAN BE SAID ABOUT GARRET AUGUSTUS HOBART IS THAT HE CERTAINLY WAS ONE.

Hobart was such a capable vice president that some people began referring to him as the assistant president. Some historians have said that Hobart had more influence over the actions of the government than any other vice president. Never heard of him? Such is the nature of the vice presidency.

Before Hobart became vice president, few people living at the time had heard of him either. He had never held a national political office, losing his one attempt at a seat in the U.S. Senate. But because he had money and he liked to spend it getting Republicans elected, Hobart was a major player behind the scenes, and with the back-room support of Republican kingmaker and party chairman Mark Hanna, he was able to grab the vice-presidential nomination.

Before being nominated to the second-highest position in the government, Hobart had been hugely successful as a corporate lawyer. He had come from a middle-class family in a small town where his father owned a general store, but by the time he received the nod from the Republicans, Hobart was one of the richest men in the country. He was the chairman of the board of directors of sixty corporations, and he owned two railroads, a water company, and several banks. Hobart was a one-man Monopoly board.

Garret Hobart was so wealthy and powerful, in fact, that he was something of a hero to President McKinley, who had been in and out of debt most of his life. McKinley's lack of financial acumen might have endeared him to the voters, however, because in 1896, not many of them had any spare change in their pockets either. During Democrat Grover Cleveland's second term as president, the country had slipped into an economic depression. Naturally, economic policy dominated the election.

The Democrats nearly succeeded in blaming the depression on the Republicans. Democratic presidential nominee William Jennings Bryan claimed that the government's gold policy—which the Republicans thought was just fine and should be left alone, especially since they had most of the gold—was causing the depression. At the Democratic National Convention of 1896, Bryan tried to make himself some sort of metallurgical martyr by proclaiming that he would not be crucified on a cross of gold. His speech electrified the nation, especially the rural poor, who were attracted by his promise of easy money and his use of religious imagery. Bryan used the popularity of his message—delivered with the fervor of a tent evangelist—to launch his nationwide campaign. In six hundred speeches he preached the evils of republicanism to five million people.

His were stirring words, but Bryan's campaign soon developed problems. Bryan didn't always have the opportunity to bathe properly between his exuberant speeches, and although he was a teetotaler, he had the peculiar habit of using gin as a deodorant. No doubt he put off many of his fundamentalist followers when he swung into town smelling like either a flophouse bum or a tenured congressman.

Another problem developed because a band of industrious entrepreneurs began traveling with the Bryan campaign train. Bryan would begin speaking on the important issue of metallurgy, and he would ask those with silver in their pockets to raise their hands. Then he would ask those with gold to raise their hands. Bryan may have been trying to make a point with this, but that didn't matter to the traveling pickpockets who appreciated Mr. Bryan's making their job much easier.

Mr. McKinley correctly decided not to try to compete with the Democratic traveling circus, and he stayed home and kept his mouth shut, as did Hobart. Not that the Republicans were passive: Theodore Roosevelt, then the police commissioner of New York, vowed to show up "on the field of battle, sword in hand" if Bryan won the election. The businessmen of the country were nearly apoplectic at the thought of a Bryan antibusiness administration. Some factory owners even told their employees that if Bryan was elected not to bother showing up for work the next day, because they would be closing the business. Against such opposition, it is no wonder that McKinley and Hobart were able to stroll into the White House by a wide margin.

AS VICE PRESIDENT, Hobart proved to be an extremely effective liaison to the legislature for the McKinley administration, because he knew how to influence congressmen. Hobart didn't rely on oratory: Ever since John Adams it was considered bad form for the vice president to make speeches, and besides, Hobart had a fear of public speaking (a strange characteristic for a politician). Instead, he gave the congressmen what they really wanted: cigars, liquor, and gambling. The senators thought Hobart was the most reasonable man they had ever had the pleasure to meet.

Hobart rented a mansion near the White House, and most afternoons, after Mrs. Hobart had thrown open every window in the upstairs of the house to allow the cigar smoke to escape, Garret turned the manse into a gentlemen's club and invited over a few dozen of his closest congressional friends for poker games and free drinks. President McKinley would often drop by and join the men in their merriment.

McKinley was known to be one of the country's friendliest presidents. He rarely forgot names or faces, and he was known for the McKinley handshake, in which he grabbed a person's elbow with his left hand while shaking hands with his right. (Most people took this gesture as an example of McKinley's good nature, but actually he found that it saved wear and tear on his hand.) Another McKinley gimmick was to wear a carnation in his lapel, take it from his coat, and insert it into the buttonhole of the coat of the gentleman he was meeting, telling the man to take the flower home to his wife.

Between McKinley's glad-handing and Hobart's freely flowing spirits, the administration was able to win friends and influence senators. The comfy congressmen were happy to accommodate their generous hosts when it came time to vote on legislation—not that that was any great inconvenience, because McKinley and Hobart enjoyed the luxury of having the Republicans control the majority of both houses.

☆ ☆ ☆

THE ONLY REAL problem that McKinley and Hobart had to tackle was what to do with the Spanish down in Cuba. McKinley was reluctant to pick a fight, but the muckraking newspapermen were screaming for a war because they knew it would help sell newspapers, and so when the USS *Maine* was blown up, McKinley gave in and sent the troops to Cuba. Vice President Hobart had been fervent in his belief that the United States should bloody the noses of the miscreant Spanish and Cubans, so much so, in fact, that when McKinley signed the declaration of war, he used Hobart's pen to write his name.

The fight was called the Spanish-American War, and it was really just an excuse to send the U.S. Army down to the tropics to beat up on some bewildered Cubans and to give Teddy Roosevelt (who was, by that time, assistant secretary of the navy) a place to ride his horse and shoot his gun outside of Washington city limits. In all, the war lasted ten weeks, and the margin of victory for the United States wasn't even as close as the final score would indicate.

Having won the war, like the dog that has finally caught the car it was chasing, everybody wondered what to do next. The question came up over what McKinley called the Philippine business. One of the spoils of battle was the deed to the Philippine Islands, which had been under Spanish control from the colonial days. Many in the country stood up and said that the United States should be a beacon of liberty and give the poor downtrodden Filipinos their freedom. Unfortunately, Vice President Hobart was not one of them. He was adamant that the Philippines had been won fair and square and that the United States should keep them. McKinley couldn't decide whether to keep the Philippines or throw them back in the ocean. Finally, after spending a night down on his knees in prayer, he said that the answer had been revealed to him, and the next morning he ordered the U.S. cartographers to add the Philippine Islands to the maps of the United States.

The Senate wasn't so sure that McKinley hadn't somehow misunderstood the Lord's will, and they put the matter of Philippine independence to a vote, which resulted in a tie. Vice President Hobart was then able to break the tie vote, which must have given him great satisfaction.

Hobart's pleasure at seeing the United States become the newest colonial power was short-lived however, because, well, so was he. The years of cigars and liquor and high living had taken a toll on Hobart's cardiovascular system. In the fall of 1898 he began having respiratory problems, and the next spring he died of a heart attack at age 55.

THEODORE
ROOSEVELT

Served with William McKinley, 1901

Republican from New York

TODAY, IF ASKED TO NAME THEIR FAVOR-
ITE PRESIDENTS, MOST AMERICANS WOULD
PROBABLY LIST WASHINGTON, JEFFERSON,
LINCOLN, AND, DEPENDING ON THEIR FLA-
VOR OF POLITICS, EITHER JOHN F. KEN-
NEDY OR RONALD REAGAN. But half a century
ago, the answer would have been quite different. Of
course, Kennedy and Reagan hadn't yet made an

appearance as presidents, but most people's short list
would have included Andrew Jackson and Theodore
Roosevelt. It is a shame that Old Hickory and the
Rough Rider have by and large been forgotten, because their brand of hands-on, mix-it-up politics
makes today's leaders look like Milquetoast, just
more small-minded politicians.

Although he is primarily thought of now as the
president on Mount Rushmore that nobody can remember, in his day Theodore Roosevelt was the star
that the political universe spun around and one of
the most popular leaders the country ever had. He
was, as H. L. Mencken said, "by long odds, the most
interesting man who ever infested the White House,
not excepting Jefferson and Jackson." He was also,
as Secretary of State John Hay said, "more fun than
a goat."

ROOSEVELT WAS BORN to a wealthy family in
New York City. He was a sickly child, and his father
encouraged him to build up his body with exercise
and boxing in order to overcome his frailty. Theodore idolized his father but was embarrassed that he
had avoided fighting in the Civil War by hiring a
conscript to take his place. Theodore's mother was a
southern belle from Georgia, and Roosevelt Sr. said
he didn't want to take up arms against his wife's family. (He may have, in fact, been a Confederate sympa-
thizer: When the family went on picnics in Central
Park, they often met Confederate agents and gave
them supplies to smuggle back south.)

Pop psychologists have theorized that it was
Roosevelt's humiliation at his father's failure to participate in the war and his own childhood frailty that
led him to find ways to prove his manhood, or perhaps it was just a natural exuberance. Whatever the

reason, once Theodore Roosevelt began his "vigorous life" he never slowed down.

Roosevelt graduated Phi Beta Kappa from Harvard, and after considering a career in law, went straight into politics. He was elected to the state assembly in 1882 at age 24 and quickly became one of the leaders. With his young wife by his side and a baby on the way, Roosevelt was settling in for a long career in state government.

Things changed quickly for Roosevelt, however, in February of 1884. Following the birth of their daughter Alice, his wife died, and then, just a few hours later, and in the same house, his mother died. Roosevelt was devastated, and he left New York State politics and headed to a ranch in the Dakotas that he had purchased a couple of years earlier as an investment with the inheritance from his father's estate.

At first, the western cowboys were amused by the sight of their Manhattan patron coming out to the Dakotas to play cowboy. Roosevelt displayed peculiar habits, at least in the eyes of the cowhands. He wore glasses, after all, and he shaved and brushed his teeth nearly every day. He avoided the rough language of the cowhands—"By Godfrey" was about the strongest thing they heard him say—and when he urged his cowhands to "Hasten forward quickly there!" at a roundup, they found the phrase so funny that for a while it became a joke throughout the territory.

But Teddy was able to win respect in the West. He worked as hard as any of his men, sometimes spending up to forty hours in the saddle on a cattle drive. He displayed courage and stood up to toughs who considered him a "dude," often using his fists but also using a rifle as a means of persuasion when the situation called for it. "That four-eyed maverick has sand in his craw a-plenty," one old cowpuncher said.

☆ ☆ ☆

ROOSEVELT EVENTUALLY RETURNED to the East and made a small fortune by writing about his western experiences. (In all, Roosevelt wrote forty books, on American history, nature, and his own adventures.) He soon remarried and again entered politics.

Despite the fact that Teddy often said he had taken the African proverb Speak Softly and Carry a Big Stick, You Will Go Far as his political philosophy, he rarely spoke softly about using a stick. Probably bored with his midlevel bureaucratic posts, TR was itching for the United States to get into some sort of scrape so that he could go riding to the rescue.

In the late 1880s he began hoping for a war with Mexico; a few years later, when that fight was avoided, he began hoping for a war with the military powers of Chile, which led Roosevelt's friends to call him the Chilean Volunteer and tease him that he should take on Chile by himself. In both cases it was his hope to raise a cavalry battalion and lead it into battle. When the United States proved reluctant to go to war south of its borders, Roosevelt began pining for another fight with Great Britain. "This country needs a war," Teddy wrote one senator, adding as extra incentive that if such a war was fought, the United States might be able to acquire Canada.

TR didn't get his wish for bloodshed, but he did move closer to the country's military might when President McKinley appointed him assistant secretary of the navy. Normally an assistant secretary has limited power, but Teddy didn't let custom prevent him from enjoying himself. Whenever the secretary of the navy stepped out of the office, even for just a short time, Roosevelt took it upon himself to take command. "The Secretary is away," TR wrote one friend, "and I am having immense fun running the navy." Once, superseding the secretary's power—not to mention that of the president—Roosevelt put the navy on alert while the secretary went to a doctor's appointment. "Order the squadron . . . to Hong Kong," Roosevelt cabled Commodore George Dewey. "Keep full of coal."

Secretary Long and President McKinley were trying to decide what to do about Teddy's impertinence when war was declared against Spain, and thanks to TR's orders, the American fleet was able to quickly defeat the Spanish in the Pacific.

With the outbreak of the Spanish-American war, Roosevelt resigned his post in the Department of the Navy and organized a cavalry unit composed of Dakota Territory cattlemen and Ivy League undergraduates. In Cuba, at the base of Kettle Hill—also called San Juan Hill—Roosevelt gave the command, "Gentlemen, charge," and waving his broad-rimmed campaign hat, he led his strange command into battle.

The press covered the exploits of Roosevelt's Rough Riders like a hometown favorite football team, and although Roosevelt had spent only a week in Cuba and seen only one day of combat, when Teddy returned to the United States, a half million people turned out in New York City to hail him as a war hero.

Roosevelt soon capitalized on his newfound celebrity. He wrote a book on his exploits called *The Rough Riders,* and within weeks of returning from the field of battle, Teddy began a campaign for the governorship of New York. Roosevelt played up his Cuban experiences, taking a patrol of Rough Riders with him to his campaign stops. At one site, one of the Rough Riders addressed the crowd, saying that Colonel Roosevelt had kept every promise he had made to his men during the war. "He told us . . . we would have to lie out in the trenches with the rifle bullets climbing all over us, and we done it. . . . He told us we might meet wounds and death, and we done it," the Rough Rider said, adding, "and when it came to that great day he led us up San Juan Hill like sheep to a slaughter and so he will lead you."

Despite such dubious testimonials, Roosevelt narrowly was elected governor. This was not good news to the longtime New York politicians. They considered Teddy some sort of lunatic, and their suspicions were confirmed when the young Republican governor put corporate antitrust reform at the top of his agenda. The leader of the New York Republican machine—none other than Thomas "Me Too" Platt—soon hatched a plan to get rid of Roosevelt.

Midway through Teddy's term, Platt approached him with the idea of running for vice president of the whole United States. Platt wanted to "kick [Roosevelt] upstairs" where he couldn't meddle in the cozy relationships the New York Republicans had with the state's large corporations. Roosevelt wasn't so naive that he didn't see through Platt's plan, but the thought of a national office intrigued him, although he would have preferred an office other than the vice presidency, complaining that if he took the office, there wouldn't be anything for him to do. "I can see nothing whatever in the vice presidency for me," he said. "It would be an irksome, wearisome place."

To reassure the administration that he wasn't about to run for a place on the ticket, Roosevelt thought that he should travel to Washington and advise President McKinley of his decision not to seek the vice presidency (although there is little evidence that McKinley asked for such an audience). Teddy was somewhat dismayed to discover how readily the McKinley administration accepted his choice. When

TR informed Secretary of War Elihu Root that he didn't want the office, Root said, "Of course not, Theodore, you're not fit for it." Secretary of State John Hay chimed in, telling Teddy that he didn't think Roosevelt could climb to the second seat because "there is no instance of an election of a vice president by violence."

Roosevelt's friend Senator Henry Cabot Lodge advised Teddy that for a man of TR's age (he was in his early forties), the vice presidency could be an effective stepping-stone to the presidency. Lodge also told Teddy that he didn't have to ruffle any feathers by saying yea or nay to the office: He could let geography make the decision for him. If you attend the national convention, Lodge told Roosevelt, the delegates will be sure to nominate you. If you don't want the nomination, simply stay home.

But Roosevelt reacted to applause much as Pavlov's hounds reacted to the dinner bell—his daughter Alice said that her father "wants to be the groom at every wedding and the corpse at every funeral"—and shortly after Republican chairman Mark Hanna called the national convention to order, Roosevelt strode into the hall waving his Rough Rider campaign hat. Immediately the crowd began cheering their hero. Over the objections of party chairman Hanna—who asked those assembled, "Don't any of you realize there is only one life between this madman and the White House?"—Roosevelt was nominated for the vice presidency on the first ballot.

When it came time to campaign, TR "hit the line hard," as he liked to say. He traveled twenty-two thousand miles and spoke to more than three million people. Humorist Finley Peter Dunne said that Roosevelt wasn't running for office, "he's gallopin'!"

☆ ☆ ☆

WHEN McKINLEY AND Roosevelt won the election, Teddy thought that he would be a "dignified nonentity for four years," saying, "I fear my bolt is shot." Asserting that the vice presidency was no place for a young man, because there was nothing to do (TR had already gone on record as saying that he didn't like to play golf), Roosevelt enrolled in law school to give himself some way to pass the time.

Roosevelt certainly didn't consider presiding over the Senate as being a good way to kill a day. He frequently daydreamed, and he himself said that he was the worst presiding officer the Senate had ever had. Still, there were those in the country who thought Teddy could be put to good use in the upper chamber of Congress. The *Philadelphia Times* wrote that if any Senator was unruly or refused to vote, "all that would be necessary . . . would be for Terrible Teddy to descend from his dais and with his own strenuous arm fire the recalcitrant into the lobby," adding, "the Senate rules should be amended as to give the vice president the needed authority."

☆ ☆ ☆

WITH ROOSEVELT SAFELY entombed in the vice presidency, some Republican leaders thought they had seen the last of him. Thomas Platt certainly thought so and traveled to the inauguration in Washington "to see Theodore Roosevelt take the veil." But Mark Hanna was still worried, and he told McKinley: "We have done the best we could. Now it is your duty to the country to live for four years."

It was not to be. Just a year later, an anarchist named Leon Czolgosz thought that "it would be a good thing for the country to kill the President," and he shot McKinley at the Pan-American exhibition in Buffalo. Roosevelt hurried to Buffalo to check on the president's condition, but after he was told by the attending physicians that the president's wound wasn't fatal, Teddy took off on a camping trip. Three days later, while Teddy was eating lunch beside a mountain stream, a man came huffing up the trail with a telegram telling the vice president that McKinley's health had worsened.

Roosevelt began a dash back to civilization and the presidency. He ran back to his base camp, where he picked up a buckboard wagon and driver. Driving fifty miles through the darkness over bumpy wilderness roads carved on the edges of the mountains, Roosevelt and his driver paused only three times to change horses. Arriving at a train station the next morning where a special train awaited him, Roosevelt learned that McKinley had died a couple of hours earlier. For Republican party chairman Mark Hanna, it was the worst situation imaginable. "Now look," he exclaimed, "that damned cowboy is president of the United States."

Under Roosevelt's direction, the national-park system was established, legislation was passed that resulted in the Food and Drug Administration, and antitrust legislation helped break up monopolies that were strangling many businesses. He sent the U.S. Navy on an around-the-world tour to show the other countries that the United States was the king of the globe, and when the U.S. Army complained of his efforts to encourage physical fitness among its officers, the president went on a one-hundred-mile horseback ride to shame them. Roosevelt promoted desegregation and invited Booker T. Washington to dine in the White House, the first time a black had been to 1600 Pennsylvania Avenue as anything other than a servant. TR even won the 1905 Nobel Peace Prize for helping to end a war between Russia and Japan.

But not all of Roosevelt's endeavors as president were as successful. He tried to have *In God We Trust* removed from U.S. coins (he thought mixing God and mammon was sacrilegious), and he even advocated simplified spelling. Responding to this last presidential proposal, the *Louisville Courier-Journal* said, "No subject is tu hi fr him to takl, nor to lo for him to notis."

His most famous act as president, of course, was creating the country of Panama and then digging a ditch through it. Even Roosevelt's own cabinet was skeptical of the president's authority to carry out the overthrow of the government of Colombia in the isthmus, and after Teddy laid out his reasons for his actions to his advisers, one of his cabinet officers remarked, "You have shown that you were accused of seduction and have conclusively proved that you are guilty of rape."

Even when he wasn't stirring the pot both at home and abroad, Roosevelt kept going with a gusto that alarmed some citizens and most Republicans. Teddy had once written, "I have scant use for the type of sportsmanship which consists merely in looking on at the feats of some one else," and he meant it. One of his favorite sports was boxing, but instead of attending heavyweight bouts, President Teddy preferred to spar with the White House aides. In one such fight, when Teddy took on a much younger army artillery officer, a blow to the presidential noggin resulted in burst blood vessels and partial blindness in one eye. In his autobiography, Roosevelt downplayed the injury, saying,

"Fortunately it was my left eye . . . if it had been the right eye I would have been entirely unable to shoot."

☆ ☆ ☆

ROOSEVELT WAS THE first "accidental president" to be elected to a term as president on his own merits, winning reelection in 1904. He declined to run for a second elected term in 1908, but in 1912 he changed his mind and decided to try for the presidency again. When the Republicans wouldn't give him the nomination (once they had the mad reformer out of the White House they weren't going to hand him the keys), Roosevelt formed his own party, the Progressive party, more popularly known as the Bull Moose party. This move only split the Republican vote, making it possible for Woodrow Wilson to waltz into the presidency.

Had he won that election, TR would have been president during World War I, which might have had an interesting effect on world history. As it was, Teddy tried to enlist at age 59 to fight in the Great War, hoping to form his own fighting group, but President Woodrow Wilson refused to let TR back in the army, much to the disgust of the old Rough Rider. Nonetheless, when the first American soldiers arrived in France, the Parisians greeted the young doughboys with the cry "Vive les Teddies!"

At the end of his life, however, Roosevelt realized that war was not just another athletic competition when his own son Quentin, who was a pilot in the Army Air Corps, was shot down and killed. That emotional blow, along with a chronic tropical infection Roosevelt had picked up while exploring the Amazon region of Brazil, reduced the man who espoused "the vigorous life" to the life of an invalid.

Roosevelt died in 1919, just months before he could begin a third run at the presidency, and his son informed the other Roosevelt offspring with the telegraphed message "The Lion Is Dead." Thomas Marshall, who was vice president at the time, said: "Death had to take him while sleeping. If he had been awake there would have been a fight."

CHARLES WARREN
FAIRBANKS

Served with Theodore Roosevelt, 1905–09

Republican from Indiana

IN SOME WAYS, CHARLES FAIRBANKS WAS SCHUYLER COLFAX: THE SEQUEL. Once again, in an apparent attempt to weigh down a popular presidential candidate, the Republicans had placed a rich, Hoosier party hack on the ticket as the vice-presidential candidate.

☆ ☆ ☆

THE MAN WHO would be TR's backup was not a firebrand reformer like Teddy. Charles Fairbanks had been born in a log cabin in the Midwest, and it must be said, Abe Lincoln was a friend of ours, and Mr. Fairbanks was no Lincoln.

Fairbanks began his career by working for the Associated Press, but he soon took up a career in law. He became a multimillionaire by offering to serve as legal counsel for failing railroad companies and then taking the companies over when they became solvent. When he moved into politics, Fairbanks used his railroad holdings to great advantage by handing out free passes on his trains to his supporters.

Fairbanks thought that he was ready for the presidency virtually from the moment he first entered politics, and he carefully planned to run for the top office in 1904, when he assumed President McKinley would retire. With that in mind,, when Republican party chairman Mark Hanna tried to offer him the vice presidency, Fairbanks turned down the lowly high office, choosing instead to hold out for a later try at the presidency. McKinley's untimely death just a year later disrupted Fairbanks's career plans. Like Levi Morton's, Fairbanks's miscalculation had cost him the presidency.

It may have seemed as though Fairbanks was boarding up the barn after the pony had fled by then accepting the vice-presidential nomination in 1904, but considering TRs penchant for risking his neck at every opportunity, Fairbanks may have thought that he had better-than-usual odds of achieving a tragic promotion.

Remarkably, in the election of 1904 TR avoided the crowds who would have cheered for the old Rough Rider and followed the tradition that said that presidents should remain above the fray and not actively stump for votes. One of the few rousing moments of the campaign came about because of a hostage situation. During Roosevelt's first term, a terrorist in Morocco named Raisuli kidnapped an American, Ian Pedicaris. President Teddy sent warships to cruise menacingly just off the Moroccan beach, and he sent a message to the leaders of Morocco: "This government wants Pedicaris alive or Raisuli dead!" Mr. Pedicaris was soon safely returned, and although the episode lost some of its glamour when it was discovered that Pedicaris was not a U.S. citizen after all but a Greek citizen who had just spent a lot of time in the United States, the phrase "Pedicaris alive or Raisuli dead!" became something of a campaign slogan for Roosevelt and Fairbanks.

Despite the lack of effort on TR's part, Roosevelt and Fairbanks won the election in a landslide. For the former vice president Roosevelt, the overwhelming margin of victory was a vindication. "I am no longer a political accident," he said.

☆ ☆ ☆

ALTHOUGH ROOSEVELT HAD said a few years before he took the second office that he thought the vice president's leadership role should be expanded so that the office-holder got a vote in the Senate and an official seat in the cabinet, by the time Roosevelt had a vice president of his own, he wasn't about to let Fairbanks even back the government down the driveway. Roosevelt considered Fairbanks a knee-jerk "reactionary machine politician," and TR made no place for him in his administration. Fairbanks was so isolated, in fact, that once when a White House chandelier persisted in tinkling—the fixture no doubt being swayed by the force of Teddy's bluster—Roosevelt told his butler: "Take it to the vice president. He needs something to keep him awake."

The only way Fairbanks was going to influence the Roosevelt administration would have been, quite literally, over TR's dead body. Fairbanks and Roosevelt nearly hated each other. Fairbanks was in concert with Senator Mark Hanna and the other big-business-friendly Republicans who thought that TR's progressive ideas—national parks, antitrust laws, regulations on the quality of food and drugs—were symptoms of some form of mental illness.

Fairbanks formed an alliance with the Speaker of the House, "Uncle Joe" Cannon, and together they conspired to try to keep Roosevelt's legislative proposals from successfully running the gauntlet of congressional committees and votes. Fairbanks promised to be "on the alert to rule any dangerous speakers out of order on the slightest context" and said that he would send "all progressive [that is, Roosevelt] measures to committee so that they never come to vote."

But Roosevelt had the power that comes from being one of the most popular presidents in history; Fairbanks had the full weight of the vice presidency behind him. It doesn't take a degree in political science to see who was going to win most of the battles. Fairbanks was never more than an irritant to President Teddy.

FAIRBANKS NEVER GAVE up on his idea that a man of his wealth and stature should become president by something akin to manifest destiny. His lust for the top office was so evident that when Roosevelt decided to take a spin on the military's newest toy—a strange craft called a submarine—humorist Finley Peter Dunne told the president, "You really shouldn't do it, unless you take Fairbanks with you" because otherwise the vice president was sure to sabotage the mission.

At the end of his term, Roosevelt declined to run for a second elected term because he had served more than half of McKinley's term and felt that he shouldn't try to hold on to the office for more than the traditional eight years. But TR was popular enough that, like Thomas Jefferson and Andrew Jackson before him, he was in a position to, for all practical purposes, name his successor. Charles Fairbanks wasn't his first-round draft pick.

Roosevelt instead chose his secretary of war, William Howard Taft (over the objections of Taft himself, who wanted to be a justice of the Supreme Court). Roosevelt could not even foresee Fairbanks continuing in his role as vice president in the Taft administration, and instead selected James Sherman of New York to be the new vice president.

The mediocre career of Charlie Fairbanks wasn't over, though. His name popped up again in the election of 1916, when he was picked to be the running mate of Republican presidential candidate Charles Evans Hughes. To their great surprise, Hughes and Fairbanks were narrowly defeated by the incumbent team of Woodrow Wilson and Thomas Marshall. The Republicans assumed that they had won the election, and apparently they weren't alone in this thought; the *New York Times* also trumpeted the fact that Hughes had won the election and was the next president. When it turned out that the incumbent Democrats Woodrow Wilson and Thomas Marshall had won reelection after all, Fairbanks pouted for two weeks before sending a congratulatory telegram to Vice President Marshall.

Charles Fairbanks, worn out from all of his electioneering, died just a year later, but because a group of citizens in a northern state named their village for the vice president, the name of the twenty-sixth vice president lives on in Alaska.

JAMES SCHOOLCRAFT
SHERMAN

Served with William Taft, 1909–12

Republican from New York

Although no one remembers James Schoolcraft Sherman these days—and there is no reason they should—he must have been some vice president. Mr. Sherman was the first vice president in U.S. history to be nominated for a consecutive term to that office by a major political party and, even more remarkable, to receive a substantial number of votes after his death.

This may have been a testament to Sherman's brilliance as the second-highest man in the U.S. federal government. More likely, it meant only that nobody really cared what kind of stiff was sitting in the vice president's chair.

☆ ☆ ☆

JOHN SHERMAN, WHO, with his pale, round face and balding pate, looked sort of like an older Charlie Brown with spectacles, was a machine politician from New York. Sherman was everybody's friend, and his disposition earned him the nickname Sunny Jim.

Although he came from a family of Democrats, Sherman was a Republican from the get go, and he had once even followed his Democratic brother as Republican mayor of his hometown of Utica. Despite his break with family tradition, Sherman was no rebel. He was Republican through to his very soul.

Such allegiance to the Grand Old Party made Sherman a favorite of the Republican congressional leaders after he arrived in Washington in 1887. During his twenty years as a congressman, Sherman was known not for his legislation but for his skill at manipulating the parliamentary rules that governed procedure. He was also pretty good at political shenanigans.

As Roosevelt and Taft began looking for a vice-presidential candidate, Sherman didn't occur to either of them. He was not known to the nation's voters, and although Roosevelt and Taft knew Sherman because he was from New York, neither thought much of him. But Sherman, it was said, was geographically gifted. Because Taft was from Ohio, the Republicans were forced to look for someone from the East to take the vice presidency, and Sherman was the only person willing to take the job who had any sort of political résumé.

When Taft and Roosevelt let it be known that
they would like Sherman to be Taft's running mate,
some wit quickly crafted the cheer "Eins, zwei, drei,
vier—Sherman is the winner here!" Through that
night the hotel corridors rang out with reveling Republicans singing "Eins, zwei, drei, vier!"

When Sherman's name was offered in nomination for the vice presidency, nobody paid much attention to the voting. It was the last day of the
convention, and most of the delegates already had
their bags packed. When Taft was introduced to the
delegates, the applause lasted a half hour (the cheers
for TR continued for more than forty-five minutes—Mrs. Taft timed both demonstrations), but
when Sherman's nomination was passed on the first
ballot, there were no cheers. Everybody just left his
seat to catch his train.

☆ ☆ ☆

ALTHOUGH TOGETHER TAFT and Sherman
weighed somewhere in the neighborhood of six
hundred pounds, they had a tough time filling the
void left by Theodore Roosevelt. After seeing the
way TR had issued orders like a foreman at the convention, some people thought that Taft would become Teddy's surrogate in the White House. Some
even claimed that Taft wasn't William Howard's real
name—it was just an acronym that stood for *Take
Advice From Teddy*. But Taft found a new group of
advisers, and he even tried to include his vice president, but, unfortunately, Sherman couldn't play ball.

The first of the problems between Sherman and
Taft came about on the golf links. Despite his heft,
Taft loved golf and claimed that it helped to keep
him at a svelte three hundred pounds. Taft's addic-
tion to this gentleman's game was so great that TR
worried that the president's reputation for spending

time on the links would cause him to lose support.
"Golf is fatal . . . ," TR wrote Taft. "Cast aside golf
and take an axe and cut wood."

But Taft refused to give up the game, and after
the election, he began inviting Vice President Sherman to join his foursome. It was rare for a president
even to acknowledge that he had a vice president,
let alone invite him along for four hours of social
camaraderie. Sherman, however, was soon to make
Taft wish he had forgotten about the foolish break
with presidential protocol.

Sherman, as it turned out, was the worst sort of
hacker. (Obviously, Sherman didn't realize the official responsibility he had to the game of golf, which
has become the national sport of vice presidents. The
vice-presidential seal should feature an eagle clutch-
ing a complete set of irons in one talon and a set of
woods in the other.) He couldn't keep up with the
putting president, and when Taft began playing golf
without inviting Sherman along, the vice-presidential feelings were bruised.

In order to give Taft some growing room, Roosevelt decided to leave the country on a much-publicized trip to Africa. When he returned and found
that the president had not followed the to-do list left
for him, TR and Taft began drifting apart. But they
continued to agree on one thing: They both held
James Sherman in open contempt.

At a dinner to honor the cardinal of New York,
Roosevelt and Taft were seated at the front table
while Sherman gave the main speech. Trying to impress the cardinal, Sherman sprinkled several quotations from the Bible throughout his speech, causing
Roosevelt to comment to Taft in a stage whisper,
"When Jim Sherman quotes Scripture the devil must
shake all hell with his laughter." Taft joined in: "I
should think it would make the cardinal feel like

goin' out of business." Later, after Taft recovered from a serious illness, he promised sarcastically to live out his term to "preserve the country from the sage of Utica."

In a last-ditch attempt to save his career, Sunny Jim Sherman managed to drive a wedge between good friends Roosevelt and Taft. Sherman thought that if he could defeat TR in a political battle, his political value would rise like stock the day after a Republican landslide. Sherman picked the state Republican convention of New York as his battleground.

Roosevelt had been asked to serve as temporary chair of the convention and probably didn't care that much when Sherman and his friends on the Republican committee pushed Roosevelt out and placed Vice President Sherman at the head of the convention. When the question of rightful chairmanship was put to Taft, he decided to remain neutral in the disagreement, which only infuriated both parties.

Roosevelt was insulted, as only a man with an ego of his size could have been. Under normal circumstances TR could have easily ignored the machinations of Sherman and his ilk. As an ex-president and the most popular man in America, it wasn't as if Roosevelt really needed to have the help of the state politicians in Albany. But when Sherman and friends trumpeted to the public that the vice president had deposed the former president, Roosevelt took the question to the delegates, who selected the Rough Rider over the moon-faced vice president. (Meanwhile, the poor New York gubernatorial candidate, for whose benefit the convention had been called in the first place, lost the election.)

In the end, the stature of Sherman or Roosevelt didn't change that much, but a large rift grew between Roosevelt and Taft. In 1912 that rift became a separation of continents when Roosevelt ran against Taft for the Republican presidential nomination. Upon losing to the incumbent Taft, Roosevelt split the GOP into two parties.

The disagreement between the two party heavy-weights doomed the Republicans' chances of winning the election, but Sherman was not to taste defeat. Instead, just a week before the election, Sherman died, when he was just 57 years old, and for once in American history, the electoral college came in handy. Because the voters were actually casting ballots for electors and not the actual men, there was no problem voting for a dead man. That argument was apparently good enough for millions of voters in 1916, because although he didn't win the election, the doornail-dead Jim Sherman still received three million five hundred thousand votes for the nation's second-highest office.

THOMAS RILEY
MARSHALL

Served with Woodrow Wilson, 1913–21

Democrat from Indiana

O NCE THERE WERE TWO BROTHERS,"
SAID THOMAS MARSHALL, THE NATION'S
TWENTY-EIGHT VICE PRESIDENT. "One ran
away to sea, the other was elected vice president, and
neither of them was heard from again."

Over its history, men have reacted to the "wholly
insignificant" office of the vice presidency in many
ways. John Adams was frustrated by it, John Cal-

houn tried to bully it, and Hannibal Hamlin and Theodore Roosevelt merely ignored it. But Thomas Marshall took a completely different tack: He laughed at it.

Marshall had a healthy sense of humor, and when he took a good look at his peculiar station in life, he couldn't help but be amused. He compared the vice presidency to the condition of a person in a cataleptic state: "He cannot speak; he cannot move; he suffers no pain; and yet he is perfectly conscious of everything that is going on about him."

Although the vice presidency often produces low comedy, it can also present tragedy. Marshall's laughter was silenced when a constitutional crisis left him pondering whether his actions could result in a civil war.

☆ ☆ ☆

TOM MARSHALL WAS a country lawyer in Columbia City, Indiana, a small burg on the prairie that considered its neighbor Fort Wayne to be the big city. He was a popular local speaker, often preaching the virtues of temperance before retiring to an evening alone with a bottle of liquor.

Marshall married late, at age 41, and his wife calmed his spirit enough that he stopped drinking. It wasn't until after his fiftieth birthday that Marshall entered politics. He had voted for the Democratic ticket all his life—his grandfather had instructed him to take his chances on Hell but not on the Republican party—and the Democrats wanted Marshall to run for a seat in the U.S. House of Representatives. Marshall declined, saying he was afraid that if he ran for Congress, he "might be elected."

In 1908 Marshall attended the Indiana state Democratic convention, and when the convention split evenly over the two leading candidates for the gubernatorial nomination, Marshall was selected. He won his seat by a large margin in a year that saw Republican presidential candidate Taft carry Indiana by fifteen thousand votes. Marshall's bipartisan popularity amidst a Republican landslide caught the attention of the national leaders of the Democratic party.

As governor, Marshall continued to make news nationally for his sweeping reforms in labor and social-welfare laws. Marshall was a compassionate man. He became famous for giving pardons to prisoners—he said he believed strongly in "the reformation of unfortunate criminals"—and the local newspapers lampooned his soft heart, showing in one cartoon a man bumping into Marshall and saying, "Pardon me, governor," with Marshall's reply: "Certainly! What crime have you committed?"

Marshall's humanity won favor with the leaders of the Democratic party, and he was offered a spot as the party's vice-presidential nominee on the Democratic ticket with Woodrow Wilson in 1912. Tom claimed not to be surprised by his nomination to the second-highest post in the nation. "Indiana," he said, was "the mother of vice presidents, the home of more second-class men than any other state."

Marshall and Wilson did not become fast friends; in fact, they could hardly have been more different. Woodrow was a dour, stern man, the expression on his face made even more severe by his ill-fitting dentures. Tom Marshall, on the other hand, was 120 spritely pounds of "glad to see ya, how ya doin'?" Wilson was the sophisticated, urbane president of Princeton University. Marshall was a shorter version of George Bailey from *It's a Wonderful Life*. Wilson considered Marshall "a man of small calibre," and he was not amused when, following their election,

Marshall sent him a book enscribed, *From your only vice.*

Wilson and Marshall probably would have lost to the Republicans that year if not for the rift between Roosevelt and Taft. At the Republican national convention, most of the delegates favored Roosevelt, and when the leaders nominated the incumbent Taft, Teddy and his followers decided to form their own group, the Progressive party, better known for its mascot, the bull moose.

While Taft and Roosevelt were wrestling on the floor of the convention, Democrats Woodrow Wilson and Thomas Marshall sneaked into the White House. Wilson and Marshall didn't have a majority of the votes, but they did have more votes than either Taft or TR, and that was good enough.

☆ ☆ ☆

AFTER TAKING THE oath of the vice presidency, Marshall took an oath of his own. He vowed to "acknowledge the insignificant influence of the office" and to "take it in a good-natured way."

Washington did not immediately know how to take its new pint-sized vice president. He first asked for a new chair at the head of the Senate, saying that the one then in use didn't allow his feet to touch the floor. Then when asked why he was able to get elected, he credited an "ignorant electorate." He also claimed not to be impressed by all the great minds assembled in Washington, saying that "the wise men remain . . . on the ends of street cars and around barber shops" back in Columbia City.

He then went on to speak on other, more serious matters. He came out against the robber barons and others of enormous wealth, saying that he believed in "vested rights but not vested wrongs." Then Marshall said the wrong thing following the deaths of

128 Americans aboard the merchant ship *Lusitania*. Marshall reasoned that as the Germans had warned that they would sink the *Lusitania* if it set sail because it was carrying war supplies, the Americans on board should have known better. The *New York Times* opined, "If Indiana cannot raise men of Presidential calibre, she should at least try to . . . train them to keep silence."

But Marshall's wit won over most people. Groups touring the Capitol would often stop and peek in his office door. He used to tell them, "Be kind enough to throw peanuts to me" and would then invite them into his office to shake hands.

When Marshall was on the road, he once noticed a police officer trailing him as a bodyguard. "Your labor is in vain," Marshall told the officer. "Nobody was ever crazy enough to shoot at a vice president." Marshall then told the officer that if he wanted to be helpful, he should go round up an assassin, because an attempt on his life would guarantee that Marshall's name would make it into the history books.

But Marshall's most famous quip came after a particularly tedious catalog of the nation's needs by a particularly bellicose senator—What this country needs is more of this! What this country needs is more of that! Marshall leaned toward an associate and said, "What this country needs is a really good five cent cigar!" The coining of this phrase may stand as the greatest accomplishment of a vice president in the nation's history.

☆ ☆ ☆

WHILE THOMAS MARSHALL was traveling the country pretending to be a vaudeville comedian, President Woodrow Wilson was attending to other important matters. Not just the great war in Europe, although there were some in the country who seemed a bit worried about that. Like other presidents had done before him, Wilson was chasing after a young widow—Edith Galt. Wilson's personal aide wrote in his journal that the president was letting the affairs of state lie fallow while he tried to win the hand of Mrs. Galt: "It seems the President is wholly absorbed in this love affair," he recorded.

The dour university president Wilson had long had a reputation as a ladies' man. Some political opponents had wanted to make a campaign issue of Wilson's affairs in the election of 1912, but Theodore Roosevelt had squelched the rumors of adultery before they reached the press. TR had claimed that what Wilson did in his personal life was irrelevant, adding, "You can't cast a man as Romeo who looks and acts so much like an apothecary's clerk."

When Wilson's wife died during his first term as president, many in Washington expected Wilson to marry his mistress, Mary Peck. Instead, just two months after he met her, and less than a year after his wife had died, Wilson asked Galt to marry him. They were married in October of 1915. Wilson's sudden marriage to Edith appeared, however, to be a campaign liability with women, one that he defused by switching his position to support women's suffrage.

☆ ☆ ☆

IN THE ELECTION of 1916, Wilson and Marshall faced stiff competition from Republicans Charles Hughes and Charles Fairbanks (it was the only time that the Democrats and Republicans nominated men for the vice presidency who were from the same state).

When the election results began coming in, it appeared that the Republicans had defeated Wilson and Marshall. Many newspapers around the country reported that Hughes and Fairbanks had won, and the news of Hughes's victory was flashed in New York's Times Square.

Even before the final results were in, the Hughes camp certainly believed they had won. Allegedly, early the next morning a reporter showed up at Hughes's room at the Hotel Astor to tell him of the late election returns. The reporter was told to leave, because "the president is sleeping." "When he wakes up," the reporter said, "tell him he's no longer president."

Even more extraordinary was Woodrow Wilson's response to the early returns. Day by day it looked as if the United States would enter the First World War, and President Wilson thought that it was no time for a lame-duck presidency. Wilson wrote to his secretary of state, asking him to resign if Hughes was in fact the winner. President Wilson planned to appoint Hughes as his new secretary of state, and then ask Vice President Marshall to join him in resigning so that Charles Hughes could immediately assume the presidency.

When the returns from California were counted, Wilson and Marshall were reelected. It wasn't exactly a mandate, but Thomas Marshall was willing to accept victory just the same. " 'Tis not so deep as a well nor so wide as a church door, but 'tis enough," he said. " 'Twill serve." Wilson and Marshall had been reelected in large part because the voters thought that in this way they could keep the United States out of war, but that was no longer possible.

During the war Vice President Marshall toured the country speaking in support of the president's decision to go to war. The *New York Times*, which had earlier been critical of Marshall, echoed the opinion of many people in the country when it said, "Thomas R. Marshall . . . is an American patriot, and the words he speaks have a sense and sanity that are urgently needed."

When the war ended, Woodrow Wilson began his battle to create the League of Nations. Wilson decided to go to Europe to present his Fourteen Points, and he asked Marshall to assume his place at the head of the cabinet in his absence. Marshall, displaying a remarkable lack of ambition, at first refused the president.

Marshall claimed that his position as the president of the Senate meant that he was a member of the legislative branch and, therefore, would violate the spirit of the Constitution if he participated in cabinet meetings. Marshall finally conceded to chair the cabinet meetings, but he said that he would not take over any of the other duties of the president unless a federal court ordered it. As a final warning to the president, Marshall joked that he would not be responsible for the actions of the cabinet while Wilson was away.

When Wilson returned from Europe and found less than overwhelming support in the Senate for his plan for international peace, the president decided to take his case to the people. In the summer of 1919 Wilson traveled across the country, delivering more than forty speeches in the intense summer heat. When he reached Colorado, Wilson suffered a stroke while addressing a crowd. That night, the president's train began speeding the chief executive back to Washington.

Although the president was near death, no one told the press or even the vice president. As the president fought for his life, the newspapers were filled with stories about how the Chicago Black Sox had thrown the World Series. When the president did not appear in public for weeks, however, rumors about his condition began flying. People noticed bars on the White House windows, and some suspected that the president had gone insane. (Actually, the bars had been installed during Teddy Roosevelt's administration to protect the windowpanes from TR's progeny.)

It became obvious to everyone that the president was unable to carry out his duties, and some members of the cabinet began planning for Marshall to assume the presidency. But blocking the way was Mrs. Edith Wilson. Although she had no legal authority to do so, Mrs. Wilson began serving as president in her husband's place. Mrs. Wilson and the president's physician refused to consider turning the presidency over to Thomas Marshall on the weak grounds that if they did so, it might take away the one thing that gave Wilson a reason to live. "I am not interested in the president of the United States," Mrs. Wilson said. "I am interested in my husband and his health."

Mrs. Wilson was supported by some members of Wilson's staff who believed that Marshall had neither the intelligence nor the ability to handle the duties of the presidency—something they had apparently not thought about when they selected Marshall to be their vice president.

Although Mrs. Wilson said she was reviewing all official papers to decide what was important enough to interrupt her husband's recuperation, many people decided that Marshall was the de facto president. Federal prisoners began sending their requests for pardons to him, and some foreign governments began corresponding with him.

For his part, despite urgings from some cabinet members and senators, Marshall refused to assume the presidency, although it appears that any court would have sustained his decision to do so. Marshall worried that he could not give the presidency back to Wilson if the president should recover. "I am not going to seize the place, and then have Wilson, recovered, come around and say, 'Get off, you usurper.' " Marshall also believed, somewhat melodramatically, that if he threw Wilson out of the presidency, some people would see it as an attempt at a coup d'état. "I could throw this country into civil war," he told his wife, "but I won't!"

That November, for at least a few hours, Marshall believed that he was the president. In the middle of a speech in Atlanta, Marshall was interrupted and told that the president had died. "I must leave at once to take up my duties as chief executive of this great nation," Marshall told the crowd. He asked those assembled to pray for him, and as he was leaving he asked the organist to play "Nearer My God to Thee."

The whole thing, however, had been somebody's idea of a joke. President Wilson was still alive. Marshall later called the prank "a most cruel hoax," and if anyone had asked, he probably would have admitted to using the same words to describe the vice presidency.

Finally, seven months after his stroke, Wilson had recovered enough to sit in on cabinet meetings, and Marshall was freed from his dilemma. Marshall spent the last year of his vice presidency in relative peace.

When Calvin Coolidge was elected to succeed Marshall as vice president in 1920, Marshall probably wasn't joking when he wrote Coolidge, "Please accept my sincere sympathies."

CALVIN COOLIDGE

Served with Warren Harding, 1921–23

Republican from Massachusetts

THE 1920S ARE THOUGHT TODAY TO HAVE BEEN A RAUCOUS TIME IN AMERICA: FLAPPERS DANCED THE CHARLESTON, college students swallowed goldfish and drank uncertain cocktails, Scott and Zelda threw each other into fountains. And Americans chose Calvin Coolidge as their vice president.

Coolidge may have been "a Puritan in Babylon,"

as one biographer put it, but he wasn't completely out of step with the times. It was, after all, also the age of Prohibition, and many Americans were horrified at the social ramifications of the philosophy of 23-Skidoo. For those people, Calvin Coolidge, the man Alice Roosevelt Longworth said had been "weaned on a pickle," was just the sort of leader the country needed.

☆ ☆ ☆

CALVIN COOLIDGE HAD a remarkable climb to the pinnacle of politics. He did little and said even less, and many people took this to mean that he was a man of immense wisdom. His career in the public arena advanced by baby steps, but it always moved forward. He began as city solicitor of Northampton, Massachusetts, and he moved steadily to mayor and then to the state legislature (where his most memorable piece of legislation was a bill that would have outlawed any automobile that could exceed twenty miles per hour on a level surface).

Coolidge confounded his political peers by always seeming to be in the right place at the right time and having new opportunities handed to him. Twenty years after he entered politics, Coolidge attained the office that should have been the zenith of his career: the governorship of Massachusetts.

It was while he was governor that Coolidge became a national figure. The city police of Boston had gone on strike, and the hooligans had a festival. For two and a half days ruffians stomped, looted, and rioted throughout the city. Finally Coolidge called in the state militia to restore order, and the mayor of Boston fired the recalcitrant peace officers. When the police complained to Governor Coolidge about his interference in their labor action, his reply made national headlines: "There is no right to strike against the public safety by anybody, any time, any-where." The effort for Calvin must have been con-siderable, because this was by far the most stirring thing he ever said.

☆ ☆ ☆

COOLIDGE WAS NO less methodical in his per-sonal life than in his professional career. He didn't marry until age 33, and even then he kept his plans to himself, not even bothering to inform his bride to be.

Calvin was shaving one day next to an open win-dow, wearing nothing but a union suit and a hat, when he heard someone laughing at him. He looked out the window and saw a young woman, Grace Goodhue, who found the sight of Cal in his long johns quite amusing. They began dating, and after discussing the matter with his grandmother, Cool-idge decided that he was ready to get married. Cal decided that a trip to his future wife's hometown was in order.

When his future mother-in-law found him sitting in her parlor reading a magazine, she asked if he was in town on business. Calvin said, "No, I came up to marry Grace." Mrs. Goodhue was surprised and asked him if he had said anything about it to Grace. Coolidge replied, "No, [but] I can wait a few days if it's any convenience."

Grace consented to be the new Mrs. Coolidge, but she may have questioned her decision when, soon after the ceremony, Calvin presented her with a suitcase filled with fiftysome pairs of worn socks and told her they needed darning.

☆ ☆ ☆

WHEN THE REPUBLICANS met in 1920, it was, H. L. Mencken said, a "carnival of bunkum."

Henry Cabot Lodge considered nominating the popular Coolidge as president but changed his mind when he discovered that the stingy Massachusetts governor lived in a two-family house. Lodge felt that any man who would be president should own his own home, and instead the Republicans chose the little-known Warren Harding as their presidential nominee.

Apparently there were some Republican bosses who longed for the good old days of the late 1800s, when holding a public office was akin to having a key to the government's treasury. They thought Warren Harding would either look the other way or be too stupid to understand what was going on. They were good judges of character. Harding, speaking the language he knew best, said on his nomination that he felt like "a man who goes in on a pair of eights and comes out with aces full."

For vice president the choice was a bit tougher. The GOP bosses wanted Hiram Johnson to be the vice-presidential candidate, but Johnson was livid at the suggestion. "We're living in a day of strange events," he said, "but none so strange as that I should be considered second to Senator Harding."

The party leaders then turned to Irvine Lenroot. Lenroot agreed to be the Republican nominee and was subsequently nominated for the post, but before the delegates could vote, a gentleman from Oregon stood on his chair and began waving his arms to attract the attention of the convention's chairman. When the chairman recognized him, expecting that he wanted the honor of seconding Lenroot, the man shouted, "I name for the exalted office of vice president, Governor Calvin Coolidge of Massachusetts!"

With this, Coolidge received the largest spontaneous ovation of his life. All of the delegates knew that Calvinistic Cal was exactly the type of man the

Republican bosses didn't want to nominate—a vote for Coolidge would mean spitting in the eye of the leaders who had been dictating the delegates' every move during the convention. Coolidge won the nomination on the first ballot. Recognizing that Coolidge's political luck had furthered his career once again, one observer said, "I wouldn't give two cents for Warren Harding's life."

When someone telephoned Calvin with the news that he was the vice-presidential nominee, Cal casually turned to his wife, Grace, and said, "Nominated for vice president."

"You're not going to take it, are you?" she asked.

"I suppose I'll have to," he said with all the enthusiasm he could muster.

☆ ☆ ☆

CALVIN COOLIDGE NEVER was mistaken for a hard worker. "Mr. Coolidge has a genius for inactivity," wrote journalist Walter Lippmann. "It is far from being an indolent inactivity. It is a grim, determined, alert inactivity." Coolidge found the vice president's schedule much to his liking, since it allowed him to get his usual eleven hours of sleep per day (which included a two-hour nap each afternoon). It is not surprising then, that unlike nearly every other vice president, Coolidge found the duties of the vice president "fascinating" and said he found the senatorial debates entertaining and instructional.

It was during his vice presidency that Coolidge became famous as Silent Cal. It was said that whenever he opened his mouth, a moth flew out; another wit commented that when Coolidge smiled, the effect was similar to that of ice breaking on a New England river. At a ground-breaking ceremony Vice President Coolidge presided over the event in typical fashion. After watching him dig out the traditional first spade of dirt, the crowd waited for the vice president to make a speech. When Cal stood there silently, the host of the event asked Coolidge if he would say a few words. Calvin looked at the crowd, pointed at the dirt he had just overturned, and said, "There's a mighty fine fishing-worm."

With that stirring message, he turned and walked off to his car.

On another occasion at a dinner party, the table was engaged in a discussion of whether it was acceptable to play golf on the Sabbath. Trying to lure Coolidge into the discussion, the hostess asked Cal his opinion on the subject. Coolidge simply said: "I had a grandmother. She was Baptist. She didn't." At another dinner party a woman told Coolidge that he had to talk with her because she had wagered that she could get Coolidge to say more than two words. "You lose," said Cal. Alice Roosevelt Longworth wondered why someone who hated small talk to such an extent would attend so many dinner parties (and Cal never turned down an invitation). When she asked him about it, the vice president replied, "Got to eat somewhere"—showing that his frugality was greater than his taciturnity.

Frugal doesn't really go far enough to describe Cal. Neither does *stingy, thrifty, miserly, prudent,* or *cheap. Coolidge* should be added to the thesaurus as a new adjective. When he began campaigning for vice president, Coolidge hadn't bought a new pair of shoes for more than two years. After he became president, Coolidge would send the White House servants out to buy newspapers. If the servants didn't promptly return his change, Coolidge would wander the White House murmuring, "Somebody owes me seven cents."

☆ ☆ ☆

QUITE THE OPPOSITE in nearly every way was President Warren Harding. As president, Harding did everything but print girlie magazines in the White House basement. Harding played poker every night, drank whiskey despite the constitutional amendment prohibiting it, chewed tobacco, and still found time to enjoy romantic liaisons with his mistress in the White House closets.

Harding pretended to preside over what was probably the most corrupt presidential administration ever. Things went along fine for a while, but eventually the manure hit the spreader. Two members of the Harding administration committed suicide, and the interior secretary resigned (he eventually went to prison—the first cabinet officer to have that honor). Naturally, President Harding was feeling a bit uncomfortable about the way things were going, and he decided he needed to go outside the city to get away from the constant pestering about the corruption in his administration. He decided to go to Alaska.

Harding began his escape, but bad news reached him in Kansas City, where he received a secret message from the White House that left him visibly shaken. A short time later he received a coded message, which must have contained more bad news that left him near collapse. When Harding reached Seattle, he became seriously ill, and his condition was considered grave by the time he reached San Francisco. Coolidge had been notified that President Harding was seriously ill, but the vice president decided to visit his father in Vermont after he was assured that Harding was recovering.

In the middle of the night on August 3, 1923, Coolidge was awakened by his father, who told him that Harding had died. After checking with officials in Washington, Coolidge thought (incorrectly) that his father, who was a notary public, could administer the oath of office. At 2:45 A.M. Calvin Coolidge was sworn in by his father as president. Papa Coolidge was so excited he sat up the rest of the night in his suit and tie. Calvin went back to bed.

When he was asked years later what he was thinking at the momentous moment when he took the oath of office as president of the United States, Calvin replied, "I thought I could swing it."

THE CAUSE OF Harding's death remains a mystery. Some thought he had a heart attack, some said it was food poisoning, and others suspected either suicide or murder by his jealous wife. However, for nearly the only time in American history, no one suspected the vice president.

Likewise, no one connected Coolidge with the corruption of the Harding administration. If Calvin had known about the sleazy dealings of the cabinet officers, he kept quiet about it. As the misdoings, including the infamous Teapot Dome scandal, became public shortly after Coolidge became president, Calvin merely said, "Let the guilty be punished."

Coolidge was popular enough that he was elected on his own to the presidency in 1924, but he declined to be renominated in 1928. By retiring early, lucky Cal escaped being blamed for the Great Depression. His retirement speech was customarily brief: "Goodbye. I have had a very enjoyable time in Washington."

After he left the presidency, Coolidge became a popular newspaper columnist. During the difficult economic times some people were comforted by Coolidge's commonsense—actually simplistic—

commentary, such as "When more and more people are thrown out of work, unemployment results." Parodying Coolidge's penchant for stating the obvious, James Thurber loved to fool his readers in Europe by concocting Coolidge proverbs, such as "A man who does not pray is not a praying man." No one on the continent was any the wiser.

When Coolidge's life came to a halt just a few years later, Dorothy Parker summed up the reactions of most by asking, "How can they tell?"

CHARLES GATES

DAWES

Served with Calvin Coolidge, 1925–29

Republican from Illinois

IF ANYONE COULD BREAK THE STEREOTYPE OF THE VICE PRESIDENT AS A STUMBLIN', BUMBLIN', FUMBLIN' FOOL, an argument could be made that it should be Charles Gates Dawes. After all, Mr. Dawes did win the Nobel Peace Prize, and he became something of a war hero for his efforts in World War I (even if it was just for his bureaucratic aptitude). Dawes was even the great-great-grandson of William Dawes, the patriot who had joined Paul Revere on his famous midnight ride.

But for those who remember their vice presidents—and believe me, the meetings are held in a very small room—Dawes is better known for his single great failure than for his triumphs. So . . .

Listen, my children, but hold your applause
for the afternoon ride of Charlie Dawes.

☆ ☆ ☆

CHARLES DAWES HAD never held public office before he became vice president. He began his career as a lawyer, but his talent was questionable, and within just a few years he was deeply in debt. He decided to change careers and was able to buy a small utility company. The company became a huge success, and Dawes parlayed his newfound fortune into a career in banking and finance.

As is common, Dawes assumed that his financial success meant that he was destined to be a leader of men, and so in 1902 he ran for the U.S. Senate. He was soundly defeated, and in a bit of hyperbole that proved that he did have a future in politics, Dawes vowed that he was finished with politics "for good and all."

Dawes had an interesting way of protecting his financial interests. Although he was a law-and-order Republican who spoke out against the Ku Klux Klan, Dawes formed his own vigilante militia to break up the activities of labor unions (his posse claimed that they were just there to support the police). Dawes paid many of the expenses of the group—which was called the Minutemen of the Constitution—and at its peak the group had nearly fifty thousand members. Backed by such strong-arm might, Dawes became one of the richest men in the country.

When World War I began, Dawes hoped to create a name for himself in the military. He asked his good friend Gen. John Pershing for a job, and Pershing eventually gave him the position of chief purchasing agent for the army. Equipment managers rarely become the heroes of the game, but it was this seemingly mundane assignment that made Dawes a national celebrity. The war itself didn't bring any special recognition to Dawes, but after the war, when Congress began paying the bills, they found a few of Dawes's purchases to be a bit extravagant (and if a group of congressmen thinks something is extravagant . . .).

Dawes was indignant at the accusation that he had not paid close enough attention to prices when he was assembling supplies for the army. "Hell and Maria!" he shouted at the congressmen, "I'd have paid horse prices for sheep if the sheep could have hauled artillery. . . . It's a hell-fire shame for everybody to be trying to pick flyspecks on the greatest army the world ever knew. We went to France to win the war and we did it!"

Many people around the country were shocked by Dawes's profanity, but even more people admired his chutzpah at facing down the committee with his underslung pipe clenched tightly in his teeth. *Hell 'n' Maria* soon became a popular phrase, as well as a nickname for Dawes.

Following this performance, Dawes was placed at the head of a commission responsible for putting together a plan to restore Europe's economy after the war. The commission's efforts became known as the Dawes Plan, and in 1925 Dawes was awarded the Nobel prize for peace for his efforts.

(Although Dawes won the Nobel prize for peace, even it held the jinx of ill fortune that seems to accompany the actions of all vice presidents. The

Dawes Plan for reparations put a huge strain on the economy of Germany, resulting in economic hyper-inflation. This allowed a demagogue named Adolf Hitler to seize power in Germany. Therefore, a case could be made that Vice President Charles Dawes caused World War II.)

☆ ☆ ☆

WHEN THE REPUBLICANS held their convention in Cleveland in 1924, it was a strange sight: Because of the Eighteenth Amendment to the Constitution, prohibiting the sale of alcohol, the delegates were forced to go through the process sober. The result, H. L. Mencken said, was "as appalling and as fascinating as a two-headed boy," adding, "a whoop for Coolidge would be as startling as a whoop for parallel longitude." Humorist Will Rogers agreed with Mencken's assessment of the convention, and he suggested that the good people of Cleveland throw open the doors of the churches in order to liven up the convention. However, if a wave of puritanism had swept the country, then the Coolidge faction was very much in tune with the times. "The man who could be a Coolidge fanatic," Mencken reported from the convention, "could also be a fanatic for double-entry bookkeeping."

The Republican leaders asked Coolidge whom he would like as his running mate, but Cal insisted that the convention should select the vice-presidential nominee. The person the Republican leaders selected was the governor of Illinois, Frank Lowden, although they had to enter his nomination over his objections. On the second ballot the delegates gave the nomination to Lowden anyway, and, proving that his was not some sort of false-humble protest, he refused the dubious honor, becoming the second man to turn down the nomination for the vice presidency by a major party after it had officially been made.

For three days the delegates tried to find another suitable running mate for Coolidge. Coolidge himself had asked Senator William Borah if he was interested in a place on the ticket, but Borah ruined his chances for the vice presidency when he asked, "At which end?"

Finally the delegates offered the nomination to Dawes. It was rumored that Coolidge was not pleased with this choice, and when Will Rogers asked Cal why he had (typically) kept quiet, Coolidge said, "Nobody told them [whom to choose] in 1920 and they did all right."

When the Democrats met to choose their combatants, they also had a difficult time coming up with a vice-presidential candidate. Will Rogers offered to save some poor Democrat the humiliation of running for the vice presidency by naming himself the candidate. Rogers claimed that he had the qualifications for the post, saying that since the largest part of the vice president's duties were to fill in for the president at dinners, he was well qualified for the job. "I am a fair eater," he said. Rogers added that he could explain the president's absence in a believable fashion, because "I am just good enough a liar to be a good vice president." There was one problem with his nomination: Rogers said that he didn't own a tuxedo and that the administration would have to buy him one because "if I went to a dinner in a rented one they would mistake me for a congressman."

DURING THE CAMPAIGN of 1924, the Republicans marketed Cal with the slogan Keep Cool with Coolidge, which pretty much summed up Cal's view of life. It seems inevitable, then, that Cool Cal and

Hell 'n' Maria Charlie were destined to collide. The first collision took place even before Coolidge and Dawes could be inaugurated.

Dawes sent a message to Coolidge that he did not think he should sit in on cabinet meetings, because it might create a precedent and future vice presidents might not be as qualified to advise the president. Dawes then sent a copy of his letter to the press. Declining the chance to sit in on cabinet meetings was a noble gesture on Dawes's part, except for two things: Coolidge had not invited Dawes to participate, and he had not even asked Dawes's opinion on the subject. Calvin Coolidge, as folks used to say about Queen Victoria, was not amused.

Then the vice president made another gaffe. Charles Dawes thought that as the incoming presiding officer of the Senate he should lay down a few ground rules. He picked his inaugural address to inform the senators on how he planned to run things.

Dawes's craw was full of the filibuster rule, the one that says that no mortal may interrupt a senator when he has his mouth fully engaged. Literally shaking his finger at the senators, Dawes warned them that if they didn't change their ways, it would "lessen the effectiveness, prestige, and dignity" of their body. "Who would dare oppose [such] changes in the rules?" he asked.

All ninety-six senators would, it turned out. Dawes had spoken blasphemy in the upper chamber. The filibuster allows nonstop talking, and nothing is more sacred to a congressman than the sound of his own voice. One senator said it was a "brutal and clownish" performance, and another said it was "Hell and Maria, and not much Maria." A third senator, put off by Dawes's arm waving and finger jabbing, said only that it was "the most acrobatic, gymnastic speech I have ever heard in the Senate."

The speech left Coolidge in the role of the bridesmaid at his own inauguration. Many reporters left the ceremonies to file stories as soon as Dawes had finished speaking, and some newspapers carried headlines eight columns wide shouting about Dawes's diatribe. Mr. Coolidge was, once again, not amused.

Less than a week after Dawes's inaugural lecture, the Washington senators taught the vice president how hardball is played in the political big leagues. Coolidge had appointed Charles Warren of Michigan to be his new attorney general, but many senators were opposed to Warren because of his ties to big business. The Senate vote on Warren appeared to be close, and President Coolidge was relying on Dawes to gather support and, if needed, to cast the deciding vote.

On the day that the appointment came up for a vote, several Democrats were scheduled to speak out against Warren. After checking with the Republican leadership, Dawes decided to turn over his seat to a president pro tem. Knowing that Dawes insisted on taking a nap each afternoon, the Democrats correctly assumed that Dawes was serenely tucked in his bed back in his hotel. The speakers waived their opportunities to speak, and the Warren appointment was called to a vote.

The Republican leaders looked as if they were watching a slow-motion train wreck. With each vote, it increasingly looked as if there would be a tie, which, if the vice president remained absent and the vote were allowed to stand, would result in a rejection of the appointment (a tie vote defeats the motion).

A call went out to the Willard Hotel to awaken the slumbering vice president. Like his great-great-grandfather Dawes, Charlie had to dash at breakneck speed to save the day. Dawes ran down the hotel corridor and out the hotel doors still trying to pull on his clothes. He jumped into a taxi, which sped him to the Capitol where a group of younger Republicans met Dawes and pulled and tugged him up the steps like a rugby scrum. Then through the Capitol halls the vice president ran, bounding up the steps and skidding down the marble corridors, until finally he made it to see . . . the gavel swing down, announcing that the appointment was defeated.

A Democratic senator who had originally voted with the Republicans had changed his vote—no doubt influenced by the Keystone Cops antics of the Coolidge clan. Warren was unemployed, Dawes had his comeuppance, and Coolidge—well, he still wasn't amused, and it was probably a good thing for Dawes that the president didn't know how to use firearms.

Where a week before the senators had grumbled under their breath about the fiery vice president, now they openly laughed at him. Remembering his puppet police force, the Minutemen of the Constitution, some people on the hill began saying that the Minuteman of Chicago was two minutes too late. Another wit hung a sign on the Willard Hotel that read Dawes Slept Here. Not surprisingly, Dawes did not play a significant role in the Coolidge administration thereafter.

☆ ☆ ☆

IN THE SUMMER of 1927, a year and a half before the terms of Messrs. Coolidge and Dawes were to end, President Coolidge called a press conference while on vacation in Rapid City, South Dakota. Meeting the reporters in the gymnasium of the local high school, instead of speaking Coolidge handed each reporter a folded piece of paper. When the reporters opened their messages, they found twelve words: *I do not choose to run for president in nineteen twenty-eight.* Coolidge would not comment further.

Coolidge had not told anyone that he had decided not to seek reelection, not even his wife. The press and the public pored over those few words like biblical scholars. Why did Coolidge not want to run? He had said "choose to run"—did that mean that he was willing to be drafted? He didn't want to run, but would he serve if elected?

Vice President Dawes had once remarked to Senator (and future vice president) Alben Barkley: "Barkley, this is a hell of a job. I can only do two things: one is to sit up here and listen to you birds talk. . . . The other is to look at the newspapers every morning to see how the president's health is." Dawes didn't know that he couldn't find out about the president's well-being in the newspapers.

Coolidge had had a reason for his strange announcement, but he never told the press, the public, or by all accounts, his vice president. Coolidge had suffered a heart attack while president, and he feared that his health would not hold up during a campaign. Charles Dawes never knew how close he had come to becoming president.

FOLLOWING HIS DEBACLE on the Senate floor just a week into his term, the *New Republic* correctly predicted, "It is extremely doubtful whether [Dawes] will again be able to get himself taken seriously in political circles." One of the senators who had witnessed Dawes's ill-fated ride read into the

congressional record this tribute to the thirtieth vice
president:

> *. . . when his statue is placed on high,*
> *Under the dome of the Capitol sky . . .*
> *Be it be said, in letters both bold and bright:*
> *O, Hell and Maria, he has lost us the fight!*

CHARLES CURTIS

Served with Herbert Hoover, 1929–33

Republican from Kansas

WHEN THE REPUBLICANS MET TO PICK A SUCCESSOR TO COOLIDGE IN 1928, HERBERT HOOVER WAS THE FRONT-RUNNER. Although he had never held elective office, Hoover had become a popular figure because he had effectively led the hunger-relief effort in Europe following the First World War.

But some hard-line Republicans thought that

anyone who spent so much time worrying about hungry people had dangerously liberal tendencies, and they opposed Hoover's nomination. The Senate majority leader, Charles Curtis, was one of those hardliners, and he asked, "Why should we nominate a man for whom we will have to apologize throughout the campaign?"

Despite the opposition of Curtis and his ilk, Hoover received the nomination for president. To balance the ticket, the Republicans decided that they needed someone who wasn't such a bleeding heart. In one of history's greatest leaps of political logic, the Republicans concluded that the person who could provide the best balance to the ticket was someone who opposed their candidate. Mr. Curtis received the vice-presidential nomination.

☆ ☆ ☆

CURTIS, 70 YEARS old and fat as a pastry, was, as one political observer wrote, "the apotheosis of mediocrity." But Curtis was also said to be "as devoted to his party as he is dull and dumb," and Will Rogers, in fact, was dismayed that the Republicans would force the vice presidency on one of their most faithful. "The Republican party owed Curtis something," Rogers wrote, "but I didn't think they would be so low-down as to pay him that way." Rogers added that Curtis had been demoted from being the leader of the Senate Republicans to "timekeeper."

Some have claimed that Curtis was the only non-white to ever hold a national executive office in the United States, but that is stretching the truth a bit. Curtis's great-grandmother was Kaw Indian, and Curtis exaggerated his Indian heritage for political benefit, even going so far as to title his official campaign biography *From Kaw Teepee to Capitol: The Life Story of Charles Curtis, Indian, Who Has Risen to High*

Estate. Truth be told, he was, as historian and author Sol Barzman wrote, "one-eighth Kaw Indian and seven-eighths incompetent."

Although Curtis served in Congress for more than thirty-five years, he never wrote a notable piece of legislation and only rarely made speeches. Instead, he was able to hold on to his seat by keeping detailed notes on every one of his constituents he met and by using these notes to win reelection. After such a bland career he was destined to become vice president, and except for Will Rogers, no one was surprised that he received the nomination.

In the election of 1928 Hoover and Curtis were never in danger of defeat. The Republicans were quite popular, and the Democrats had not helped their own cause when they nominated Al Smith, a Catholic, for president. In the hinterlands of the country, the fundamentalist Protestants howled in protest over the Catholic at the head of the Democratic ticket. The Democrats and Al Smith, one radio evangelist said, stood for "card playing, cocktail drinking, poodle dogs, divorces, novels, stuffy rooms, dancing, evolution, Clarence Darrow, overeating, nude art, prize-fighting, actors, greyhound racing, and modernism."

But in the end, it was the prevailing prosperity, not paintings of nude poodle dogs playing poker, that doomed the Democrats. "You can't lick this prosperity thing," Democrat Will Rogers groaned. Hoover and Curtis won easily.

EVEN WHEN HE held the second-most-powerful position in Washington as chief of the upper chamber, Charlie Curtis had remained the "regular of regulars," just another of the congressional guys. But when he was elevated to the lofty position of vice president, a change came over Curtis. When one senator greeted his good friend as Charlie, Curtis bristled and said, "I want you to address me as Mister Vice President." Curtis even considered his post too refined for shaking hands with black constituents.

Curtis's sister Dolly Gann joined in with Mister Vice President in demanding appropriate reverence. Because Curtis's wife had died five years before he became vice president, Dolly Gann took her place as Curtis's hostess and unofficial campaign adviser. In this role, Dolly demanded that she receive as much esteem as the vice president himself.

This caused quite a bit of commotion for those in Washington who were concerned with social protocol (this being the predominant contact sport in the District of Columbia before the advent of the Redskins). Customarily, the vice president's wife was elected president of the Senate Ladies Luncheon Club, but the senators' wives refused to seat the mere sister of a vice president. This act became the Fort Sumter of Washington society, and a war of manners was on.

Leading the opposition was Alice Roosevelt Longworth, daughter of Teddy Roosevelt and wife of the Speaker of the House, Nicholas Longworth. Mrs. Longworth felt that she was the nation's second lady, and the only condition under which she and her husband would attend state dinners was if she enjoyed a higher rank (that is, was seated closer to the president at formal dinners) than the upstart Dolly Gann. (Alice later claimed that the issue had been blown out of proportion and that the actual reason she and her husband sent their regrets to state affairs was that, in the midst of Prohibition, Mr. Longworth did not care to attend dinners where no alcohol was to be served.)

The vice president appealed to the outgoing secretary of state, who advised the vice president to issue a formal letter to the State Department stating that Mrs. Gann was his official hostess. Curtis promptly did so, but his act was voided when the new secretary of state said, after consulting with President Hoover, that the State Department had no jurisdiction in the matter. Meanwhile, the clerks of the Supreme Court began researching the problem. Just as in Andrew Jackson's administration, the serious work of the federal government ground to a halt until the problematic issue of social etiquette could be solved.

Senator Norris, ridiculing the standstill, wrote to the secretary of state, saying, "The League of Nations, the World Court . . . are all important and may affect the peace of the civilized world, but they sink into insignificance and fade into oblivion when compared to the great question that is now agitating the whole world as to where the Vice president's sister should sit at the dinner table."

The *Cleveland Plain Dealer* suggested that the issue be settled by a version of musical chairs, with the fastest getting to sit wherever they pleased. This opinion was seconded by the *Chicago Tribune*, which even found political precedent for the idea, claiming that when he was president, Thomas Jefferson would have the dinner bell rung and his guests would have to scramble to be seated.

Senator Norris reentered the fray, wondering what was to happen to Dolly's husband. "I refuse to abandon him in this crisis," Norris wrote. "I do not intend to let this matter rest until I am assured that he will have at least a snack wherever he goes."

Bloodshed was avoided when a matter of somewhat greater importance forced something of a truce: In October of 1929 the stock market crashed, signaling the beginning of the Great Depression.

☆ ☆ ☆

DESPITE THE SOBERING effect the depression had on most Americans, Charles and Dolly continued to eat, drink, and be merry. Dolly, for her part, claimed that the whole thing was a figment of people's imagination. In one speech given on behalf of the Hoover administration, she announced that the depression, such as it was, had ended. This inspired at least one newspaper to run the headline DOLLY CALLS IT OFF!

The vice president was no more sympathetic to the fears of American workers. When thousands of World War I veterans demonstrated in Washington, demanding food and jobs from the government they had risked their lives to defend, Curtis became scared for his own safety and ordered two companies of U.S. Marines to shoo the protestors away from his office. (This didn't end the old soldiers' protest, and a few days later President Hoover ordered Gen. Douglas MacArthur to break up the demonstration, which MacArthur did by using troops and tear gas. It's no wonder the Republicans were not able to regain the White House for another twenty years.)

When Curtis went on a cross-country campaign trip for the 1932 election, hecklers in the crowds asked why he didn't try to help the veterans. Curtis lost his cool. "I've fed more than you have, you dirty cowards!" he shouted, adding, "I'm not afraid of any of you!" (In response the crowd began cheering for Hoover's opponent in the upcoming election, Franklin Roosevelt.) In another campaign speech on the same swing through the countryside, Curtis responded to hecklers by saying that if the people in the country had a better understanding of economics, they wouldn't be in such a fix. The citizens, he said, were just "too damn dumb" to understand what was going on.

The voters weren't too dumb to know a pompous ass when they saw one, and Curtis soon became the subject of satire. In 1931, a musical featured a fictional vice president named Alexander Throttlebottom as a supporting character. It was widely thought that Throttlebottom was based on Hoover's bumbling vice president.

Of Thee I Sing was written by the successful team George S. Kaufman and Morrie Ryskind with a score and lyrics by George and Ira Gershwin. In the play, Throttlebottom is awarded the vice presidency when names are drawn out of a hat and, as one of the characters says, "this fellow lost."

At first Throttlebottom worries about taking the job, because he's afraid his mother will be hurt, but the conflict is resolved when it is agreed "she'll never hear about it." After Throttlebottom accepts the nomination and wins election, he spends most of his time feeding pigeons in the park. He is denied a library card because he can't come up with two references, and he is able to get into the White House only by joining a guided tour.

The play opened to reviews of the raving sort. The *New York Times* said that the play was "funnier than the government and not nearly so dangerous." The *New Yorker* said the play was "a Washington merry-go-round with a hey nonny nonny and a ha-cha-cha." *Of Thee I Sing* had enough nonny nonny to win a Pulitzer Prize in 1932.

Despite the ridicule, in 1932 enough Republicans thought Curtis was speaking the truth that he was renominated as Hoover's running mate. The voters didn't feel the same way, and Curtis and Hoover were promptly booted out of office by an angry electorate.

THE ALSO-RANS

Some of the Men and
Women Who Dared
to Be Second—and Failed

Losing a political race is usually a setback in a politician's career, but when it comes to the vice presidency, coming in second (or would that be fourth?) can actually give a career a boost. The office holds the most danger for the presidential nominees who make the selections. Although they try to follow the surgeon's credo First Do No Harm, sometimes this is easier said than done. Some tickets have had to look long and hard to find someone who could be a junior partner to their presidential nominee.

The cliché that politics makes strange bedfellows is never more true than when the vice presidency is involved. Over the course of history some unusual combinations have cropped up, and some unlikely people have tried for the office. Following are some who in this century dared to be second but didn't quite make it:

☆ FRANKLIN DELANO ROOSEVELT. In the presidential election of 1920, the Democrats nominated James Cox, governor of Ohio, for president and picked as his running mate the little known secretary of the navy, Franklin Roosevelt. Although Cox and Roosevelt lost the election to the Republican tandem of Warren Harding and Calvin Coolidge, the nomination elevated Roosevelt's political stature, and his vigorous appearance on the campaign trail—he wasn't paralyzed by polio until a year later—would help Roosevelt overcome his image as an invalid in the 1932 election.

☆ JOHN FITZGERALD KENNEDY. In 1956, John Kennedy decided that the road to the Oval Office ran through the vice presidency, and at the urging of his father (and with his father's considerable financial support), he set out to grab a place on the ticket.

Joseph Kennedy tried to help his son by offering to pay for a campaign for Lyndon Johnson if Lyndon would try for the presidential nomination and pick JFK as his running mate. The race for the Democratic vice-presidential nomination was close that year, but on the second ballot LBJ convinced his fellow Texans to go for the Harvard fellow, and Johnson stood and said, "Texas proudly casts its vote for the fighting sailor who wears the scars of battle." Despite Lyndon's help, JFK lost the nomination to Tennessee's Estes Kefauver.

It was a fortunate loss, as it turned out. Kennedy had come close enough that most Americans watching in their living rooms became used to the idea of JFK as a national leader, but by losing the nomination, Kennedy avoided being labeled a loser in the Republican avalanche.

☆ THOMAS EAGLETON. In 1972, Democrat Thomas Eagleton of Missouri was George McGovern's running mate. For some reason, during his first news conference following his nomination, Eagleton felt the need to share the information that he had been hospitalized three times for psychiatric treatment and that he had undergone electric-shock therapy. He emphasized, however, that he had recovered.

Suddenly Eagleton, who had been almost as unknown as Agnew had been in 1968, became a household name for all the wrong reasons. McGovern displayed that he did have at least one quality that would serve him well as president: the ability to talk out of both sides of his mouth about his vice president. McGovern held a press conference to say that he was behind Eagleton "one thousand percent"—and then promptly dumped him.

McGovern had so much difficulty finding a new running mate that the Democrats investigated whether the law required him to have a vice-presidential candidate at all. A sign was placed in the Senate cloakroom listing a phone number for anyone interested in the job to call (most people considered this a joke; others weren't so sure). Finally McGovern chose Ted Kennedy's brother-in-law, Sargent Shriver, as his running mate.

☆ GERALDINE FERRARO. In the presidential election of 1988, Democratic nominee Walter Mondale made vice-presidential history by selecting Geraldine Ferraro, U.S. representative from New York, as his running mate. Ferraro was the first woman to be named to the presidential ticket of a major political party.

Ferraro's spouse, John Zaccaro, would have set a new precedent had his wife been elected. Although through history almost no vice presidents have been allowed to sit in on presidential cabinet meetings, in an interview in *Redbook*, Zaccaro said that if Geraldine were elected, he would sit in on cabinet meetings in the Mondale administration. "Even if they didn't like it, I would sit in," Zaccaro said. "I would insist on being there."

Although Ferraro was the first woman to win a nomination, other women have been seriously considered for the office. In 1948 Harry Truman said that he wouldn't mind running with Eleanor Roosevelt as his sidekick. In 1988, Republican George Bush said that Elizabeth Dole was a possibility for the office (as was her husband, Senator Robert Dole). In 1956, Clare Booth Luce, Republican representative from Connecticut and wife of *Time* magazine founder Henry Luce, made it known that she was interested in the job if Nixon weren't renominated.

Also listed as a possibility for the Republican nomination in 1952 was Republican senator Margaret Chase Smith. During the convention, one bumbling reporter asked Smith what she would do if she won the nomination as vice president and found herself sleeping in the White House. Smith handled the question with aplomb: "I'd go straight to Mrs. Truman and apologize," Smith said. "Then I'd go home."

JOHN NANCE

GARNER

Served with Franklin Roosevelt, 1933–41

Democrat from Texas

ACTUS JACK GARNER GAVE UP HIS LIFE'S DREAM—BECOMING SPEAKER OF THE HOUSE—TO BECOME VICE PRESIDENT OF THE UNITED STATES, a decision he later said was the "worst damn fool mistake I ever made."

☆ ☆ ☆

JOHN NANCE GARNER was the oldest son of a Confederate soldier. At one time he thought he was going to be a baseball player and even played semi-pro ball for a while, but when that didn't work out, he decided to attend Vanderbilt University. Garner found that his fourth-grade education didn't adequately prepare him for the Harvard of the South, however, and returned to Texas after just a month of college. Lacking a proper education, Garner decided that a career in law would be the best thing for him, and he was able to pass the bar and join a local practice.

When he was in his early twenties, Garner was told that he had tuberculosis, and he decided to move to the southwest Texas town of Uvalde, near the Mexican border, where he hoped the drier air would restore his health.

It has been said that the only two things that prospered in Uvalde were the cactus and John Garner, and this is at least true for Garner. Cactus Jack gained a reputation as a skilled horse trader, and he acquired three banks, several businesses, and thousands of acres of land, all while maintaining his law practice.

When Garner was 25 years old, he became a judge in Uvalde, and from there he moved to the Texas legislature. In 1902 Garner decided to run for the U.S. House of Representatives, and he won election to the house that he would make a home for years to come. Garner rarely returned to his home district to campaign, and he seldom gave speeches. After he had been reelected to his House seat for the fourth time, he even admitted that he had never set foot in five of the counties in his district.

Garner didn't work any harder in Congress. He almost never made speeches and he authored little notable legislation. A critic once said that Garner advanced in the House mainly because of the obituary column, but Garner had more going for him than seniority: He also depended on poker and bourbon. Garner played so much poker with his House colleagues that his yearly winnings often exceeded his salary. Garner also liked to imbibe bourbon and branch water with his fellow congressmen, a practice he liked to call "striking a blow for liberty" but that others might have called "violating the Constitution," since for many of his years in the House the Eighteenth Amendment was in full effect.

Garner's congenial meetings with what he called the Board of Education helped him to overcome his reputation as "another cow thief from Texas." Thanks to his Board meetings, Garner was able to win enough friends that by 1929 he was elected House minority leader.

For years Garner had hoped to someday become Speaker of the House. When the Democrats won a majority of the House (by a single seat) in 1931, this dream became a reality for Cactus Jack. Garner didn't forget about his friends or their Board meetings once he attained this powerful post. At closing time in the House, Garner would say: "Boys, let me stick my finger in the mouth of my pet snake and see if he'll bite me this afternoon. Because if he does, as he has in the past, I will be in need of the cure, and we will have to go to the Board of Education room and take care of the situation pronto." Garner and his pals may have not been the most diligent in performing their duties on behalf of the American public, but they never missed one of their Board meetings.

☆ ☆ ☆

ONCE HE REACHED his goal of becoming House Speaker, Garner should have stopped climbing, but he became greedy and just a year later decided to try for the presidency.

Garner had been talked into running for president by William Randolph Hearst, who needed a president who would follow his lead. Hearst bought time on the large NBC radio network to allow Garner to express his views. Garner was able to gain much support for his run for the presidency but not as much as Franklin Delano Roosevelt (whom H. L. Mencken referred to as "Roosevelt minor"). Neither man, however, had enough votes to win the nomination.

Roosevelt's backers appealed to Hearst to switch his support from Garner to FDR. After gaining concessions from Roosevelt, Hearst called Garner and told him to give his delegates to Roosevelt, which Garner did.

Although he had won the nomination, Roosevelt still needed Garner's help. Roosevelt's urbane and liberal outlook meant that he was vulnerable in the conservative South. More important, FDR needed Garner to run with him on the ticket to show the voters that the Democrats were one big, happy family. For the sake of his party, Garner agreed to give up his powerful position as Speaker of the House to take on the neutered vice presidency.

Although vice-presidential nominees have long been expected to campaign tirelessly for their ticket, Garner continued his congressional practice of not campaigning. To the chagrin of FDR, Garner made but one, solitary speech on behalf of the party. Garner told Roosevelt that he need not worry: "Hoover's making speeches, and that's enough for us."

☆ ☆ ☆

FOLLOWING THE ELECTORAL victory of Roosevelt and Garner in November of 1932, Cactus Jack nearly succeeded to the presidency before he even became vice president. Just two weeks before the inauguration, an immigrant named Joseph Zangara decided to travel to Washington to kill President Hoover. When he learned that Roosevelt would be in his hometown of Miami, however, Zangara changed his mind and decided to kill FDR instead. "Hoover and Roosevelt—everybody the same," he said later.

Zangara was a mere five feet tall, and when he attended Roosevelt's speech, he found that he couldn't see over the crowd. When Roosevelt finished his speech, Zangara climbed on a chair and fired five shots as dignitaries crowded around Roosevelt to shake his hand. Roosevelt was unharmed, but Anton Cermak, the mayor of Chicago, was killed. If Zangara had succeeded in killing president-elect Roosevelt, under the Constitution, John Nance Garner would have been sworn in as president in his place.

ONCE HE BECAME vice president, Garner quickly learned that he didn't enjoy presiding over the Senate as much as he had taking charge of the friendly confines of the House. When the Kingfish, Senator Huey Long of Louisiana, baited Garner by asking him how he should vote if he was half for a bill and half against it, Garner's angry reply was: "Get a saw and saw yourself in half. That's what you ought to do anyway." Garner also refused to carry on the traditional evening socializing expected of vice presidents, saying that the vice presidency was an eight-to-five job. But despite being uncomfortable in the upper chamber of Congress, Garner proved invaluable to Roosevelt by helping to smooth the way in Congress for FDR's radical New Deal legislation.

In 1936 Roosevelt and Garner were renominated by the Democrats. A national poll by the *Literary Digest* showed that Republicans Alf Landon and Frank Knox were about to reclaim the White House for the GOP. But the poll was fantastically wrong—Roosevelt and Garner won by the widest margin ever up to that point. Following this prediction, some wags said that the old saw As Maine Goes, So Goes the Nation should be changed to As Maine Goes, So Goes Vermont.

After the election, however, the professional relationship between FDR and Cactus Jack took a turn for the worse. Garner grew concerned as Roosevelt's New Deal proposals became increasingly liberal, and he warned FDR that the boys up on Capitol Hill were becoming alarmed. "Mr. President, you've got to let the cattle graze," Garner advised.

Not having an agricultural background, Roosevelt apparently didn't understand what Garner was getting at and decided that he would actively oppose the reelection of any Democrats who weren't ardent New Deal supporters. This upset Garner, but Cactus Jack and the other congressional leaders were stunned when FDR announced the next phase of his plan: The Supreme Court had been declaring a good deal of the New Deal unconstitutional, and FDR wanted to bench the Supreme Court by naming six new justices.

Garner thought the idea stank, and he let everyone know by walking through the Capitol holding his nose and giving a thumbs-down sign when the idea was mentioned. When Roosevelt's legislation for reforming the Supreme Court was about to come to a vote in the Senate, Garner said his ears were "buzzing and ringing" from all the hullabaloo, and he decided it was time to take a vacation back home in Texas (thus avoiding having to vote on the measure in case of a tie). An angry Roosevelt ordered Garner to return to Washington, saying that it wasn't a good time to "jump ship," but Cactus Jack decided to stay in Texas.

When Garner did return to Washington, he found himself increasingly locked out of the president's inner circle. Franklin Roosevelt knew that a person who had been paralyzed by polio could die suddenly and, partially because of this, had made sure that his vice president was always part of the workings of the executive office. In 1938, however, Roosevelt and his cabinet officers became frustrated by Garner's active opposition to their policies. Instead of telling the vice president he was no longer welcome at their meetings, Roosevelt and his cabinet set up a ruse. The official cabinet meetings became what one cabinet officer called "delightful social occasions." The real discussions were held after Garner left the room in what Garner called Roosevelt's "prayer meetings."

Garner said that he thought that Roosevelt was "the most destructive man in all American history." Roosevelt wasn't a big fan of Garner's either, and he was particularly upset when Cactus Jack greeted the king of England by slapping him on the back.

But the final blow came when Roosevelt let it be known to the Democratic leaders in 1940 that he wouldn't mind running for a third term. The conservative Garner thought that this was blasphemy. "I wouldn't vote for my own brother for a third term," he said.

Garner backed up his words with actions by running against Roosevelt for the Democratic presidential nomination. Garner didn't fare nearly as well as he had in 1932. At the convention, 61 delegates voted for Garner; 946 voted for FDR. Garner didn't take the defeat well; he went home to Texas and refused to return to preside over the Senate for the remainder of his term.

☆ ☆ ☆

ALTHOUGH CACTUS JACK was 72 years old when he returned to Texas, he was still as vigorous and as feisty as ever. Democratic politicians began making regular pilgrimages to Garner's ranch. When Lyndon Johnson stopped by, Cactus Jack told him—Texan to Texan—what he thought of the vice presidency. Reporters later said that Garner had said that the office "wasn't worth a bucket of warm spit," but he wasn't actually that polite. Despite the advice, Lyndon went on to accept the vice presidency.

On Garner's ninety-fifth birthday, President John Kennedy called while he was in Texas to wish Garner a happy birthday. "You're my president and I love you," Garner told JFK. "I hope you stay in there forever." Kennedy was killed later that day.

Garner, who had begun his career campaigning by stagecoach, died in 1967 just two weeks short of his ninety-ninth birthday.

HENRY AGARD

WALLACE

Served with Franklin Roosevelt, 1941–45

Democrat from Iowa

 ENRY WALLACE IS THE VICE PRESIDENT
WHO MAY NOW BE SHIRLEY MACLAINE.
Wallace was an independent thinker, and he loved
tinkering with mystical religions and alternative political philosophies. He was immersed in mysticism
and New Age thinking back when Catholicism was
considered a fringe religion.

This would seem to make Wallace an unlikely

politician, but as the television hucksters say, wait, there's more. Wallace also thought that Stalin's Soviet Union would make a swell model for governments in the post–World War II world—a belief that earned Wallace a scarlet *C* (for Communist) in the minds of most people.

So how did such a person become vice president during one of the most sober periods of American history? Easy. One of the most popular presidents in the country's history, Franklin Delano Roosevelt, said, "they will go for Wallace or I won't run, and you can jolly well tell them so."

☆ ☆ ☆

ONLY ONE THING can be said with certainty about Henry Agard Wallace: If he didn't *make* a difference, at least he *was* different. Unlike other aspiring politicans who studied law and the ways to maneuver around it, Henry Wallace went to college to study animal husbandry. Wallace soon gave up that glamorous field, however, for the excitement of corn genetics. Wallace had come from one of the country's foremost agricultural families—his grandfather founded the magazine *Wallace's Farmer*. Henry disproved the conventional wisdom that a good-looking ear of corn was a better ear of corn, and he started a company to market his new, improved (albeit homely) ears, called the Hi Bred Corn Company. Wallace eventually took over the family farm journal, and it was his fervent editorial support of U.S. farmers that drew the notice of Franklin Roosevelt, who asked Wallace to be his secretary of agriculture.

From such a background one might assume that Henry was an earnest midwestern hayseed who had done good. But Wallace wasn't the rock-steady conservative type most people think of when they consider folk from the heartland. Wallace had what his friends generously called a curious mind. In the words of a person not so close to him, Wallace was a "queer duck."

When he wasn't concentrating on plant chromosomes—an interest that he continued even after entering politics—Wallace spent his time searching for eternal truth. At various times he tried on the cloaks of Presbyterianism, Judaism, Buddhism, Roman Catholicism, Humanistic Darwinism, Muhammadanism, Zoroastrianism, and Christian Science. He was also known to be not much fun.

Such extracurricular activities usually do not make for a long career in politics (outside California, of course), but they worked well for Wallace, because he came within a few months' time of being the president of the most powerful nation in the world.

☆ ☆ ☆

OF THE PRESIDENTS who were so popular that they were able to pick their successors—Thomas Jefferson, Andrew Jackson, Theodore Roosevelt, Franklin Roosevelt, and Ronald Reagan—FDR certainly had the most creative choice: He picked himself. This wasn't an easy sell to all the Democrats. Vice President John Nance Garner decided to abandon ship over Roosevelt's decision (although it was a case of jumping before being pushed, because Roosevelt wasn't going to ask him to run on the ticket again anyway), and many other Democrats had to be hoodwinked into believing that this was what all the party faithful wanted.

But Roosevelt's effort to get his party to conveniently forget about 150 years of presidential tradition was not the most difficult task he faced at the 1940 Democratic convention. The hardest thing was to convince everyone to let Henry Wallace run on the ticket with him.

The governor of Oklahoma told newsmen that Wallace was his second choice for the vice-presidential nomination. When they asked him who his first choice was, the governor replied, "Anyone—red, white, black, or yellow—that can get the nomination." This feeling was seconded by nearly everyone at the convention. The Democratic national chairman told Roosevelt that most people considered Wallace "a wild-eyed fellow" and said that "it would be a terrible thing to have him become president."

Roosevelt was beside himself over the convention's attitude on Wallace. He tried a maudlin play for sympathy, telling the party chairman: "You know, a man with paralysis can break up at any time. While my heart and lungs are good . . . nothing in this life is certain." This hardly reassured the delegates.

Roosevelt then became angry, and as opposition to Wallace grew, FDR wrote out a five-page message to the convention to be delivered in the event that Wallace was denied the party's nomination for vice president. It said that "it would not be best to straddle ideals. . . . Therefore, I give the Democratic party the opportunity to make that historic decision by declining the honor of the nomination for the presidency. I so do."

Whether Roosevelt was bluffing, no one will ever know, but just by writing out his message he gave the party leaders a good scare. FDR sent Eleanor to the convention in Chicago to try to calm the nerves of the delegates, which she did. Following her speech to the convention supporting Wallace, he was given the second place on the ticket. Still, the mood of the delegates was such that the leaders of the convention decided not to let Wallace make any sort of acceptance speech.

☆ ☆ ☆

WALLACE SOON PROVED to be a potential liability to President Roosevelt in the fall presidential campaign, thanks to a group of letters that were sent to various newspapers. During one of Henry's walks along the razor's edge, he had met up with Nicholas Konstantinovich Roerich, who claimed to be the leader of a group called the White Brotherhood of the East (he was also, conveniently, its sole representative). Roerich told Wallace that during his travels through Kashmir, Turkestan, and Tibet, he had discovered an ancient Buddhist document that told that as a young man, Jesus Christ had visited India and Asia before he began his teachings in the Middle East. During his sojourn there, Christ had supposedly created thousands of paintings that were evidence of his visit.

Wallace not only believed Roerich but also thought that Roerich's search for additional evidence was worthy of government funding. Since Wallace was secretary of agriculture, he sent Roerich to Mongolia to find proof of Christ's travels—although this wasn't the official explanation for Roerich's trip. Officially, USDA agent Roerich was traveling through Asia looking for new strains of forage crops.

Things took a bad turn for Roerich and Wallace (especially Roerich) in the middle of the trip, however. Not only was Roerich unable to pick up the scent of the Lord's two-thousand-year-old trail, but he was arrested by the Chinese, who thought that this strange character wandering around the countryside asking ridiculous questions was some sort of spy. Even more dangerous for Wallace's political future, while Roerich was away from the United States, he was charged with tax evasion. With Roerich in big trouble at home and abroad, Wallace abandoned him, firing him from the USDA and stopping all his funds.

Roerich had had a few followers in the United States besides the secretary of agriculture, however, and they saw an opportunity to seek vengeance for Wallace's callous treatment of Roerich when Wallace received the vice-presidential nomination. Roerich's followers hoped to embarrass the candidate by releasing some letters that Wallace had written to the shaman. The letters contained some cryptic passages that would have frightened the conservatives (and many liberals) right out of their union suits. "I have been thinking of holding the casket—the sacred, most precious casket," Wallace wrote. "I have thought of the new country going forth to meet the seven stars under the sign of the three stars. And I have thought of the admonition 'Await the stones.'"

Participation in a cult religion was bad enough, although most reasonable people know that very few politicians are eligible to be Baptist deacons. But another letter could have been even more damaging to the campaign, since it was allegedly written from Wallace to Franklin Roosevelt. That letter said that the administration "must deal with . . . the flameless ones, who with their one last dying gasp will strive to re-animate their dying giant 'Capitalism.'" This sentiment, which apparently revealed Wallace as a socialist, would have damaged Roosevelt as well, since the president had said that Wallace was the best man in the country to carry on his policies if he were to die.

Why were the letters not made public before the election? Mainly because they were so outlandish that most newspaper editors didn't believe they were real, especially after Wallace strongly denied having anything to do with them. And because the letters were typewritten, no one could dispute Wallace's claim. (No doubt, too, there were some aides in Roosevelt's administration working overtime to pressure the newspaper publishers not to run stories on the letters.)

Despite Wallace's denial, he apparently was the author. In her autobiography, Eleanor Roosevelt said that he had written the letters, adding that Wallace was simply too idealistic to be a good politician.

☆ ☆ ☆

ROOSEVELT DIDN'T IGNORE Wallace the way most chief executives ignore their second in command. In fact, Roosevelt appointed Wallace to the Board of Economic Warfare, the group charged with purchasing all the supplies for the military during World War II. It was an amazingly important job for a vice president.

Soon, however, the vice president's Board of Economic Warfare ran into trouble. Wallace wanted to send free food to the rubber-plantation workers in South America, believing that the laborers would work harder if they weren't hungry. Others in the Roosevelt administration, chiefly the secretary of commerce, thought that the primary reason the rubber-plantation employees were working at all was to buy food, and that if the United States just gave it to them for free, they would spend all their time taking siestas.

Naturally such an anticapitalist gesture brought Wallace to the attention of the House Committee on Un-American Activities, which reported that the vice president's Board of Economic Warfare employed "pinkos, nudists, Communists, and world-savers." This was of much concern to the Roosevelt administration. In order to end the bad press about the vice president's plaything, FDR simply took it away from him and left Wallace with no more duties than those of the standard-issue vice president.

Wallace did not take to these duties well. He closed John Nance Garner's popular bar in the vice president's office, and he rarely invited senators up to see him there. He insulted the senators even more by frequently falling asleep in the Senate chambers while the congressmen discussed some point or another.

Wallace was no slacker, though. He believed that World War II offered the opportunity for the nations of the world to re-create themselves into something he called the New Frontier (a phrase that John F. Kennedy would later borrow as the title for his governmental policies). In promoting his ideas Wallace wrote three books and numerous magazine articles. He also found time for public speaking—a favorite topic being the benefits of Soviet Communism, particularly as practiced by Joseph Stalin. Wallace held that American capitalists, in contrast, were "midget Hitlers." These socialist sentiments might have been quite amusing if he had been a professor down at the local community college, but Wallace was vice president during a world war, serving under a president who had serious health problems—something that terrified the leaders of the Democratic party.

The Democratic insiders nudged, shoved, and cajoled Roosevelt into dropping Wallace from the ticket in 1944. Roosevelt had promised the nomination to Wallace, but that didn't really matter, since he had led several other men to believe that they would also be his running mate that year. Finally, Roosevelt agreed to let the Democratic convention decide whom to select, and the unpopular Merchant of Globaloney, as Wallace was known, was quickly dumped from the ticket.

Henry Wallace went on to serve in Roosevelt's fourth term and in the Truman administration as secretary of commerce, but Truman had to fire Wallace early on. Wallace's constant stroking of Joseph Stalin was making it difficult to get the Soviet leader to take Truman's anti-Communist stand at face value.

In 1948 Henry Wallace formed his own political party, the Progressive party, and they selected Wallace as their candidate for president, with Glen "The Singing Cowboy" Taylor as their vice-presidential candidate. Instead of splitting the Democratic party, though, as most Dewey Republicans had hoped, Wallace's socialist wallowings made Truman look positively conservative and helped save the election for the Democrats. Wallace found just more than a million fellow pinkos, nudists, Communists, and world-savers to vote for him for president.

☆ ☆ ☆

THE WORLD TODAY would be a different place if Franklin Roosevelt had died just a few months earlier, before the end of World War II and before the other Democrats convinced him to dump Wallace. If Henry Wallace, instead of Harry Truman, had met at Potsdam with Joseph Stalin, millions more people may well have lived under Stalin's totalitarian jackboot.

Although it had taken considerable work to get Roosevelt to drop Wallace from the ticket, nearly everyone thought it was worth the effort. The chairman of the Democratic National Committee, Robert Hannegan, knew what a great service he had done for his nation. "When I die," he said, "I would like to have one thing on my headstone: that I was the man who kept Henry Wallace from becoming president of the United States."

HARRY S TRUMAN

Served with Franklin Roosevelt, 1945

Democrat from Missouri

JUST EIGHTY-THREE DAYS AFTER BECOM-ING VICE PRESIDENT, HARRY TRUMAN RECEIVED A TELEPHONE CALL FROM THE WHITE HOUSE WHILE HE WAS PLAY-ING POKER with a few of his old buddies from Congress. The caller told Truman to drop every-thing and go to the White House immediately. "Jesus Christ and General Jackson," Harry said to his card-playing friends, "something must have happened."

When Harry arrived at the White House, Eleanor Roosevelt told a shocked Truman that President Franklin Roosevelt had died. Incredibly, despite the country's being involved in a two-theater world war and his own failing health, President Roosevelt had not kept his vice president apprised of the state of the world. The small man from Missouri had no idea of the enormity of the task before him. But, no doubt, Eleanor did.

"Is there anything I can do for you?" Truman numbly asked Mrs. Roosevelt.

"No, Harry," Eleanor said. "Is there anything *we* can do for *you*? You are the one in trouble now."

The first full day of Truman's presidency was Friday the thirteenth—the same day Truman learned that something called the Manhattan Project was close to creating an incredibly destructive weapon called the atomic bomb. That day Truman held a press conference and told reporters how he had felt the night before when he learned that he was president. "I don't know whether you fellows ever had a load of hay fall on you," Truman said, "but when they told me yesterday what had happened, I felt like the moon, the stars, and all of the planets had fallen on me. . . .

"Boys, if you ever pray," Truman said, "pray for me now."

☆ ☆ ☆

HARRY TRUMAN WAS the oldest son of a Missouri farmer and the stereotypical four-eyed, piano-playing mama's boy. Even he admitted that when he was growing up, he was "kind of a sissy."

Truman didn't go off to college—the last chief executive to miss that academic rite of passage. He wasn't uneducated, however. It has been reported that Harry read all three thousand books in the Independence, Missouri, library when he was growing up, including the encyclopedias.

Truman had hoped to make his living as a piano player, but it was apparent that this wasn't where his fortune lay. Nothing else seemed to work out for the young man either: He tried being a bank clerk, mailroom clerk, railroad man, postal worker, and road-crew foreman, all without success. He then went home and tried to help out the best he could around the family farm. As with Ulysses Grant, it always took the crucible of war to let the true measure of Harry Truman shine through.

Although he was nearly turned down by the army for what they called flat eyeballs, Truman was accepted into the National Guard as a lieutenant. Although his first duty was to man the canteen, when World War I began, Harry found his place in a field-artillery unit. Eventually promoted to major, Truman was involved in much serious fighting, including the Meuse-Argonne offensive.

After the war, Harry was able to capitalize on his military success when he returned to Missouri. One of his war buddies asked him to help in setting up a haberdashery, but the men were better at cannon fire than they were at shirt sales, because the business went belly-up within three years. Truman's partner declared bankruptcy. Truman refused to do the same, even though his bills totaled nearly thirty thousand dollars. Instead he worked for many years to pay his debts.

Another of Major Truman's soldiers happened to have an uncle who was involved in politics, and when Harry needed a job, Tom Pendergast helped Harry get a job as county administrator. Pendergast was the powerful boss of one of the largest political machines in the Midwest. Eventually he decided that he needed an "office boy" in the U.S. Senate, and he thought the short piano player from Independence was just his boy. Everybody was surprised that Pendergast had picked Harry Truman as his choice for the Senate seat, but nobody was as surprised as Truman himself. With the backing of the Pendergast machine, Truman's election was a fait accompli.

Senator Truman confounded Pendergast by developing a reputation for honesty and common sense. Although Truman was a part of Pendergast's machine, Harry never let the machine become a part of him. Not even his political enemies could question Truman's honesty. This also meant that Harry wasn't a favorite of Pendergast, who called Truman the contrariest man alive. Fortunately for Truman, Pender*graft* was sent to prison after being found guilty of bribery and fraud, and Truman was free to be his own man in Washington.

In the Senate, Truman made his mark as the head of a committee charged with overseeing the war effort. Truman was diligent in his work, driving more than thirty thousand miles to visit defense facilities to inspect their efforts. He also read the proceedings of a similar Senate committee that had been in place during the Civil War—the transcripts of which take up five feet of shelf space. Because of his efforts the United States was able to save fifteen billion dollars. Near the war's end, the Washington journalists voted Harry Truman second only to FDR in assisting the war effort.

☆ ☆ ☆

AS THE ELECTION of 1944 approached it was obvious to Roosevelt's White House advisers and to the leaders of the Democratic party that they needed a new vice president. Not only did they consider

Henry Wallace an unstable and dangerous man, but they knew what almost no one else in the country knew: Roosevelt was about to die, which meant that the voters weren't selecting just a vice president but the man who would soon be the new commander in chief.

Roosevelt was aware of the political situation enough to know that Wallace had to be dumped, but he had a problem saying no to anyone who asked for his vice-presidential endorsement. Jimmy Byrnes, one of Roosevelt's White House aides who pined for the nomination, got wind of FDR's courting of other candidates and telephoned the president to ask him about it. Roosevelt assured Byrnes that he was still the top pick. "You are the best-qualified man in the whole outfit," Roosevelt told him. "You must not get out of the race." Byrnes, who assumed that the nomination was his, asked his good friend Harry Truman to nominate him at the Democratic National Convention.

Then Roosevelt took a shining to Supreme Court Justice William O. Douglas. Douglas had high qualifications for the vice presidency, though they did not include his wisdom from sitting on the nation's highest court—that would be of little use to a vice president. Instead, as Roosevelt said explaining his selection of Douglas, "He is good in a poker game and he tells good stories."

But the man whom Roosevelt's advisers—chief among them the head of the Democratic National Committee, Robert Hannegan—really wanted for the vice presidency was Harry Truman. After much arm-twisting and inside maneuvers the committee convinced FDR to give the vice-presidential nomination to Truman. But before anything was to be arranged, Roosevelt had one last concern: "Clear it with Sidney," he instructed. Sidney was Sidney Hillman—head of the Congress of Industrial Organization's Political Action Committee (PAC)—who apparently had considerable say in how the country was governed. Once organized labor had given its approval to Truman, the next thing to do was to convince Truman to accept the vice presidency. This was more difficult than Hannegan and the other Democratic leaders had anticipated.

Many delegates, especially the labor leaders, still hoped to renominate Henry Wallace for the vice presidency. When one pro-Wallace demonstration threatened to buoy Wallace all the way to the nomination, Hannegan had to act quickly. He ordered the doors to the convention hall thrown open, which flooded the floor with spectators, diluting the strength of the demonstration (and causing such heat that many women fainted). Hannegan then rammed through a vote to adjourn that day's meeting (his selective hearing didn't allow him to hear the majority of people who voted no to the motion) and sent an aide with a fire ax to tell the organist that he would chop through the amplifier cords if the organist didn't stop playing "Iowa—That's Where the Tall Corn Grows."

That ended the last gasp of Wallace's dubious reign as vice president, but Hannegan then faced the even larger task of convincing Harry Truman to take the job. When Hannegan first approached Harry and told him that he was Roosevelt's choice for vice president, Truman characteristically responded, "Tell him to go to hell."

Truman, who had once said that the vice presidency was as useful as "the fifth teat on a cow," wanted no part of the office.

That was that, Hannegan thought. "It's all over," he said. "Our candidate won't take it." But Franklin Delano Roosevelt had faced greater difficulties than a small reluctant senator. Roosevelt telephoned Truman and Hannegan, and, talking loud enough for Truman to hear, asked, "Bob, have you got that fellow lined up yet?"

"No," Hannegan said. "He's the contrariest Missouri mule I've ever dealt with."

"Well, you tell him that if he wants to break up the Democratic party in the middle of a war, that's his responsibility!" Roosevelt shouted, and then hung up.

Truman was stunned. "My God," Harry said, "if that is the situation, I'll have to say yes, but why the hell didn't he tell me in the first place?"

☆ ☆ ☆

TRUMAN WAS A popular vice president in the Senate, not only because he was one of their own, but more important, because he reopened John Nance Garner's liquor cabinet and reconvened the Board of Education meetings in the vice president's office.

As for himself, Truman didn't much like to sit around listening to the senators bloviate. "I am trying to write you a letter," Harry wrote to his mother from the Senate chambers, "while a windy Senator . . . is making a speech on a subject with which he is in no way familiar."

On the afternoon of Roosevelt's death, the White House staff had difficulty coming up with a Bible for Truman to use in the swearing-in ceremony (confirming the suspicions about the Roosevelt household held by many Bible-belt Americans). Finally, someone found a Gideon Bible that had been left in one of the guest bedrooms, and Harry became president.

Following the ceremony, Truman returned to his apartment to tell Bess and later that evening went to his neighbor's apartment to eat a roast-beef sandwich and tell him the news. The pace of Truman's life would soon pick up considerably. Within the first 120 days of his presidency, Truman oversaw the surrender of Hitler's Nazi regime; he ordered two atomic bombs dropped on Japan and presided over the terms of that country's surrender; and he helped push through the creation of the United Nations.

And that was that. With former vice president Harry Truman leading the way, the country stepped into the modern world.

Although Truman had made decisions far greater than those most presidents had ever faced, there was some early difficulty getting people to believe that he really was president. Truman once told an aide about a presidential appointment, and when the aide asked if the president had made the appointment before he died, an irritated Truman said, "No, he made it about half an hour ago."

Even worse were those who continued to try to become president after it was clear that Harry was indeed the number one man. Truman had appointed Jimmy Byrnes—his old rival for the spot as FDR's running mate in 1944—as secretary of state, but Jimmy B. was pouting, and he often refused to consult with his president before he acted. Things became so bad that during one press conference a reporter asked Truman if he supported a position taken by his State Department.

Soon, however, people became accustomed to, if not comfortable with, the short, bespectacled man in the Oval Office. As president, Truman gained support for his refusal to make excuses. The Buck Stops Here read the message on his desk, which was paired with his equally famous saying, If You Can't Stand the Heat, Get Out of the Kitchen. And fathers around the country agreed with Harry's response when a reporter gave a scathing review of his daughter's singing recital: "I never met you, but if I do you'll need a new nose and a supporter below."

(Harry Truman always used a fair amount of pepper in his speech, something that regularly caused him to be criticized. Richard Nixon, for his part, said that Harry's language was a menace to children. Truman's daughter Margaret apparently agreed with Nixon: When Harry told her that he was going to teach his grandchildren how to talk, she said, "The hell you will!" A newspaper columnist once suggested that children who imitated what he called Trumanisms should have their mouths washed out with bourbon. Still, Harry did his best to keep his tongue under control. When a woman complained to Truman's wife about Harry's use of the word *manure*, a story goes, Bess reportedly said, "You don't know how long it took me to get him to say manure.")

In his accidental term as president, Truman had many successes: He passed landmark civil-rights legislation—someone once said that FDR was for civil rights, but "Truman means it"—he oversaw the creation of NATO and the Marshall Plan, and he stared down the Soviet Union with his airlift of supplies to Berlin. Such wide-ranging and thoughtful leadership would be completely alien to most politicians of recent vintage, but Harry always said he didn't try to do what people thought he should do but what he believed was correct. He liked to quote Mark Twain, who had said: "Always do right. This will gratify some people and astonish the rest."

But after Harry squeaked by in the election of 1948 to gain his own term as president, the wheels seemed to come off. He invented something called the limited police action, which most other people called the Korean War, a type of engagement in which the United States decides to fight but promises not to win.

While Harry was trying to contain the Communists on the Korean peninsula, Republican senators Joseph McCarthy and Richard Nixon thought they smelled Commie blood in the Truman administration, and although McCarthy just saw shadows (and really wasn't looking for anything more), Senator Nixon did find at least one Communist spy in Truman's State Department.

As if unpopular wars and hidden Communists weren't enough, Truman also had problems with a more traditional scandal—good old corruption. Some ten million dollars was missing from the Department of Agriculture, and even the Justice Department had legal problems of its own. Although the scandals didn't touch Truman, he decided not to press his luck by running for president a second time.

Because of what the Republicans called "Korea, Corruption, and Communism," Truman's reputation as a leader was tarnished for many years. But in the 1970s, shortly after Truman's death, a favorable biography of Truman, *Plain Speaking*, helped to rehabilitate his standing among U.S. presidents. The book was released during the height of the Watergate scandal, and many readers were nostalgic for Truman's no-nonsense style during the time of another great crisis. Soon bumper stickers began appearing on automobiles around the country with a message that would have warmed Harry's crusty heart: America Needs You, Harry Truman.

ALBEN WILLIAM

BARKLEY

Served with Harry Truman, 1949–53

Democrat from Kentucky

IN THE PRESIDENTIAL CAMPAIGN OF 1948, NOBODY, NOT EVEN HIS OWN MOTHER-IN-LAW, thought that the accidental commander in chief, Harry Truman, could be elected to the presidency on his own merits. People said such things as "We're just mild about Harry" and "Don't shoot the piano player, he's doing the best he can"—and that was at the *Democratic* National Convention.

The Republicans, for their part, went around acting as though their presidential candidate, Thomas Dewey, were running unopposed, which some Democrats suggested wouldn't be a bad idea. Since Truman is going to be defeated anyway, they reasoned, why bother to pay for a campaign? And the Republicans got their gibes in, too, saying, "To err is Truman" and "What would Harry Truman do if he were alive?"

Naturally, no one with anything resembling a political résumé wanted to be associated with the Truman candidacy, which they assumed was a ship looking for a place to founder. Poor President Harry was having a difficult time trying to find someone to be his vice president. He offered the vice presidency to Supreme Court Justice William O. Douglas, but Douglas declined, telling a friend he had no intention of being second to a second-rate man.

The reigning Senate majority leader, Alben Barkley, however, was interested in taking the job, despite, as Barkley put it, the vice presidency's being passed around "like a cold biscuit." Barkley wasn't forced into some form of political maneuvering to gain the second spot on the ticket. He simply picked up the telephone and called Truman and said that he was interested. "Why didn't you tell me you wanted to be vice president?" a relieved Truman shouted back.

☆ ☆ ☆

ALBEN BARKLEY WAS the last of the nation's executive officers to have been born in a log cabin. Barkley's father was a dirt-scrabble Kentucky tenant tobacco farmer, and the son's future was anything but certain. But Barkley was determined to receive an education, and while a teenager he took a job as a janitor at a nearby college in order to pay his tuition.

(Years later, after Barkley rose from janitorial duties to the much easier life of a vice president, the college honored its favorite son by putting up a banner that proclaimed Barkley Swept Here.) Following his graduation and a brief stint in graduate studies at Emory University, Barkley was admitted to the Kentucky bar in 1901.

Alben Barkley was blessed with a pair of leather lungs and the natural inclination to exercise his larynx at every opportunity. He was known to be among the best hog callers in the Bluegrass State, and he admitted to "a natural inclination to start making a speech anytime I saw as many as six people assembled together."

With such innate talent it was no surprise that Barkley gravitated toward a career in politics. After a few local political positions, Barkley was elected to the U.S. Congress in 1912 and was sent to the Senate fourteen years later.

Barkley had little of a strong, personal political philosophy, but his loud voice and witty speech made him a popular fellow to have around, and the voters regularly renewed his employment—just another "professional jobholder," groused H. L. Mencken. Barkley was able to hang around long enough to rise to the position of Senate majority leader in 1937.

The Democrats found Barkley's oratorical skills useful in the golden age of radio, and the senator from Kentucky became a frequent speaker at Democratic National Conventions. He was tapped to deliver the party's keynote address three times and even took part in Roosevelt's stunt to gain a third Democratic nomination by announcing that FDR had no intention of running (even though as leader of the Senate, Barkley had to know Roosevelt's true intentions).

Barkley had long served as what he admitted was

"sort of a rustic, amiable errand boy for the [Roosevelt] White House." This gave Barkley the reputation of a lapdog, which, naturally enough, meant that he was always a contender for the vice presidency. But Barkley showed that he had backbone—quite a stiff one—when he stood up to President Roosevelt and resigned as senate majority leader after Roosevelt harshly criticized Barkley's effort at pulling together a budget. Roosevelt quickly apologized, Barkley was soon reelected by his colleagues as majority leader, and although the episode ruined Barkley's chances at a spot on the Roosevelt ticket in 1944, his reputation as Bumbling Barkley was put to rest for good.

☆ ☆ ☆

BARKLEY HAD SEVERAL reasons for wanting the vice presidency in 1948. For one, he was the chairman of the Committee to Inform the Vice-Presidential Nominee, and his nomination made his task of breaking the news to some poor soul much easier. More important, at age 70, Barkley was considered by most people too old for the presidency, but he was considered plenty vigorous for the lower standards of the second office.

Considering the dismal chances most people were giving Truman of being elected president that year, it may have been that Barkley never expected to give up his powerful seat in the Senate. It was reported that at the convention even Barkley doubted that Truman could be elected. H. L. Mencken, attending his last political convention, said that Barkley had the air "of a country pastor preaching the funeral services of a parishioner plainly bound for hell."

But when Barkley gave a keynote speech using the phrase *Give 'em hell!* the campaign had its theme, and Harry and Alben, the two oldest men ever to share a presidential ticket, took off around the country on an amazingly vigorous campaign. Despite his age, Barkley was a tireless campaigner for Truman. In the first "prop stop" campaign trip, Barkley boasted of traveling 150,000 miles in six weeks. (Since this works out to more than thirty-five hundred miles per day, it can only be assumed that most of Barkley's campaign events consisted of a touch-and-go at the airport.)

Nearly everyone in the country, including Harry Truman's mother-in-law, was shocked to learn that Truman had defeated Dewey (the reportage of the *Chicago Tribune*—DEWEY DEFEATS TRUMAN—notwithstanding). For the two small-town candidates who had been underestimated most of their lives, the victory must have been especially sweet.

☆ ☆ ☆

HAVING RETIRED FROM the stress of trying to lead the Democratic portion of the Senate, Barkley decided that he was free to have a rollicking good time as veep (an endearing term coined, in fact, by Barkley's proud grandson). Barkley presided over his former colleagues often with his tongue firmly in his cheek. When one senator complained to Barkley that another senator had yawned during his speech, Barkley ordered that "the yawn of the Senator from Illinois will be stricken from the record."

Barkley—the oldest vice president in history at age 71—also found that being vice president was a good way to meet women. He often posed for pictures with beauty queens, not passing up the opportunity to give them a buss on the cheek, something he referred to as "this osculatory business." Barkley's wife had died a few years before he became vice president, and the nation was amused by reports of Barkley's courting of younger women. Barkley downplayed his reputation as a septuagenarian lothario: "When I was in the House I was told that the difference between the House Foreign Affairs Committee and the Senate Foreign Relations Committee was that senators [and, presumably, vice presidents] were too old to have affairs. They only have relations."

He finally fell in love with a 38-year-old woman from St. Louis, and he spent much of his time in the Senate writing mash notes to her. "I would have done anything, even the most outrageous sort of filibuster, to keep the senators talking so I could get my love letters written," he said. Four months later the vice president married his sweetheart, becoming the only vice president to enter into matrimony while serving in that office.

Barkley's retirement into the vice presidency was nearly interrupted in tragic fashion. In 1950 Harry Truman had to vacate the White House because the old building was about to fall down, and he took up residence in the nearby Blair House. Truman was in his bedroom taking his customary afternoon nap when he heard a commotion and an exchange of gunfire on the street below. Instead of diving under his bed, Truman went to the window to watch what was an assassination attempt on his own life. Two Puerto Rican radicals, Griselio Torresola and Oscar Collazo, had decided to kill President Truman to bring attention to their movement to gain independence for their homeland. Torresola and Collazo had bought new suits for the event, and they had taken a tour of Washington to learn where the president was staying. On November 1 the two men tried to shoot their way into Truman's suite.

As guards yelled at Truman to "Get back, damn it! Get back!" there was a fusillade of gunfire. One of the gunmen wasn't stopped until he was partway up the steps to Truman's suite. In just more than two minutes approximately thirty shots were fired, killing one of the guards and one of the would-be assassins. Truman later claimed he wasn't worried that he would be killed. "I never had bad luck," he said.

Had Barkley become president he would have been just as uninformed about the affairs of state as Harry Truman had been when he became president. Truman had said that he intended to keep Barkley updated on events, and he had created a position for the vice president on the National Security Council, but as with most vice presidents, Barkley was out of sight and out of mind. Barkley compared himself to a catcher in nighttime baseball game after the lights have gone out. He said he never knew what the pitcher was going to do next.

☆ ☆ ☆

WHEN TRUMAN DECIDED not to try for another term as president in 1952, the 74-year-old Barkley thought he'd try for the office on his own but found little support for his candidacy outside his home state of Kentucky. He left politics for a while, but he wasn't ready for retirement. In 1954 he ran for and won a seat in the Senate. Thus, the former senate majority leader and president of the Senate became just another junior member of that body.

Two years later, in a speech at Washington and Lee University, Barkley said that his lowered station in government suited him just fine. "I am willing to be a junior [senator]. I am glad to sit on the back row," he said. "I would rather be a servant in the House of the Lord than to sit in the seats of the mighty." With that proclamation, Barkley fell dead of a heart attack.

RICHARD MILHOUS NIXON

Served with Dwight Eisenhower, 1953–61

Republican from California

IN CALIFORNIA IN 1945, A GROUP WITH THE OMINOUS NAME *THE COMMITTEE OF ONE HUNDRED* CIRCULATED A WANT AD IN THE STATE. The advertisement said that the committee was looking for "any young man, resident of the district, preferably a veteran, fair education, [with] no political strings or obligations." They wanted a

"Congressman candidate with no previous political experience."

The person the committee chose for the assignment was a 33-year-old lawyer from Whittier, California. Thus began the political life of Richard Milhous Nixon, and as those political philosophers the Grateful Dead would say, what a long, strange trip it's been.

"Richard Nixon," Harry Truman once said, "is a shifty-eyed, goddamned liar, and people know it." Although many Americans would agree with Harry's assessment, it doesn't provide a complete picture. Nixon was more than just a man who told a few fibs. He was perhaps the nation's greatest practitioner of the black art of politics since Alexander Hamilton. For nearly half a century Nixon has been able to grab headlines and be a part of the political process.

Nixon's later debacle as president tends to overshadow his earlier career, but before Richard Milhous Nixon became the most disgraced president in U.S. history, he was one of the most visible—and controversial—vice presidents our country has ever had.

☆ ☆ ☆

NIXON FIRST TRIED his hand at politics at Whittier College. While a senior there, he ran for class president on a platform promising a monthly dance—despite the fact that dances were banned by the school administration. Nixon not only won the election but convinced the school's administrators to allow social mixers.

Nixon had always been quite serious about his schoolwork, and when he attended Duke Law School, his grindstone-scarred nose earned him the nickname Gloomy Gus. When he was a third-year law-school student, Dick became so concerned about his academic status that he broke into the dean's office hoping to get a glimpse of his class standing. He saw that he was at the top of his class, and he managed to escape punishment.

Following his graduation, Nixon attempted to peddle his sleuthing skills to the FBI, but they declined the opportunity to make Dick a G-man. (Nixon had a penchant for odd career choices: He once modestly suggested "I would have made a good pope," and in a recording at the Richard Nixon Library, he says that if he had been born later in the century, he would have liked to have been a rap star.) He was likewise turned down for a job by a New York law firm, so he returned to Whittier and joined a law firm there.

Back at Whittier, Nixon met Pat Ryan, a local teacher and part-time actress. He was so smitten with her that he announced on their first date that he intended to make her his wife. She wasn't sure, but Nixon was so confident that he even drove her to and picked her up from her dates with other men. They did finally marry in June of 1940.

After a failed attempt to run a frozen-orange-juice business with other local entrepreneurs, in 1942 Nixon joined the navy, where he served as a paper pusher in the South Pacific. His military career aided his future political career in one important aspect: Dick was an accomplished poker player, and he used the several thousands of dollars he won from fellow swabbies to finance his first political race.

After Nixon responded to the advertisement of the Committee of One Hundred, he based his first campaign for the U.S. House of Representatives on fighting Commies and liberals, saying that he was fighting against "lip-service Americans," a theme he would rely on for many years to come.

Nixon stayed true to his campaign promise to scour the government of Communists with his efforts on the House Committee on Un-American Activities. Testifying before the committee, Whittaker Chambers, a *Time* magazine editor and, at that time, an acknowledged ex-Communist, accused a State Department official, Alger Hiss, of being a coconspirator. Hiss denied even knowing Chambers, but Nixon knew a too-slick lie when he heard one. Nixon dogged Hiss, poking holes in his testimony that he had never even met Chambers. President Harry Truman derided the Nixon investigation, calling it a red herring, but it turned out that Nixon was at least partially correct.

Eventually, Hiss was convicted of perjury and sent to prison. Nixon's triumph had been dramatic, and it gained the young congressman national support within his party.

In 1950, at the age of 38, Nixon decided to parlay his popularity into an attempt on a Senate seat. He defeated Helen Douglas for the seat by painting her as a "pinko" who was soft on Communism, although the evidence for that accusation was slight. Nixon referred to his opponent as the Pink Lady and distributed campaign fliers attacking Mrs. Douglas that were printed on pink paper. The infamous Senator Joseph McCarthy joined the fray, telling Californian voters that a vote for Nixon's opponent would be a vote for the "Commicrat party of betrayal." Disgusted with Nixon's low-road campaign tactics, a Southern California newspaper nicknamed him Tricky Dick, a handle that would stick to Nixon throughout his career.

☆ ☆ ☆

AS THE PRESIDENTIAL election of 1952 approached, both the Democrats and the Republicans pleaded with Gen. Dwight Eisenhower to be their party's candidate for president. The general wasn't much involved with politics—he had voted for the first time in his life just four years before in the presidential election—and although he was interested in becoming president, Eisenhower wasn't even sure to which party he belonged. Finally, he apparently took stock of himself—career military man, avid golfer, no terrific compassion for the downtrodden—and decided he'd sign up with the Republicans.

Eisenhower was surprised to learn that as the presidential candidate he would be able to select his running mate, but when aides asked him if he favored anyone, Ike pulled a list of names out of his wallet. At the top of the list was the young Dick Nixon, and he was given the vice-presidential nomination.

On the campaign trail Nixon fought like a bulldog. He promised that the presidential contest would not be "a nicey-nice little powder-puff duel," and he meant it. Nixon called Stevenson Adlai the Appeaser and said that Stevenson had a Ph.D. from the "College of Cowardly Communist Containment." When Stevenson said that he had a plan for ending the Korean War, Nixon declared that the patriotic thing to do would be to share the plan immediately with the Joint Chiefs of Staff so that they could stop the fighting (a position that Nixon apparently forgot when, as a presidential candidate in 1968, he claimed to have a secret plan to end the Vietnam War).

Nixon would soon be forced into a completely defensive posture, however. In September 1952, the *New York Post* published a story headlined: SECRET RICH MEN'S TRUST FUND KEEPS NIXON IN STYLE FAR

BEYOND HIS SALARY, and Nixon was knocked back on his heels. The story reported that during his two years as a senator, Nixon had taken more than eighteen thousand dollars from unnamed supporters to pay for personal expenses.

The fund, as it later turned out, was not secret, not illegal, and at the time, not even considered highly unethical. It was independently audited and used only for campaign expenses. In fact, Democratic presidential candidate Adlai Stevenson had a much larger fund of his own and one that appeared to be far less on the up-and-up. The Democratic vice-presidential candidate even used a slush fund to keep his wife on the campaign payroll.

But for the Eisenhower campaign, just the aroma of scandal would be a disaster. The campaign had focused on three things—Korea, corruption, and communism, which they called K_1C_2—and even if Nixon's fund wasn't technically a case of corruption, that point was sure to be a subtlety lost on the American public. Eisenhower wondered how his campaign could attack the corruption in Washington "if we ourselves aren't as clean as a hound's tooth?"

Nixon tried to dismiss the scandal by saying that it was just another Communist plot to discredit him. At a campaign stop in Oregon he shouted that his wife didn't have a mink coat but "a good Republican cloth coat" instead. It soon became obvious to many people in the Eisenhower campaign, however, that the slush-fund peccadillo was about to blow up their campaign.

Many people, including Adlai Stevenson, were calling for Nixon to resign from the campaign. Even the *New York Herald Tribune*, considered the mouthpiece of conservative Republican power brokers, said, "The proper course for Senator Nixon . . . is to make a formal offer of withdrawal from the ticket."

Nixon said later that he had been prepared to resign from the ticket in order to save himself from the indignity of being dumped, but he wanted to hear his future from the mouth of the general himself. Eisenhower's ability to dodge a question by burying his answer under an avalanche of qualifications and platitudes would become well-known after his election, but when Nixon confronted Ike, he grew frustrated with the general's evasiveness. Finally, Nixon exploded in a way that no one probably had with Eisenhower in many years: "General, there comes a time in matters like this when you've got to piss or get off the pot."

Eisenhower's advisers decided that it was time for Nixon to make a national mea culpa. The Republican National Committee bought a half hour of television time—immediately following the immensely popular Milton Berle show—to allow Nixon to plead his case directly to the American public. Eisenhower's aides hoped to force Nixon to sign his own death certificate, because they told him that if after the speech six out of ten people supported him, he would be dropped from the ticket, but if nine out of ten people supported him, he could stay on.

Apparently, this plan didn't seem foolproof enough for those Republicans who wanted to dump Dick, and just one hour before Nixon was to go on the air, one of Ike's aides telephoned Nixon and told him, "At the conclusion of the broadcast tonight you should submit your resignation." Nixon declined to say whether he agreed with the plan, only answering: "You will have to watch the show to see. And tell them I know something about politics, too."

There was a danger that Nixon would lose control while on camera. He had had only four hours' sleep the night before, and after receiving the telephone call from Ike's headquarters telling Dick that they were, in effect, deserting him, Nixon had received a telegram from his Quaker mother telling him that she was praying for him. The possibility was high that he would either explode in anger or break down in tears.

As the television lights came on, Nixon looked hesitant and his voice was hoarse. But within a few minutes, he had control of himself and his audience. Nixon laid bare his finances and said that he drove a modest 1950 Oldsmobile. He dragged out his wife's "Republican cloth coat" again, saying that although it wasn't a mink, "I always tell her that she'd look good in anything." As the speech went on, Nixon picked up confidence and steam. He attacked Commies. He attacked Democrats. He attacked Commie Democrats. He attacked Democratic slush funds. The high point of the speech came when, in a masterpiece of convoluted logic, he claimed that his opponents were trying to throw his little girl's puppy out on the streets, and he would have no part of it:

> One other thing I probably should tell you, because if I don't, they'll probably be saying this about me too. We did get something, a gift, after the election [Nixon was getting ahead of himself; he meant the nomination] . . . You know what it was? It was a little cocker spaniel dog . . . black and white spotted. And our little girl—Tricia, the six-year-old— named it Checkers. And you know, the kids love that dog, and I just want to say this right now, that regardless of what they say about it, we're going to keep it.

Ike watched the speech from a campaign stop in Cleveland. He made no comment, but the others in the room knew how Eisenhower felt. In attacking the Democrats' slush fund, Nixon proposed that all candidates for president and vice president fully disclose their financial records, as he was doing in his speech. Ike knew, as did Nixon, that this would be embarrassing for the general, who had been showered with gifts and enjoyed tax privileges after he returned home from World War II.

And Nixon had even more surprises for Ike. When Nixon finished his speech by asking people to write the Republican National Committee and tell them whether he should stay on the ticket, he effectively took his political fate out of the hands of the Eisenhower camp. Nixon had many friends on the Republican National Committee, and they weren't about to drop him from the ticket, especially after the party faithful were moved to write in to support the young senator from California and his wayward puppy. The general who had directed the largest military operation in history had been effectively outflanked, and he knew it. No matter what Eisenhower thought of Tricky Dick, he would have to live with him now.

For his part, Nixon thought that he had blown it, and afterward he said, "I was an utter flop," adding that the only votes he would get would come from the canine contingent. A few people agreed with Nixon's early assessment, and some compared Nixon's speech to a soap-opera confession. Many people thought it was just another slick attempt by Nixon to worm his way out of a tight spot. As Lyndon Johnson liked to say about Nixon's speeches, "Boys, I may not know much, but I know the difference between chickens--t and chicken salad."

But the Checkers Speech, as it came to be known, was an overwhelming hit—such a masterful performance, in fact, that it even gained a review in the show-business newspaper *Variety*. The speech had been the highest-rated show in television up to that point, reaching more than sixty million people. It was the first time (and only time to date, thank goodness) that a cocker spaniel was used in American electioneering as a political hostage, and thousands upon thousands of letters and telegrams poured into every Republican enclave in the country supporting the beleaguered vice-presidential candidate.

Eisenhower quickly adjusted to the political reality that Nixon would remain his vice-presidential nominee. When he greeted a teary-eyed Nixon the next day, Ike put his arm around Nixon's shoulders and shouted, "Dick, you're my boy!" Ike and Dick went on to win the election by a large margin.

AS OPPOSED TO most vice presidents, Nixon claimed to love the office. He said that unlike the House and Senate, "in the vice presidency you have an opportunity to see the whole operation of government and participate in its decisions." Exactly what decisions Nixon was participating in he did not say.

As vice president, Nixon continued his attack on Communists and Democrats, two groups he had trouble distinguishing, calling the Democratic party the party of treason. The Democrats said that Nixon was representing "McCarthyism in a white collar." Nixon fired back that an attack on him was an attack on "the millions of Americans who work for a living in our shops and factories."

Unfortunately the high-minded political discussion was interrupted by Ike's faulty ticker. In September 1955, Eisenhower had a severe heart attack, and for a few moments it looked as if Nixon might become president. Eisenhower instructed the National Security Council and the cabinet to continue meeting in his absence. Then, the following June, Eisenhower experienced an obstructed bowel and had to be rushed to the hospital for an emergency operation. Officially Nixon served as acting president during the weeks that Ike was unable to attend to his duties. But in reality, Eisenhower's chief of staff, Sherman Adams, was serving as president. This wasn't a big secret: Some smart alecks asked what would happen if Adams died and Eisenhower had to become president.

Despite his physical problems, in 1956 Eisenhower decided that he would like to serve a second term as president, but he wasn't sure he wanted Dick Nixon to go along for the ride. Ike thought that Nixon would be a poor president, and he was realistic enough about his health to know that his vice president could be promoted before his second term expired. Eisenhower tried to ease Nixon off the ticket in 1956 by offering him his choice of cabinet posts, with the exceptions of the head of the State or Justice departments.

Eisenhower didn't hide his plans to dump Dick. At a press conference Ike said that Nixon would have to "chart his own course." Despite Eisenhower's obvious hints for Nixon to remove himself from the vice presidency, Nixon decided to stay the course and remain on the ticket. He even cleaned up his act and, if not becoming statesmanlike, at least acted less like a Chicago ward captain. Reporters dubbed Dick the New Nixon. (It was hard to tell whether they meant this sarcastically.) The new, different Dick could have stayed his old self and it probably wouldn't have changed the election results, because nearly everyone in the country liked Ike, and he won reelection by nearly ten million votes.

☆ ☆ ☆

NIXON'S SECOND TERM as vice president was the most eventful of any chief magistrate-in-waiting in American history. The first crisis came in November 1957, when the old soldier, Dwight Eisenhower, suffered his third major illness while president. This time Ike had a stroke, and he became frustrated about his poor health. "If I cannot attend to my duties, I am simply going to give up this job," he said. "Now that is all there is to it." Sherman Adams called Nixon to brace him for what he thought was coming. "You may be president in the next twenty-four hours," Adams said.

As it turned out, Ike's stroke was relatively minor, but because of his increasingly frequent, serious health problems, Eisenhower decided to draw up an official memorandum that would make Nixon "acting president," but not the country's official president, if Eisenhower were forced to retire because of poor health. This seemed to fly in the face of more than one hundred years of presidential precedent—ever since Vice President John Tyler had overruled John Quincy Adams following the death of President William Henry Harrison, the creature of "acting president" had failed to exist. The Speaker of the House, Sam Rayburn, spoke out against the memorandum, calling it unconstitutional. Nonetheless, the next two presidents, Kennedy and Johnson, followed Ike's lead and crafted similar directives.

Nixon hoped to escape the pressures of Washington in 1958 with a goodwill tour of South America, but it quickly turned into a tour of ill will instead. In Lima, Peru, Nixon was greeted at San Marcos University by a stone-throwing Communist mob. Nixon yelled at the crowd that they were "the worst kind of cowards!" and had his message translated into Spanish. When Nixon reached his hotel, he was greeted by another unruly collection of Commies, and when one man spit in his face, Nixon returned his assault with a sharp kick in the shins. In his famous book *Six Crises*, Nixon said, "Nothing I did all day made me feel better."

Nixon and his wife, Pat, then traveled to Caracas, Venezuela, where they were met with anger and violence. Leaving the airport, Nixon's limousine was stopped by a greeting committee who beat on the car with sticks and pieces of metal pipe and rocked it in the apparent hope of turning it over and setting it on fire. The protesters broke through one of the car's windows, and the shattering glass cut the vice president's face. A Secret Service agent, assuming that all of the passengers in the limousine were about to be killed, drew his revolver, saying that if they were all to die, he was going to take a few Commies with him.

Finally the limousine began to move and, using its wipers to clear the windshield of spit, was able to deliver the vice president and his wife to their hotel. Once safely ensconced, Nixon canceled his other appearances and thereby avoided assassination, because still another mob had prepared a bomb that was to go off at a wreath-laying ceremony. President Eisenhower was afraid that Vice President Nixon would have trouble leaving the country safely and ordered two companies each of Marines and paratroopers to a ship stationed thirty miles off the Venezuelan coast to rescue the vice president and his entourage if needed. Fortunately, Venezuelan authorities cleared a corridor to the airport by using tanks and tear gas, and the Nixons were able to return home.

Although some Americans viewed the trip as a "diplomatic Pearl Harbor," fifteen thousand well-wishers greeted Nixon at the Washington airport when he arrived, and his courage on the trip won him the highest approval ratings of his career.

Nixon would soon increase his popularity by standing up to yet another bully, Soviet premier Nikita Khrushchev. In July of 1959, Nixon was sent to the Soviet Union to christen a cultural-exchange exhibit in Moscow. Part of the exhibit was a model of a typical American home, complete with a color television. As Nixon and Khrushchev toured the exhibit, the Soviet premier seemed determined to provoke a fight with the vice president. Pausing in the model kitchen, the two superpower leaders argued over whether Sears or the Red Army built washing machines that made clothes whiter and brighter. Khrushchev jammed his finger into Nixon's chest and said that he wanted to compete in washing machines, but that "your generals say we must compete in rockets."

Nixon gave as good as he got from the Soviet premier, with both men shaking their fingers at the other, and the entire episode was captured on film. When the tape was shown back home, the American public loved the sight of its vice president standing up to the belligerent Soviet leader. The Kitchen Debate, as it became known, established Nixon as a world leader—after all, would Khrushchev have bothered to argue about frost-free refrigerators with some low-level bureaucrat?—and helped Nixon win the 1960 Republican presidential nomination.

☆ ☆ ☆

IN THE PRESIDENTIAL election of 1960, when Vice President Nixon faced off against Massachusetts senator John F. Kennedy, it was time again for Richard N. (as in *new*) Nixon. This Nixon was not the mudslinging Tricky Dick nor the handwringing "acting president" but a cool, confident world leader.

It might have worked, but Nixon was up against greater odds than he realized. For one thing, President Dwight Eisenhower gave only lukewarm support to the idea of a job promotion for his vice president, saying at one point that he had trouble believing "he [Nixon] *is* presidential timber." Additionally, Jack Kennedy was the handsomest presidential candidate since the Republicans had nominated the philandering Warren Harding in a cynical (and successful) attempt to get women's votes. Kennedy's good looks and charm played well to the television camera. Nixon, on the other hand, was trying to act cool, and on the already cool medium of television, he came across icy cold. Nixon's television appearances opposite Kennedy in a series of three televised debates, in fact, mortally wounded his candidacy.

The 1960 presidential election was one of the closest in the twentieth century. Nixon lost to Kennedy by less than 0.2 percent of the popular vote. There were many accusations at the time that the Democrats had stolen the election, especially in Lyndon Johnson's home of Texas and in Chicago mayor Richard Daley's Illinois. The *New York Herald Tribune*, in fact, planned a series of articles on voter fraud in those two states until they were called off by Nixon. "No one steals the presidency of the United States," Nixon said. He added, "Our country can't afford the agony of a constitutional crisis—and I damn well will not be a party to creating one just to become president."

Nixon appeared equally gracious when he later told a Kennedy White House staff member that he wished that he had said some of the things that JFK had said during his inauguration. The staff member asked Nixon if he was referring to Kennedy's famous line *Ask not what your country can do for you, but what you can do for your country*, but Nixon said that wasn't the part. What he envied, Nixon said, was "the part that starts *I do solemnly swear*."

☆ ☆ ☆

AFTER LOSING THE presidential election of 1960, Nixon did not rest for long. He thought that if he were to be elected governor of California, the nation's most populous state, that would give him a boost on a second assault on the presidency in 1964. Unfortunately, Dick's plan was dashed when he unexpectedly lost the election. It was an embarrassing defeat for Nixon. Just a couple of years earlier he had been an international political figure. Suddenly he couldn't even get elected governor of his home state.

A disconsolate Nixon refused to appear at a press conference to concede defeat. When an aide told him that members of the press were waiting for a statement, Nixon said, "Screw them." He then changed his mind and stalked into the pressroom. "Now that all of the members of the press are so delighted that I've lost, I'd like to make a statement of my own," he told a room of startled reporters. "For sixteen years you've had a lot of fun. You've had an opportunity to attack me and I think I've given as much as I've taken. . . . But as I leave you I want you to know how much you're going to be missing. You won't have Nixon to kick around anymore, because, gentlemen, this is my last press conference."

Nixon's retirement from politics was short-lived, however. In the next few years the former vice president toured the country campaigning for Republican congressional candidates, gaining both chits and news clips in the process. By 1968 Nixon was once again ready to enter the gridiron of national politics, and that year he captured the Republican nomination for president.

As Calvin Coolidge had been in the 1920s, in 1968 Richard Nixon was a man for the times. Most Americans were horrified by the riots and disruptive behavior of college students, and they were looking for a new national sheriff to come in and restore order. Aided by the fact that the Democrats were floundering, with President Lyndon Johnson's refusal to run and Bobby Kennedy's assassination, Nixon turned out to be "the one" for a majority of voters.

☆ ☆ ☆

NIXON'S FIRST PRESIDENTIAL administration was overshadowed by the Vietnam War and the widespread student protests that accompanied it, and he spent a good deal of time trying to figure out quite what would make the students go away. But it was in his second administration that Dick really had his hands full. His vice president was accused of taking bribes in the White House basement and was eventually convicted of felonious tax evasion; his campaign aides were caught breaking into the Democratic national election headquarters. There were wiretaps, cover-ups, and general dirty tricks; ignored subpoenas; suspicious transfers of money, which included possible tax evasion by Nixon; and eventually, and not surprisingly, impeachment proceedings against President Nixon himself.

Nixon was not able to convince the citizens of the country when he publicly announced "I am not a crook." Finally, after months of suffering in political purgatory, on August 8, 1974, Tricky Dick Nixon became the first U.S. president to resign.

☆ ☆ ☆

GIVEN ALL THE Sturm and Drang of Nixon's political career despite seas settling and the smoothing of water with the passage of time—if most Americans were asked to name a single lasting benefit of the Nixon's years of public service, they might be tempted to repeat the words of President Eisenhower, who, when asked in 1960 if he could name any positive contributions made by Nixon in his eight years as vice president, said, "Well, if you give me a week, I might think of one."

LYNDON BAINES
JOHNSON

Served with John Kennedy, 1961–63

Democrat from Texas

WE WANT SONNY-BOY FOR VICE PRESI-
DENT. GO FETCH HIM FOR ME," was how one
of Lyndon Johnson's aides predicted that Johnson
would order him to line up John F. Kennedy as his
vice-presidential nominee in the 1960 race.

The quote showed Johnson's disregard for all
things Kennedy. Johnson really did call JFK Sonny-
boy, and he considered him a rich kid whose daddy

bought his prominence in government. "It's the god-damnedest thing," Johnson told biographer Doris Kearns. "Here was this whippersnapper, malaria-ridden and yellah, sickly, sickly. He never said a word of importance in the Senate and he never did a thing. . . . His growing hold on the American people was simply a mystery to me."

Equally mysterious to the supporters of the urbane and eloquent John Kennedy was the popularity of the rough and crass Lyndon Johnson. Despite their disregard for each other's abilities, without their strange symbiotic relationship, neither man probably would have made it to the White House.

☆ ☆ ☆

BOTH OF JOHNSON'S grandfathers and his father had served in the Texas state legislature, so from the moment he was born, Johnson's parents had high expectations of him. For the first three months of his life they called him Baby—they were sure that he would grow up to be a U.S. senator, and they wanted a name that sounded senatorial. Lyndon seemed to fit the bill.

Growing up in Johnson City—a town named for his grandfather—Lyndon wasn't known so much for his good grades in school as for his bad behavior: When he was eight years old, his report card showed all As except for a C in deportment, and he was kicked out of dancing classes for being mean to the girls. After LBJ graduated from high school, he took off with five friends to find fortune in California, but within two years the prodigal Johnson was forced to hitchhike back home flat broke. He finally entered Southwest Texas State Teachers College, where he was assistant to the president (who accused him of trying to run the entire college).

After teaching for a year, Johnson took a job as

secretary to a Texas congressman, a position that gave him a lust for Washington power. The congressman's wife had her husband fire Johnson because she thought that LBJ was trying to steal her husband's job. Johnson was able to win his own seat in the House of Representatives in 1937.

By 1940 Johnson decided that he was ready for the U.S. Senate. He lost a close race that year but learned an important lesson. It has been said that Johnson went to bed on election night of that year five thousand votes ahead and woke up ten thousand votes behind. In the future, Franklin Roosevelt advised the young congressman, "sit on the ballot box." It was a lesson Lyndon would learn well.

☆ ☆ ☆

ALTHOUGH HE LOST his bid for a place in the Senate, Johnson had not been forced to give up his seat in the House of Representatives. As World War II approached, Representative Johnson boasted that if war came, he would not sit out the battle behind a desk in the Congress but would join the boys in the trenches to fight for freedom. When the Japanese attacked Pearl Harbor, several people reminded Lyndon of his promise to fight, and Johnson enlisted in the navy at the rank of lieutenant commander.

Although his longtime mistress Alice Glass later said that LBJ spent most of his military career taking voice lessons and practicing photographic poses in Los Angeles, Johnson did serve as an "observer" (also known as a passenger) on one bombing mission over New Guinea. In Johnson's lone escapade in the South Pacific he saw only thirteen minutes of combat, during which, he claimed, his airplane was attacked by fourteen Japanese Zeros. Although there is no evidence that Johnson played any significant role in the battle (which some have suggested was pure fantasy), he managed to get himself awarded a Silver Star for bravery. After President Roosevelt ordered Johnson and the other soldier-playing congressmen to get back to work in Washington, Johnson had the medal presented to himself over and over at various public ceremonies.

☆ ☆ ☆

IN 1948 JOHNSON prepared for a second assault on the Senate. Lyndon had learned about hard-ball politics during his first Senate campaign, and he proved to be quite creative when it came to campaign maneuvers. LBJ chartered a helicopter, called the *Johnson City Windmill*, to take him around to his various campaign stops. If he was on his way to make a speech and he saw a group of people clustered on the ground below, Johnson would simply hover over the startled folks and yell over the microphone, "Hello down there . . . this is your friend Lyndon Johnson." One critic said that *Johnson City Windmill* was the name of both the aircraft and its occupant.

Johnson won the election by just eighty-seven votes, forever earning him the nickname Landslide Lyndon. Interestingly, in one South Texas county, Johnson had picked up an extra two hundred votes in a recount. Even more incredible, all two hundred votes were written in the same ink, in the same handwriting, and were in *alphabetical order*. Years later one of Johnson's aides admitted the obvious: They had stolen the election. "Of course they stole the election," he said. "That's the way they did it down there."

One of the people who voted for Johnson in that election was the grandfather of conservative icon William F. Buckley. Bill Buckley thought it quite amazing that his grandfather had voted for the Democratic Johnson—especially since his ancestor had died in 1904. "I am very proud of my grandfather's sense of civic obligation," Buckley said.

Landslide Lyndon entered the Senate to mocking applause for his narrow and suspect victory, but he was able to win over so many senators that he was elected minority leader just five years into his first term. Two years later, when the Democrats won control of the Senate, Johnson was voted majority leader. Johnson was just 46 years old, the youngest person ever to lead the upper chamber of Congress.

IN 1960 JOHNSON thought he had a strategy that would ultimately land him in the White House. Instead of entering the presidential primaries, where Hubert Humphrey and Jack Kennedy were tussling for the most votes, LBJ decided he would wait until just before the convention to announce his candidacy and then ride into the convention hall as the Texan in the white hat who would save the Democratic party from certain defeat in the fall. Johnson waited until just five days before the convention to announce that he was running for president. What he hadn't counted on was the strength of Kennedy's victories in the presidential primaries. By the time Johnson announced his candidacy, Jack Kennedy had virtually locked up the nomination.

On the road to the nomination, Kennedy had held out the vice presidency to a number of people. One senator said, "If they called a meeting of all the people to whom they've promised the vice presidency, they couldn't find a room in Los Angeles large enough to hold it in." But when Jack mentioned the vice presidency to Lyndon, Johnson quickly accepted. Later Kennedy would say that he hadn't actually meant to offer the vice presidency to Johnson: "I just held it like this," Kennedy said, pretending to hold an object next to his chest, "and he grabbed it." And although his brother Bobby was vehemently opposed to having Lyndon take the vice presidency—he even went to Johnson's hotel room and told him to give it back—Jack saw the pragmatic advantages of a Kennedy-Johnson ticket.

At first glance it seems strange that Johnson would want the vice presidency or that Kennedy would offer it to him. After all, Johnson already held the powerful position of majority leader of the Senate (he said that he had no inclination to "trade a vote for a gavel"), and he hardly seemed to fit into the collection of Harvard chums with whom JFK intended to surround himself. But in reality, both men depended on Johnson's being vice president. Kennedy needed the southern votes that Johnson could deliver—especially in Texas, where Johnson could work his magic to pad the total with Lazaruslike votes. As for LBJ, his reign in the Senate as majority leader was in jeopardy because of the influx of liberal Democrats. The vice presidency allowed a way to escape an embarrassing political defeat. It was also a low-risk maneuver by Johnson, since he had convinced the Texas state legislature to allow him to run for both vice president and Senator in that fall's election. (He won both races, and considering Lyndon's powers of persuasion, it is incredible that he didn't try to hold on to both seats simultaneously.)

Kennedy also had other reasons for wanting Johnson on the ticket. He was afraid that Johnson would be a constant burr under his saddle if he stayed on as the head of the Senate; JFK hoped to replace Johnson with someone whom, in his words, he could "trust and depend on." (Apparently Kennedy didn't think these qualities were as important in a vice president.) Kennedy thought the vice presidency was a like an attic where he could lock Lyndon away. "The vice presidency doesn't mean anything," he explained to one of his aides. "I'm 43 years old, and I'm the healthiest candidate for president of the United States. I'm not going to die in office."

☆ ☆ ☆

IN ACCEPTING THE vice presidency, Johnson had said, "Power is where power goes." But when it came to vice presidential power, this wasn't true—even for Lyndon Baines Johnson.

One of Johnson's first acts as vice president was to draw up a list of things that he saw as his new duties and send it over to the Kennedy boys at the White House. The list said that the vice president would be in charge of several of the smaller federal agencies, such as NASA, and that they would report to him. Instead of telling Lyndon what a ridiculous idea it was, JFK took the safest route and simply ignored the memorandum.

Johnson next tried to claim that he should continue as the leader of the Senate Democrats, a job that traditionally went to the Senate party leader. The senators, some of whom had supported Johnson for president over Kennedy, told Lyndon to his face to forget about such a scheme.

Vice President Johnson did manage to win one concession. When he had been Senate majority leader, he had furnished his office in such lavish fashion that it was known throughout Washington as the Taj Mahal of Capitol Hill. Instead of moving into the extravagant office, as was his right, the new majority leader, Mike Mansfield, graciously allowed LBJ to continue to conduct business there.

Johnson was virtually powerless, and he knew it. He told friends that he was nothing more than a neutered "cut dog," but he did find one way to continue to get his mug in the newspapers and on television. As vice president he was the chairman of the Aeronautics and Space Council, and when the seven *Mercury* astronauts became national celebrities, Lyndon was right there with them, even sharing astronaut John Glenn's glory by riding with him in a New York ticker-tape parade.

Locked out of power in Washington, Johnson decided to hit the road. President Kennedy wanted Johnson to tour Southeast Asia, but Johnson was reluctant to visit war-torn Saigon. "Don't worry, Lyndon," Jack Kennedy teased. "If anything happens to you . . . , I'll give you the biggest funeral Texas ever saw." Reporting from South Vietnam, Johnson said that "the battle against Communism must be joined in southeast Asia," but he also told Kennedy, "American combat troop involvement . . . is not desirable."

Johnson continued to travel. In Pakistan he casually invited a camel driver to visit him in Washington sometime (and was quite amused some months later when the Pakistani did just that). In a restroom in Thailand, Johnson displayed his Texas manhood and asked his guests, "Don't see 'em this big out here, do they?"

While in India, Johnson whooped inside the Taj Mahal, hoping to hear his echo, and he walked through the slums handing out campaign pencils with Compliments of Your Senator, Lyndon B. Johnson, Your Friend written on them. "If Lyndon forgets and asks for votes," John Kenneth Galbraith, the U.S. ambassador to India, told the translator, "leave that part out." Later, while having an audience with the pope at the Vatican, Vice President Lyndon gave His Holiness a plastic bust of his Texas self.

Lyndon's international escapades were sharply criticized by Kennedy's collection of Ivy League advisers, who liked to call LBJ Uncle Cornpone. They suggested to Kennedy that he not allow Johnson to travel to any developed countries.

Johnson, for his part, was as contemptuous of the White House staff as they were of him. He called the Kennedy aides the Georgetown jelly beans and said that they "didn't have sense enough to pour piss out of a boot with the instructions written on the heel."

Since Johnson wasn't allowed to do much back-room politicking in Washington, he began trying to mediate some of the squabbles between politicos back home in Texas, but his heavy-handed meddling only did more harm than good. In November of 1963, President Kennedy decided to travel to Texas as a means of restoring order among the Democrats there.

On their trip, Johnson and Kennedy flew in separate airplanes and traveled in separate automobiles as a security precaution. It turned out to be needed. In Dallas, riding just two cars behind Kennedy's convertible limousine, Johnson watched President Kennedy's horrifying murder.

Johnson's limousine followed Kennedy's as they raced to Parkland Memorial Hospital. Secret Service agents had shoved Johnson to the floorboard of his car as the shooting began, and an agent lay on Johnson all the way to the hospital. Johnson stood by at the emergency room as doctors tried to revive Kennedy, but after a half hour, one of Kennedy's press aides told Johnson, "Mr. President, I have to announce the death of President Kennedy." Lyndon Johnson took the oath of office on board *Air Force One*, with Jacqueline Kennedy standing beside him, still wearing clothes stained with her husband's blood.

Johnson had feared that there was some sort of plot and that there might be several assassins or that the shooting might have been the opening volley in a modern war. As he took the oath of office he was anxious to leave the vulnerable Dallas airport. Upon finishing the oath, his first words as president were, "Now let's get airborne."

☆ ☆ ☆

AS PRESIDENT, JOHNSON always considered the entire United States of America his own, one time even referring to the "State of *My* Union Address." Once, after reviewing a group of marines, Johnson began to step into the wrong helicopter but was corrected by an officer who said, "That's your helicopter over there, sir." "Son," Johnson replied, "they're all my helicopters."

Johnson wasn't imperial, he just thought of all Americans—of whatever color, it should be pointed out—as his children. Johnson wanted nothing but the best for them, and to prove it he came up with a plan called the Great Society. Johnson introduced civil-rights legislation in an effort to put an end to discrimination, he began a War on Poverty, he increased the amount of money going to education and Social Security, and he took steps to improve the nation's environment. Lyndon Johnson might have lived up to his dream to be the country's greatest president—"the greatest of the whole bunch of them," as he often said—if it hadn't been for Vietnam. Lyndon's ego led him to send U.S. fighting men into a war that he knew was unwinnable. It was bloodshed that delivered the presidency to Lyndon Johnson, and, in the end, it was bloodshed that took it all away.

HUBERT HORATIO
HUMPHREY

Served with Lyndon Johnson, 1965–69

Democrat from Minnesota

WHEN LYNDON JOHNSON BEGAN LOOK-
ING FOR SOMEONE TO SHARE THE TICKET
WITH HIM IN 1964, nobody had any doubt about
the kind of person Lyndon would want. "I want
loyalty," the earthy Johnson often said about his
subordinates. "I want him to kiss my ass in Macy's
window at high noon and tell me it smells like roses."

Considering the way Lyndon treated those who worked for him, he probably wasn't joking.

It was obvious to most people who were able to read newspapers that the most logical choice for vice president was Hubert H. Humphrey—the only person qualified to be vice president and still willing to agree to LBJ's job description—but Lyndon Johnson didn't want to make things so simple. He knew that as long as he could keep people guessing, he held the spotlight. Naturally this little game of I've Got a Secret drove political pundits and junkies nuts as they tried to answer the question, "If not Hubert, who?"

Even Lyndon's brother, Sam Houston Johnson, was dying to know whom LBJ was going to pick. As he states in his book *My Brother, Lyndon*, Sam assumed that Lyndon would pick Hubert Humphrey as his vice president, but he wasn't sure that Lyndon had made up his mind, so he decided to trick LBJ into giving himself away.

Sam started his fraternal fact-finding mission by suggesting to LBJ the least likely person being considered—Senator Pastore of Rhode Island—saying that he thought Pastore would make a good vice president. "God damn it, Sam Houston, what in hell's gone wrong with you?" Lyndon roared. "How could an Italian from a dinky state like Rhode Island possibly help me?"

Sam then suggested that Adlai Stevenson might help Lyndon with the country's intellectuals. "Don't need him," Lyndon said. "With Barry Goldwater running, I look like a Harvard professor to the eggheads."

Many people thought Eugene McCarthy was a front-runner for the job, including McCarthy himself, Sam Houston said. But McCarthy's holier-than-thou personality raised Lyndon's fur. "There's something sort of stuck-up about Gene," Lyndon said. "You get the impression that he's got a special pipeline to God and that they only talk Latin to each other."

Then what about an urban mayor, such as Chicago's Mayor Richard Daley? Sam asked.

"With Goldwater running, I don't have to worry about the big-city vote," Lyndon said.

"Well, hell, Lyndon, that only leaves Hubert, and you sure ain't picking him, are you?" Sam asked. "He's a damned maverick."

"Damn it, Sam Houston, you've got him all wrong!" yelled Lyndon. "Hubert's a good man. I've made a goddamn Christian out of him!"

Sam Houston thought he had cornered his brother on his choice for vice president. "So your mind's made up?"

"Not yet," Lyndon replied. "I want to talk to some more people."

☆ ☆ ☆

HUBERT HUMPHREY WAS always an ambitious person. From the moment his father dropped him off at the University of Minnesota with the encouraging words "Good-bye. Good luck. Grow up," Hubert was trying to make something of himself.

Humphrey was forced to abandon his schoolwork and return to help out in his father's pharmacy during the depression, but when the 24-year-old escorted a group of Boy Scouts from his hometown to Washington, D.C., for a tour of the city, Humphrey decided to give up the pharmaceutical life. "I set my aim at Congress," Hubert wrote his wife from Washington. "Don't laugh at me, Muriel . . . I know others have succeeded. Oh, gosh, I hope my dreams come true."

Hubert reentered college at age 26 and was able

to graduate with honors in just two years with a degree in political science. Humphrey went on to teach at St. Paul's Macalester College, and in 1943, at age 32, he attempted to put his scholarship to work by running for mayor of Minneapolis. He narrowly lost that race but was elected mayor in 1945.

Humphrey's position as mayor allowed him to become a delegate to the Democratic National Convention in 1948, and the ever-loquacious Humphrey couldn't pass up an opportunity to pontificate. The Democratic party had tried to appease people on both sides of the civil-rights issue, but Humphrey urged the Democratic party to adopt a less mealy-mouthed position. "The time has arrived for the Democratic party to get out of the shadow of states rights and walk forthrightly into the bright sunshine of human rights!" Humphrey said.

Thanks to Hubert, the Democratic party's platform was overruled by the delegates, which resulted in a party split led by "Dixiecrat" Strom Thurmond. Strom stormed out of the convention, taking his fellow Southerners with him, and they formed their own party to challenge incumbent Harry Truman in the fall presidential election. (The split actually helped elect Truman that fall, because it made him seem moderate by comparison.) Humphrey became so popular for his stiff stand against racial discrimination that the people of Minnesota rewarded him that fall by electing him to the U.S. Senate.

It was in Congress that Humphrey became known for his energetic elocution. "Hubert Humphrey talks so fast," Senator Barry Goldwater once said, "that listening to him is like trying to read *Playboy* with your wife turning the pages." Humphrey himself once said that it took him more than three minutes just to clear his throat, and stories about Humphrey's windiness have become part of congressional lore. Representative Gerald Ford claimed that the first time he heard Humphrey speak, Hubert was "in the second hour of a five-minute speech." Ford said, "I asked the fellow next to me what followed Senator Humphrey. The fellow looked at his watch and said, 'Christmas.' "

Even Humphrey's good friend Lyndon Johnson was frustrated at his inability to get Hubert to shut up once in a while. Ever the Texas ranch hand, Lyndon Johnson often said that he could have come up with a mighty good hybrid politician "if I could just breed [Hubert] to Calvin Coolidge."

Humphrey's verbal prowess earned him more than just the admiration of other verbose congressmen. Increasingly, Hubert became the voice of the liberal wing of the Democratic party. He came up with the idea of Medicare, and years before John F. Kennedy claimed it for his own, Humphrey introduced a bill proposing the peace corps.

Not all his ideas were so successful or highminded. At one point, Humphrey gave in to the 1950s red scare and introduced legislation that would have outlawed the Communist party in the United States, a law so obviously wrongheaded that even J. Edgar Hoover considered it a bad piece of legislation.

Humphrey drew enough attention to himself that in 1952—just four years after he won national office as a U.S. Senator—he ran for president. Humphrey's campaign didn't go any farther than the Minnesota state line, but he had gained enough power that he was able to marshal the necessary Senate votes to elect his good friend Lyndon Johnson majority leader. Johnson appreciated Humphrey's efforts, and he said that Hubert was his liaison with the left wing of the Democratic party, or, as LBJ put it, "my link with the bomb throwers."

In 1956 the ever-ambitious and optimistic Humphrey made a play for the vice presidency, but when that failed, he merely began gearing up for an attempt at the presidency in 1960. Humphrey did well enough in that bid to become the nominee of the Democratic party until he ran into a mountain in West Virginia—a mountain of Kennedy money. Humphrey was bitter that JFK had used his fortune to bury Humphrey's campaign in an avalanche of television ads: "Anybody who gets in the way of papa's pet is going to be destroyed," he said. Instead of battling Richard Nixon for the presidency (which he would get the chance to do eight years later), Humphrey returned to the Senate.

☆ ☆ ☆

HUMPHREY AND JOHNSON had been close friends from the time they entered the Senate together. LBJ had always been something of a mentor to Humphrey, and the two were so close that Lyndon and Lady Bird spent the evening with Hubert and Muriel Humphrey the day after Kennedy's assassination.

It therefore came as something of a surprise to Humphrey, and to many others, that Johnson was even considering picking someone else as his vice president during the campaign of 1964. But Lyndon Johnson knew that he held the attention of the press and of the political world as long as he delayed making his vice-presidential choice, and he thus began what one newspaper columnist called the splendid tease.

Besides Hubert, at least one other person was eager for the vice presidency: John Kennedy's brother and the attorney general, Bobby Kennedy. Kennedy, whom LBJ referred to as the little squirt, was the one person Lyndon Johnson did not want to get the job. To extinguish any chance that Bobby might slide into the vice president's chair, Johnson issued a statement that said that "it would be inadvisable for me to recommend to the convention any member of the cabinet" because he relied so much on their judgment. Bobby later jokingly apologized to his cabinet colleagues for "taking so many nice fellows over the side with me."

Johnson's splendid tease worked to perfection; daily the new reports wondered whom Lyndon was going to pick for vice president. It was probably the most fun he had the entire time he was president.

One hot, humid afternoon in Washington, Johnson decided to talk on the record to the press about his choice for vice president. In typical LBJ style, he took the opportunity to torment his guests. Johnson went out into the ninety-degree heat, and with the panting reporters in tow, he began walking briskly around the White House. Johnson raced around the White House as the reporters struggled to scribble on their notepads. Round and round he went, fifteen laps in all, before finally stopping to give the press something worthwhile to write about. Johnson told the members of the press the qualities he looked for in a vice president: complete loyalty, constant acquiescence, and the ability to keep his trap shut at all times (this last one almost wrecked Humphrey's chances for the job). One senator later said that Johnson didn't want a vice president, he wanted "a trained seal."

When Eugene McCarthy heard Lyndon's list of vice-presidential qualifications, he sent a telegram to President Johnson saying that the president could take his vice president's job and shove it off on somebody else. Somebody like Hubert Humphrey, McCarthy suggested.

The press and the public weren't the only ones

Johnson teased about the announcement—Humphrey himself had to endure a fair amount of harassment. Not only did LBJ neglect to let Humphrey in on his ruse, but during one state dinner the president leaned across the table and loudly asked Humphrey if he thought Mike Mansfield would make a good vice president. Finally, Lyndon decided to end his game and tell Hubert that he was the one after all. But, of course, even this Johnson could not handle graciously.

Humphrey was summoned to Washington, but when he got there, LBJ was concerned about the timing of his arrival. Lady Bird was about to arrive at the Democratic National Convention in Atlantic City, and Johnson was afraid that the sight of Humphrey arriving at the White House might cause the television cameras to ignore Bird and focus on Hubert. Johnson ordered Humphrey to take an hour-long tour of the many monuments around Washington, and once Humphrey's limo was allowed to enter the White House gates, Johnson kept Hubert waiting in the driveway for an hour. Hubert dozed off while sitting in the driveway, and he was awakened by Johnson's own oversize paw shaking his shoulder.

Johnson was unapologetic for his handling of the ordeal. After he asked Humphrey to be his vice president, he told Hubert, "If you didn't know you were going to be vice president a month ago, you're too damn dumb to have the office."

☆ ☆ ☆

ONCE HE BECAME vice president, Hubert supported LBJ with typical Humphrey hyperbole, calling Lyndon Baines Johnson the greatest president in the history of the country.

Although that was exactly the type of tail wagging

that Johnson had expected out of his vice president, he still wasn't about to throw him a bone. Humphrey had assumed that he would be a player in the Johnson administration—after all, Johnson had relied on him in the Senate, and Johnson himself knew what it felt like to be shut out of White House decisions as vice president. But Lyndon barely tolerated Vice President Humphrey.

Once Johnson did give Humphrey five minutes to address the cabinet—"*five minutes,*" Johnson emphasized, keeping his eye on the second hand of his watch—but when Humphrey wasn't able to finish his point in the allotted time, Johnson stood up and shoved the vice president out of the room.

In private Johnson was even crueler to his vice president. Johnson had once talked Bobby Kennedy into going hunting with him in Texas by insulting his masculinity, and he pulled the same trick on Humphrey. When the softhearted liberal balked at shooting two deer, Johnson told him to kill the beasts and prove that he was as much of a man as a Kennedy. At another visit to the Johnson ranch, Lyndon dressed the vice president up in an ill-fitting cowboy outfit, complete with an oversize ten-gallon hat, and paraded him in front of a group of reporters. Johnson then roared while his vice president struggled to ride a spirited horse.

But as embarrassing as these episodes were for the vice president, the greatest indignity of all was Johnson's insistence that Hubert not speak out against him about the war in Vietnam. Humphrey might have become president in 1968 if he had voiced his views about the Vietnam War earlier in the campaign. Before he became a candidate for president that year, he had been a great early supporter of Johnson's war in Southeast Asia. "This is our great adventure," Humphrey said, "and a won-

BLAND AMBITION ☆ 332

derful one it is." In another speech he claimed that if we didn't stop the Communists from taking Saigon, "they'll be in Honolulu and San Francisco."

Despite this public pandering to the president, after his election to the vice presidency Humphrey began to have doubts about the U.S. military involvement in Southeast Asia. He began crafting memos to the White House on war policy but stopped when President Johnson told him, "Hubert, we don't need any more memos." At one point Johnson became so worried that his vice president would speak out against the war that he insisted that Humphrey submit a travel request every time he wanted to leave town, which Johnson would personally approve or disapprove before giving Hubert the keys to *Air Force Two*.

When the unpopular war ended any chances that President Johnson would be reelected, Vice President Humphrey jumped into the race for the presidency. "Here we are, just as we ought to be," the ebullient Hubert cried, announcing his decision to run for president. "The people, here we are, the way politics ought to be in America, the politics of happiness, the politics of purpose, and the politics of joy."

Joy was not what the campaign of 1968 was about. After all, Humphrey had entered the presidential race only because incumbent Lyndon Johnson had been humiliated in the New Hampshire primary and had withdrawn from the race, and because the next presumptive nominee, Robert Kennedy, had been assassinated in Los Angeles. The politics of joy never made an appearance in 1968; instead, it was the year of the politics of confrontation.

Thousands of hippies and yippies and people of other flavors had shown up at the Democratic National Convention in Chicago that summer to protest the Vietnam War. They were met by thousands of National Guardsmen and twelve thousand Chicago policemen, all of whom were set on preventing any sort of disturbance. Since disturbing things is pretty much the point of being a protester, it was inevitable that the two groups would have differences. For the better part of a week the convention was the site of riots and violence.

Humphrey was ensconced inside the barbed-wire-protected convention hall, but even he was not protected from what was happening on the Chicago streets. Watching the fighting between the protesters and the policemen from his hotel window, the vice president was teargassed and had to take a shower to rid himself of the chemical that was burning his eyes and skin.

It was no wonder that what should have been the crowning moment of his life—receiving his party's nomination for president—instead left him, he said, "heartbroken, battered and beaten." On the campaign trail things got even worse for Humphrey. The familiar protest jeer "Hey, Hey, LBJ—How many kids have you killed today?" was coupled with "Dump the Hump! Dump the Hump!" and the vice president was compared to Adolf Hitler for his support of the Vietnam War.

Finally, realizing that his support of his president's war in Vietnam was costing him votes, Humphrey began to waffle about the threat that he had once said would soon have Commies riding the cable cars in San Francisco. Near the end of September, Hubert made the bold claim, "The President has not made me his slave and I am not his humble servant." A week later he said that if he were president, he wouldn't drop bombs on Vietnam (a position that caused eleven senators in the South Vietnamese government to endorse Richard Nixon for president).

But it was too late for Humphrey; he had publicly supported his president's foreign war for too long. Because Humphrey had placed greater emphasis on being vice president than on following his beliefs and speaking out against the Vietnam War, he joined Lyndon Johnson in seeing his political career, as well as his position in history, be napalmed to near ruin.

SPIRO THEODORE
AGNEW

Served with Richard Nixon, 1969–73

Republican from Maryland

DURING THE SECOND ADMINISTRATION OF THE NIXON-AGNEW TEAM, RICHARD NIXON STOOD UP IN FRONT OF THE NATION AND SAID, "I AM NOT A CROOK." Spiro Agnew stood up before the nation and said, Well, I, er, maybe I am.

Agnew's political career was remarkable. In just ten years he had gone from being vice president of the Baltimore Kiwanis club to being vice president of the United States. But he was accused of taking kickbacks and bribes along the way and evading income tax. "Spiro Agnew," said Tennessee senator Albert Gore, "was this country's greatest disaster next to Vietnam."

☆ ☆ ☆

SPIRO THEODORE AGNEW was the son of Greek immigrant and restaurant owner Theofrastos Spiro Anagnostopoulos, but he never considered himself a member of an ethnic minority. He was raised as an Episcopalian, and his friends knew him as Ted instead of Spiro.

His political rise was swift. He was a Republican in a state dominated by Democrats, and the GOP offered the least resistance to a quick rise to the top. In 1966, Spiro was elected governor of Maryland. None of this was enough to catch the attention of the national Republican leaders. But as with Calvin Coolidge, a tough position during a riot brought him the vice presidency.

Following the assassination of Martin Luther King, Jr., Baltimore was one of several cities rocked by violent disturbances. After the rioting, when black leaders met with Agnew to explain the causes of racial discontent, Agnew replied that what the city needed was a get-tough policy on rabble-rousers and malcontents. He also chastised a police officer who had refused to shoot a fleeing looter who had stolen a pair of shoes. Agnew declared that the police officer's decision not to fire displayed the kind of "insidious relativism that has crept into our thinking," because, Agnew presumed, the officer would have shot if the thief had stolen something really valuable, such as a diamond ring. Agnew's take-no-prisoners views on inner-city crime were popular with whites concerned about what was happening in urban America and began to gain him minor attention nationally.

As the time for the presidential conventions drew close, both political parties were in chaos, as was nearly every social institution in the country. Out of this chaos rose the phoenix of American politics, Richard Nixon. In 1968 Nixon returned to the top of the Republican party with the nomination for president.

Nixon wanted two things in his vice-presidential nominee: He wanted a "political eunuch" so that he wouldn't have to share the spotlight with anyone (perhaps he remembered how he himself had drawn negative publicity to the Eisenhower campaign), and he wanted someone who was a "centrist" to help woo voters who considered Nixon's archconservative image a bit too dark. One of Nixon's speech writers thought that he had just the person Nixon was looking for. The aide, a young man named Patrick Buchanan, began clipping newspaper stories about the governor of Maryland, Spiro Agnew, to send to Nixon. Influenced by Buchanan's urgings, Nixon began seriously considering Agnew for the second spot on the ticket.

The day after he received the Republican nomination for president, Nixon met with reporters to announce the name of his running mate. The name Nixon mentioned was so unfamiliar and foreign sounding that the national joke that summer was "Spiro who?"

In Atlanta that week, a reporter asked pedestrians what Spiro Agnew was. The answers included "Some kind of disease," "It's some kind of egg," and of course, "He's a Greek who owns a shipbuilding firm." Nobody knew who Spiro Agnew was. The *Washington Post* said that Agnew's candidacy was "perhaps the most eccentric political appointment since the Roman Emperor Caligula named his horse a consul." Even one Nixon aide revealed, "I'm from Maryland, and I have trouble remembering his name."

Being unknown is not a large disadvantage to becoming vice president, however. After all, when FDR had announced his choice for vice president, a member of his staff had bellowed, "Who the hell is Harry Truman?" The problem, at least for Richard Nixon, was that the people would soon discover who—and what—Spiro T. Agnew was.

In a state that Agnew called Illi-*noise*, he made a crack about "a Negro, an Italian, a Greek, and a Polack." Next, on a campaign plane, he noticed a sleeping reporter and asked, "What's the matter with the fat Jap?" Then, when asked why he didn't spend more time campaigning in inner cities, Agnew replied, "If you've seen one slum, you've seen them all." The press portrayed Agnew as being in a stumbling march from gaffe to blunder. (At one rally someone held up a placard that said Apologize Now, Spiro, It Will Save Time Later.)

The Democrats tried to gain some votes by making Agnew's nomination to the vice presidency a campaign issue. In one television commercial, the screen flashed *Agnew for Vice-President?* as canned laughter played in the background. At the end of the commercial a voice said, "This would be funny if it weren't so serious."

Agnew may not have succeeded in winning over any Democratic supporters, but he did keep conservatives from bleeding the Republican party to death by running to vote for George Wallace. Nixon won three key states in the South and won the election. However, the citizens of Maryland refused to believe that favorite son Spiro was worthy of standing that close to the presidency. Maryland voted for Humphrey.

☆ ☆ ☆

AGNEW BEGAN TO come out of his vice-presidential nap slowly in the fall of 1969 by attacking the people who had spent so much time criticizing the Nixon administration. He first called the intellectuals of the country an "effete corps of impudent snobs." He said that it was time to "sweep that kind of garbage out of our society." Then in a televised speech he attacked the television-news media, saying that their coverage of the Vietnam War was based on "instant analysis" and "querulous criticism" and suggested that the evening news say only good things about the president.

Newsweek responded that Agnew's views had an "odor of sanctity . . . mingled with the burning tar of demagoguery," and the race to the thesaurus was on. "Supercilious sophisticates," Spiro spat. "Hopeless, hysterical hypochondriacs of history," he heaved. "Pusillanimous pussyfooting," "vicars of vacillation," and "nattering nabobs of negativism," added Agnew. The same Middle Americans who had just discovered the wonders of polyester went just as wild over Agnew's tacky politics of polysyllables.

Although freshman-composition professors were running for cover at the alliteration, a great number of Americans (at least those who were able to make their way through the thicket of repeating vowels and consonants) backed Spiro's policies of a limited press, support for the Vietnam War, and putting minorities in their place. Agnew's supporters—his Silent Majority—were transfixed that someone smart enough to use such big words could hold some of the same bonehead views that they did.

At his zenith, the speaking invitations poured in at more than fifty per day, and his popularity with the *Reader's Digest* literati was such that one national Gallup poll found that Agnew was the nation's third-most-admired person, trailing only President Nixon and evangelist Billy Graham.

(Agnew's popularity was crystalized in the form of the Spiro Agnew watch. A joke was going around the country that Spiro was such a "Mickey Mouse" choice for vice president that the famous Disney character was seen wearing a Spiro Agnew watch. An entrepreneurial California physician heard the quip and decided to manufacture such a timepiece; it featured a caricature of Agnew wearing star-spangled shorts and shoes, pointing out the hours and minutes with crossed arms. Thousands bought copies of the watch, which sold for $14.95 in 1970. The vice president seemed to be the only one who failed to see the humor—he filed a suit, claiming that his likeness couldn't be used without his permission. The suit was settled when the doctor agreed to turn a portion of the profits over to charity.)

However, just as with any fad, within two years the novelty of Spiro Agnew had worn off. Nixon had tried to capitalize on Agnew's speaking style by sending him out to attack the Democratic congressional candidates in the fall of 1970. The people of America had laughed when Agnew bared his teeth at unnamed members of the press and the eastern intelligentsia, but when Agnew began naming names, even mentioning their own representatives to Congress, his shiny armor became tarnished.

Although Democrats had always considered Agnew a buffoon, Agnew's career began snowballing downhill when fellow Republicans began snickering at him (even White House aides referred to Spiro as the clown). It seems that Agnew had a bad habit of

hitting spectators with his golf shots, and this made
him the source of jokes in what should have been a
Nixon stronghold, the nation's country clubs. Republican joke *meister* Bob Hope said, "When Agnew
yelled 'Fore!' you never knew whether he was telling
someone to get out of the way or predicting how
many spectators he would hit with the shot."

Many people thought that Nixon would dump
Agnew from the ticket when he ran for reelection in
1972, and Nixon didn't say anything to counter the
gossip. Finally, just a short month before the Republican convention in August of 1972, Nixon announced that he had again chosen Spiro Agnew as
his running mate. It was to be an easy election; in
fact, it couldn't have been any easier had Nixon and
Agnew picked their own challengers—which, to
some degree, they did.

CREEP, the apropos acronym for the Republicans' nefarious Committee to Reelect the President,
and other Nixon aides did everything from the criminal, such as breaking into the Democratic headquarters; to the slimy, such as passing around anonymous
documents that claimed that Scoop Jackson was a
homosexual; to the truly stupid, such as sending
unordered pizzas to the headquarters of Senator Ed-
mund Muskie. Thanks to the committee and the
general ineptitude of the bumbling McGovern
Democrats, Tricky Dick Nixon and Agnew were reelected by the second-largest margin in the nation's
history. It was the first time that two former vice
presidents were placed in the top two positions in the
government. That fact alone should have tipped off
the nation that the executive branch was about to
enter its darkest hour. By the time the next presidential election came around, neither Nixon nor Agnew
would be in office, both having been forced to resign
in disgrace.

☆ ☆ ☆

THE REPUBLICANS' DIRTY tricks began to come to light in 1972, and soon after the election the investigations, and the cover-ups, were on. There were scads of scandals, and Nixon's presidency was in jeopardy. In order to save himself, Nixon decided to hang his vice president and leave the corpse twisting in the wind.

It seems that Agnew was accused of taking bribes and kickbacks and extorting money and services while serving as a Baltimore County executive and continuing his life of corruption later as governor of Maryland.

The Justice Department had been investigating Spiro Agnew, and only a political naïf would think that Nixon didn't have full knowledge of, and substantial control over, this investigation. No doubt, had he wanted to, Nixon could have withheld the announcement of the investigation for some time. But Nixon needed some relief from the daily headlines announcing new accusations of an unscrupulous White House, so he ordered the investigation made public, and as a coup de grace, he ordered Agnew to make the announcement himself. In August of 1973, Spiro Agnew told a shocked nation that he was being investigated by the Justice Department for several impeachable offenses. But Agnew told the public, "I have nothing to hide."

Nixon let Agnew run from the press like a wounded animal for two months in order to keep the public's attention off the Watergate break-in. At the end of September, Agnew had one last hurrah when he spoke to a group of supporters—the National Federation of Republican Women. Agnew became emotional over the support given him by the beehived women (who were waving signs that read Spiro Is Our Hero), and shouting with the fervor of an evangelist, he ended his speech with the refrain "I will not resign if indicted! I will not resign if indicted!"

Two weeks later he was not only indicted but also convicted, disgraced, and forced to resign. Although he pleaded nolo contendere to only one charge of tax evasion, the judge hearing his case allowed more than forty pages of criminal activities to be read into the record. The judge also asked Agnew if he realized that his plea was an admission that the Department of Justice "is possessed of sufficient evidence to prove its case beyond a reasonable doubt." Agnew replied, "I do."

Because of his position as vice president, Agnew did not have to serve out his term sitting in a prison cell. Agnew was fined ten thousand dollars and placed on probation. He resigned as vice president that same day. (Technically, Agnew was not vice president when he pleaded no contest to the felony charge. Following the recommendation of the attorney general, Agnew had ordered that his resignation be sent to Secretary of State Henry Kissinger just minutes before he presented his plea in court so that, officially, it could not be recorded that a vice president of the United States had been convicted of a felony.)

Despite this apparently unremorseful admission of guilt, years later Agnew would insist that he was innocent of all charges. In 1980 Agnew released a book, *Go Quietly . . . Or Else,* that was dedicated to singer and tough guy Frank Sinatra, who had loaned Agnew nearly a quarter of a million dollars for living expenses and fines after his conviction. In the book Agnew said that he had lied in court and in his farewell address, writing, "I am innocent of the allegations against me which compelled me to resign from the vice presidency in 1973." Agnew further

claimed that he resigned, despite his innocence, because Nixon's chief of staff, Alexander Haig—who
Agnew said had acted as chief executive while Nixon
was paralyzed by the Watergate scandal—threatened that if he did not do so, things would get "nasty
and dirty." Agnew wrote that he believed at the time
that his life might be in danger. "[The] directive was
aimed at me like a gun at my head," Agnew wrote.
"I was told, 'Go quietly . . . or else.' "

Agnew later became an "international consul-
tant." In one instance, according to Sidney Blumen-
thal's book *Nixon*, Agnew's consulting involved acting
as a middleman for the sale of $181 million's worth
of military uniforms from then Romanian dictator
Nicolae Ceausescu to Iraqi leader Saddam Hussein.

☆ ☆ ☆

Vice President Agnew's farewell speech in October of 1973 showed none of the fire of his earlier
diatribes. Agnew said that he had been charged with
"permitting my fund-raising activities and my con-
tract-dispensing activities to overlap in an unethical
and an unlawful manner," adding, "perhaps, judg-
ing by the new, post-Watergate morality, I did." Apparently thinking that his resignation would cause
widespread concern among the citizenry, Agnew
added a quote from James Garfield, who had reportedly quieted an anxious crowd after the death of
Abraham Lincoln by saying, "Fellow citizens, God
reigns, and the Government in Washington still
lives."

Agnew was oblivious to the irony; he didn't realize that those were exactly the two reasons why he
was no longer in office.

GERALD RUDOLPH
FORD, JR.

Served with Richard Nixon, 1973–74

Republican from Michigan

FTER SPIRO AGNEW RESIGNED, RICHARD NIXON NEEDED A SPECIAL PERSON TO TAKE OVER AS HIS NEW VICE PRESIDENT. At first Gerald Ford didn't make Nixon's top three choices of possible executive officers for the nation, but Nixon was forced to take a second look at Ford. The press was trying to carpet bomb the Oval Office, and Nixon and his merry band needed someone with the image of a Boy Scout to save their administration. In their time of darkest need they turned to Jerry Ford. There was a cool irony to this. More than once, Nixon had laughed at the idea of Ford becoming president. "Can you imagine him sitting in this chair?" he had joked with Nelson Rockefeller.

It is said that God looks after fools and democracies, and that must have been the case in 1974 when Gerald Ford became president. The United States needed a break from the dark remnants of the 1960s and the Watergate years of the early 1970s; the country had had enough of political assassinations, tear gas, body bags, and wiretaps. People wanted to do truly stupid things like dance to BeeGees hits and make macramé plant holders. Jerry Ford was the nice neighbor who said he would watch things for a while while the country went for a small vacation. Folks were free to enjoy disco, "Charlie's Angels," and leisure suits while Jerry Ford kept the chair warm in the Oval Office.

☆ ☆ ☆

GROWING UP IN a middle-class home in Grand Rapids, Michigan, Gerald Ford was the prototypical all-American boy. He had a dog named Spot. He was so good at that Boy Scout thing that he achieved the rank of Eagle Scout.

But Ford's childhood wasn't completely idyllic. He had actually been born Leslie Lynch King, Jr., after his father, who soon ran off and left Mrs. King and her baby boy. When Mrs. King remarried and became Mrs. Gerald Rudolf Ford, she renamed her 2-year-old son after her new husband. Gerald Ford, Jr., didn't know about his true father until he was 12 years old. He met him for the first time a few years later when Leslie King, Sr., drove up in an expensive Lincoln to the restaurant where Jerry worked, said

"I'm your real father," gave Jerry twenty-five dollars, and drove off. Ford would see his father only once more in his life.

In later years Gerald Ford was often thought of as someone who was clumsy and none too bright, but his early life certainly didn't support this assessment. Ford wasn't uncoordinated. He played football at Michigan and was not only named the team's most valuable player his senior year but was also asked to join both the Detroit Lions and the Green Bay Packers. Even while he was president, he was the most aerobic chief executive since Teddy Roosevelt.

And although he never claimed to be an intellectual, Ford certainly wasn't stupid—he graduated in the top third of his class at the University of Michigan (remember, he did this while on an athletic scholarship, so expectations were subterranean), and he again finished near the top of his class when he attended law school at Yale University. But because Ford went around Capitol Hill saying things like "If Lincoln was alive today, he'd be spinning in his grave," many people thought, as Lyndon Johnson often said, that Jerry Ford had "spent too much time playing football without a helmet."

What Ford was, truth be told, was goofy (as might be expected from a guy who—so it was said—was left-handed when he was sitting and right-handed when he was standing). He was a big, lovable lug who would never be the lead but always in the supporting cast.

Ford didn't immediately take to politics: Jerry Ford began his career in front of a camera. While a student at Yale in the early 1940s, Ford was dating a fashion model, and through her connections Ford began modeling clothes himself. He even appeared in *Life* magazine and on the cover of *Cosmopolitan*.

Ford stopped dating his model friend, however,

and soon after was called into service in World War II. He served in the South Pacific as athletic director aboard an aircraft carrier (you there, straighten your back on those push-ups), taking part in most of the major battles in that theater and winning ten battle stars.

Once he returned to civilian life in Grand Rapids, Ford began dating a divorced dancer named Betty Bloomer. They were soon married, and following their wedding, rather than head for a romantic hideaway, Jerry took his new bride to a Michigan football game. (This would have been completely understandable if the Wolverines had been playing Ohio State or Notre Dame, but Michigan was playing Northwestern, for goodness' sake. He at least could have taken off at halftime.) After the game, Jerry took Betty to hear a speech by Republican presidential candidate Tom Dewey.

Soon after, Ford successfully ran for a seat in the U.S. House of Representatives, a job he would keep for the next twenty-four years. It was there that Ford first earned his reputation as an intellectual lightweight. Once when President Lyndon Johnson hoped to win Ford's vote on an important piece of legislation, Johnson told one of his aides who had a toddler son to take some of the boy's blocks up to the Capitol "and explain to Jerry Ford what we're trying to do." Whether Ford's intellectual liabilities were real or imagined, he was successful enough in his tenure in the House to be elected House minority leader in 1965, a position he held until called for duty as vice president.

☆ ☆ ☆

FROM THE TIME he entered the House of Representatives, Gerald Ford was a friend and loyal supporter of Richard Nixon. Ford had supported Nixon in 1956 when Eisenhower was considering dumping Dick from the Republican ticket, and he had been one of the first Republicans to endorse Nixon's 1960 presidential candidacy. In 1968, before he selected Spiro Agnew as his running mate, Richard Nixon had asked Gerald Ford if he would be his vice-presidential candidate. Ford declined Nixon's offer, but nonetheless Ford was a loyal member of Nixon's team. When in 1970 the Democrats in the Senate successfully denied the confirmation of two of Nixon's appointments to the Supreme Court, Ford launched a ridiculously partisan effort to impeach Supreme Court Justice William O. Douglas, the most liberal justice on the Court. It was not one of Ford's finer moments.

This type of loyalty was just what Nixon was looking for in a replacement for Spiro Agnew in October 1973. Nixon reportedly told an aide that Ford could be used as a "tool" and said that all they had to do was "wind him up and he'll go 'arf, arf.' " Nixon's chief of staff, Bob Haldeman, said that Nixon also considered Ford an insurance policy against impeachment, reasoning that the members of the House who had worked with Ford would never place him in position to become president.

When Nixon told Ford that he was the choice to replace Spiro Agnew, the president did not heap praise on the congressman's accomplishments. In fact, he told Ford that he would not support a Ford candidacy for president in 1976 but that he planned to support former Texas governor John Connolly instead. Tricky Dick also told Gerald Ford that there was nothing to this Watergate business, and Ford, showing that Lyndon Johnson's assessment of him might not have been too far off, assumed that a president wouldn't lie to his vice president to be.

Ford was immediately on the front lines defending the bunkered Nixon administration. The vice president urged people to take the long view. "When you look back on the past years of the Nixon administration . . . , Watergate is a tragic but grotesque sideshow." Soon, however, Ford began wondering if Dick really was the innocent, blue-suited Mother Teresa that he claimed to be. After massive staff firings, subpoenas, and numerous press revelations, Jerry began to think that there might be something to this Watergate thing.

Although he tried to deny it, in his off-the-cuff remarks Ford began to waver in his support for the president. When the *New York Times* complained that the vice president's positions on the president's complicity were nothing more than a series of "zigs and zags," Ford offered the weak defense that "a zigzagger makes touchdowns."

When Nixon was shut out in the Supreme Court eight to zero over whether he had to turn over the secretly recorded White House tapes, Nixon's chief of staff, Al Haig, decided it was time to cut a deal with the vice president. It was simple: a pardon for Nixon in exchange for the presidency. Ford told Haig he would consider the arrangement. Haig also advised Vice President Ford that it would be in his political best interest to stop defending Nixon's innocence. Ford didn't distance himself too far from the Nixon administration, but when asked, he did admit that he thought that Nixon would soon be impeached.

On August 9, 1974, Richard Nixon could no longer deny the reality that his presidency was doomed, and he resigned rather than become the first U.S. president to be convicted on articles of impeachment. Thus, later that day, the first man ever to be appointed, instead of elected, to the vice presidency became chief executive of the most powerful democracy in the world.

☆ ☆ ☆

AFTER SURVIVING THE long-drawn-out ordeal in which President Nixon played hide-and-seek with the Constitution in the Oval Office, the entire nation breathed a sigh of relief when they saw Jerry Ford. The morning after he became president, Ford forgot that he was in the public eye and went to the front door in his pajamas to fetch the newspaper from the front lawn. He then proceeded to make his own toast for breakfast, and when his golden retriever Liberty made a mess on the carpet, Ford told his staff that he would clean it up, saying that "no man should have to clean up after another man's dog."

After six years of looking at Dick Nixon's ominous five-o'clock shadow, the entire country went around saying, "Is this guy great or what?" Then Ford fumbled the ball. On September 8, 1974, a quiet Sunday morning, President Gerald Ford shocked the nation by saying that he was granting former president Richard Nixon a "full and free pardon" for "any and all crimes."

The national outrage was immediate and intense. Ford's press secretary, Jerry ter Horst, resigned because of the injustice of sending Nixon's White House aides to prison without punishing the former president. It turned out that Ford had not even consulted with his attorney general about the legality of his pardon, and Ford took the extraordinary step of appearing before the House Judiciary Committee to explain his actions.

Everyone assumed there had been a deal. After all, Ford and Al Haig had discussed such a scheme almost to the letter. But Ford insisted that the pardon was his own idea. Despite his denials, the episode had the aroma of a bargain struck, and Ford's political future was mortally wounded.

In the end, Ford's pardon of Nixon, however unjust it may have been, did help the nation to move beyond Watergate, just as Ford had said it would. It also saved the country from the indignity of having a former president sent to jail. Was the country really ready for the sight of former president Richard Milhous Nixon sitting on a prison cot wearing a numbered chambray shirt and playing mournful tunes on a blues harp? Probably not.

FROM THE TIME he pardoned his former boss, the wheels came off the presidential Ford. Domestically, things were in a mess. High inflation threatened to destroy the savings Americans had struggled to put away. Ford thought he had something to offset the complex economic problems that were causing the devaluation of the nation's currency. Perhaps inspired by the infernal yellow smiley Have a Nice Day buttons that were so popular at that time, President Ford decided that the best way to counter the complex economic forces that were driving prices up was to get everyone to wear little buttons that said WIN (Whip Inflation Now). At least the pins didn't cost much.

Ford wasn't much more successful in foreign affairs. When the U.S. merchant ship *Mayaguez* was captured by Cambodia in 1975, the subsequent rescue operation caused more casualties among the marines than there were *Mayaguez* crew members. Despite this, Ford would later point to the rescue operation as an example of his crisis management while in the White House.

As if these dubious achievements weren't enough to cause concern, Ford began to stumble, literally, to cause concern, Ford began to stumble, literally, everywhere he went. He fell down airplane steps, ski courses, and staircases. Ford's unsteadiness became a running joke on a new television show called "Saturday Night Live" and helped launch the career of comedian Chevy Chase.

In 1976 Ford attempted to be elected to the presidency on his own merits, but his blunders continued. The most extreme occurred during a presidential debate with Jimmy Carter, when Ford boasted, incredibly, that "there is no Soviet domination of Eastern Europe and there never will be under the Ford administration." This gaffe might have been dismissed as a slip of the tongue, but in answering follow-up questions during the debate, and in statements released the following day, Ford dismayingly insisted that he was correct. Not surprisingly, Ford lost the 1976 election to the little-known Jimmy Carter.

Ford retired to make a fortune by sitting on the boards of American corporations and to make a nuisance of himself on the nation's golf courses. His short terms in the executive offices were tarnished because of his quick and presumptive pardon of Richard Nixon and his inept attempts at leadership. But at the very least, most Americans would agree with Jimmy Carter, who said in his inaugural address that he wanted to "thank [Gerald Ford] for all he has done to heal our land."

THIS ISN'T THE WHITE HOUSE

The Home of the

Vice President

The White House, first occupied by President John Adams in 1800, is one of America's most familiar institutions. But what about the home of the vice president? Where is his house? Until 1977, when Walter Mondale moved into the official vice-presidential residence, it was wherever the poor vice president could lay his head. Some vice presidents, such as Garret Hobart, were wealthy enough to buy temporary homes in Washington, but most were forced to live in rented rooms in nearby hotels or inns. Spiro Agnew, for example, dropped his suitcases in the Sheraton's Washington hotel.

For many years vice presidents made their bed (figuratively speaking) in the Willard Hotel. The Willard has nearly as much history as the White House itself. It was in this hotel that "The Battle Hymn of the Republic" was written; that Lincoln spent the night before his inauguration, sneaking through the doors disguised in women's clothes; and that the term *lobbyist* was coined, because President Ulysses S. Grant used to meet petitioners in the lobby. While the Willard was home to Vice President Calvin Coolidge, he discovered that a vice president isn't even king in his own rented castle.

Once a small fire caused the evacuation of the hotel in the middle of the night. Coolidge grew tired of waiting outside, and he started to reenter the hotel. A fireman stopped Coolidge but let him proceed when Cal informed the man that he was the vice president. Before Coolidge could actually enter the hotel, however, the fireman stopped him again and asked, "What are you vice president of?"

"I am vice president of the United States!" Coolidge said.

The fireman ordered Cal to get back with the rest of the crowd, saying, "I thought you were vice president of the hotel."

That sort of disrespect changed in 1974, when Congress ordered the chief of the Naval Observatory to give up his government-supplied home and turn the keys over to the vice president. Although the admiral protested that the house would make a poor residence for the vice president since the roof leaked, the home lacked air-conditioning, the wiring was a fire hazard, and the fireplaces didn't work (unfortunately, the admiral wasn't exaggerating) Congress decided that the home was fit for vice-presidential habitation.

The mansion is a Queen Anne–style home, a type of architecture emphasizing a combination of shapes and styles. Built in 1893, it has twelve rooms and six bathrooms (by comparison, the White House has 132 rooms and 20 bathrooms), although Dan and Marilyn Quayle remodeled a portion of the mansion, adding on new bedrooms for their family. The house sits in a twelve-acre parklike estate and comes complete with a staff of six navy stewards, who serve as butlers, and other assorted staff members such as gardeners and cleaning staff.

Gerald and Betty Ford were the first vice-presidential family scheduled to move into the house, but President Nixon resigned before they had the chance, and they were able to move up to a much nicer home on Pennsylvania Avenue. The next vice-presidential family, the Rockefellers, politely told the U.S. government, "Thanks, but no," to using the house. They already had a home in Washington, and it was much larger and nicer. (Later, when Rockefeller removed himself from the Republican ticket in 1976, the *Washington Star* joked that Nelson just couldn't bear to "face that spooky old house.")

Although the Rockefellers didn't choose to move into the mansion, they did try to redecorate. The Rockefellers decided to donate some of their personal furniture and artworks to the home to be enjoyed by future guests. Unfortunately, the Rockefellers were art snobs, and what they considered pleasing to the eye many other people considered downright ugly.

One gift was a surreal brass-and-walnut bed with mink trim by artist Max Ernst, which was titled "Cage Bed with Screen." A bed with a name and an attitude isn't what most people had in mind for the vice president, however, and eventually the Rockefellers decided that if nobody liked the bed, they would buy it back. Being Rockefellers, they later sold the bed at a Sotheby auction for a substantial profit.

The three vice-presidential families who have lived in the house since have all left their mark. Walter Mondale's family planted a vegetable garden and buried their family dog on the grounds. The Mondales also began a collection of books about U.S. vice presidents and placed the collection prominently in the living room. (A copy of this book will be donated to that collection.)

George Bush and his wife, Barbara, helped guide the house through much-needed renovations. The Bushes also added antiques and a horseshoe pit. Dan and Marilyn Quayle, the most recent vice-presidential family, not only decided to extensively remodel the house but also chose to turn the estate into Club Quayle by adding a twenty-five-thousand-dollar putting green and a swimming pool.

NELSON ALDRICH
ROCKEFELLER

Served with Gerald Ford, 1974–77

Republican from New York

NELSON ROCKEFELLER WAS BORN WITH A SILVER SPOON IN HIS MOUTH, AND HE DIED WITH HIS WING TIPS OFF, in the company of a young female assistant. Both events made the front page of the *New York Times*.

From beginning to end, Nelson Rockefeller was never out of the public eye. He was born in 1908 on the birthday of his grandfather, John D. Rockefeller, who had been one of the great robber barons of the nineteenth century. By the time Nelson Rockefeller was appointed vice president, his total assets were estimated at $1.034 billion, easily making him the richest person ever to hold an executive office. But money couldn't buy the one thing Nelson Rockefeller wanted. No, not love—if you're a billionaire, there are plenty of people around willing to take care of that. Despite the fact that Nelson divided the world into two groups—"we the wealthy" and "those who work for us"—he always wanted to have the top political prize: the presidency of the United States. He would have to settle for the consolation prize.

☆ ☆ ☆

NELSON ROCKEFELLER ALWAYS lived a bizarre and protected life. Although he liked to brag about how he had roller-skated to school as a child, he neglected to say that a chauffeured limousine always crept along the curb behind him, ready to pick him up and ferry him to school should he tire. Later, when he was denied admission to Princeton University because of his poor prep-school grades, Nelson applied to Dartmouth College by going to see the college president personally. Needless to say, Dartmouth decided that it would be good to allow him to enroll.

After graduating, Nelson went to work in the family business, where he became known for successfully leasing the office space in Rockefeller Center by convincing those who traded with the many Rockefeller businesses to sign on the dotted line. From there he went to work at his family's plantation in Venezuela.

When he returned to the United States, Nelson decided that his time spent in South America made him an expert in U.S.–Latin American relations, and he took his ideas straight to the top, to President Franklin Roosevelt. Roosevelt gave Rockefeller his start in public service by appointing him assistant secretary of state for Latin America, a post Rockefeller held until 1944.

Rockefeller moved in and out of Washington jobs until 1958, when he was elected governor of New York. He had needed the governorship to build the credibility that would allow him to run for president, and he began working on his first presidential campaign just six months after winning his first elected office.

Although Nelson tried for the Republican presidential nomination in 1960, 1964, and 1968, he never found enough people who wanted a Rockefeller as president to win the nomination. Instead, he spent his years serving as governor of the Empire State, which he lorded over like a benevolent royal master. True, he built universities, parks, and roads, but he also sent taxes skyrocketing, and he built a complex of state-government offices that were derided as Rocky's Follies, as a type of monument to his reign.

The largest crisis of his career came in September 1971, when inmates at the Attica state prison took hostages following a riot. Rockefeller was worried that a poor handling of the situation would ruin his reputation—"Nelson Rockefeller will be there on world television as the man who failed," he said—and so he sent a thousand policemen storming into the prison. The resulting battle cost the lives of more than forty men.

As a young man, Nelson had often played tennis with Vice President Henry Wallace, who was always hanging around the Rockefeller estate because he had nothing better to do. That experience, combined with Nelson's ego, meant that he would never settle for the vice presidency.

Nelson Rockefeller had been offered the vice presidency previously, first by Richard Nixon in 1960 and then by Democrat Hubert Humphrey in 1968. (Rockefeller wasn't just offered the vice presidency because of his leadership abilities. Because of the importance of New York in any election, it is almost automatic that the governor of the state is considered a leading candidate for the vice-presidential nomination. Not surprisingly, New York has given the nation more vice presidents than any other state.) Each time, he had dismissed the office, saying haughtily that a Rockefeller "wasn't built for standby equipment." But by 1974, his equipment was 66 years old, and Rocky began to face the reality that vice president was about as high as he could hope to go. This time, when Gerald Ford asked him if he were interested in the job, Rockefeller said yes.

ALTHOUGH HIS ENORMOUS wealth clearly gave Nelson a leg up on the world, it is still somewhat surprising that he was able to get elected to any office at all, considering how out of touch he was with virtually every American who wasn't a billionaire. "Take an average American family with an income of one hundred thousand dollars . . . ," Rockefeller once said in his most famous illustration of just how out of touch he was. And once, during a campaign trip in 1968, a reporter mentioned to Rocky that with all of his private jets and security people, he traveled like James Bond. When Nelson responded with a blank expression, the reporter said, "You know, James Bond. 007. Sean Connery," to which Rockefeller asked, "How many delegates does he have?"

mistaking Her Majesty's secret agent for yet another poor soul out on the rubber-chicken circuit.

Rockefeller's oblivion to the concerns of the world often made the jobs of his aides much more difficult. His speech writers, for example, were forced to put stars at each end of the sentences that were supposed to be jokes so that Rockefeller wouldn't read right through them. Even at that, Rocky flubbed his lines. In his fascinating book *The Imperial Rockefeller*, former speech writer Joseph E. Persico says that he once wrote Nelson the lines: "As soon as I leave all of you tonight, I will engage in an ancient ritual of the Jewish people. I'm going to Miami Beach." But when he delivered the speech, Rockefeller changed the joke to: "As soon as this evening is over, I am flying directly to Miami Beach. Unfortunately, I won't be staying at the Fontainebleau."

Rockefeller didn't believe that his enormous wealth removed him from the voters or that it was a disadvantage in holding positions of leadership. In fact, he didn't agree with the conventional wisdom that pulling one's self up by the bootstraps built character. Nelson said that people who made their own way in life were hindered by "their working-class resentments." The wealthy, Rockefeller said, were much more generous and progressive.

In fact, the Rockefellers, including Nelson, were known as philanthropists, although the degree of their sacrifice was sometimes questioned. Rockefeller's family had designated a portion of their money to the public good, and with that much money, even a dollop can do amazing things. Thanks to the Rockefellers, land was purchased for Jackson Hole and the Great Smoky Mountains National Park, Colonial Williamsburg was restored, as was Versailles, and untold medical and scientific breakthroughs were achieved. Rockefeller admitted one time to an aide that he had once financed a movie, mainly agreeing to fund the project just so that he could get the pleading director out of his office and finish his lunch. The director was Orson Welles, and the movie was *Citizen Kane*. Rockefeller added that he had never had any interest in seeing the film.

☆ ☆ ☆

AFTER THE RESIGNATION of Richard Nixon, President Gerald Ford looked for a person to serve as his vice president. Ford assembled a list of more than three hundred national Republican leaders, including all of the Republican members of Congress and Republican governors, and asked them each to submit the names of three potential vice presidents. More than nine hundred nominations were passed along to Ford: Leading the balloting was George Bush, followed by Nelson Rockefeller, Barry Goldwater, and Ronald Reagan. When word got out that Bush led the straw poll, several Republican leaders called Ford to advise him not to pick Bush, whom they considered an unfocused lightweight. Ford apparently followed their counsel, because in short time he offered the position to Rockefeller.

Rockefeller became the appointed vice president of an appointed president, one who had himself been named at the last minute by a president enduring an impeachment battle. It was not the best example of democracy in action.

Because of his inherited wealth, Rockefeller had always felt he was superior to nearly every man he met. He did not change his attitude when dealing with the president, especially since the president was Jerry Ford. Shortly after becoming vice president, Rockefeller assembled his staff writers to help draft Ford's State of the Union address. Ford had not asked for any assistance—Rockefeller had just assumed that he could do a better job than Ford. (Ford wasn't the only president to receive this type of treatment. When President Nixon asked Rockefeller to travel on a goodwill mission to Latin America, Rockefeller not only sent the president a letter listing his terms for making the trip but also had his staff draft a reply for President Nixon to send back to him.)

Vice President Rockefeller never considered Gerald Ford a great man. "He's no Roosevelt," Rocky would say as an insult, which, for a Republican, may actually have been a compliment. On one occasion, Rockefeller damned the president with faint praise, saying, "If it took a football player who played center without a helmet to pull us through, I say, thank God we've had him to lead the team."

But even Ford was somewhat awed by the power of his vice president. During his vice presidency, Rockefeller had decided to have his private estate, Pocantico, dedicated as a national historical landmark. Pocantico was a capitalist's palace. In the house, which was named Kykuit (Dutch for "lookout"), were hundreds of original artworks, including a Gilbert Stuart painting of George Washington and one of Rodin's first sculptures. The doors of Kykuit would not be thrown open to tourists, however. Rockefeller just wanted the designation for his own edification. And to make the occasion more special, he had the president, Jerry Ford, go to his house to deliver the dedication personally.

When he wasn't having his house made into a national landmark, Vice President Rockefeller busied himself with other small projects. When Rocky read a newspaper article mentioning the difficulty the Danes were having with Greenland, Rockefeller sent a memo to one of his aides asking, "Why don't we buy it?" It wasn't clear whether by *we* Rockefeller meant himself or the U.S. government.

Rockefeller also spent much of his time as vice president trying to make the vice presidency a better place. He had the vice president's official seal redesigned (which he paid for personally), and he donated furniture and paintings for the home on the grounds of the Naval Observatory that had been assigned to the vice president (although he refused to move in to the vice president's mansion because his Washington mansion was much nicer).

Rockefeller had time to spend on such petty matters because he had few duties as vice president other than attending funerals of foreign dignitaries. Once when asked how President Ford used him, Rockefeller responded, "It depends on who dies."

On two occasions, Rockefeller nearly became president. Within two weeks, Ford was the victim of two assassination attempts. The first occurred in Sacramento, California, when Lynette "Squeaky" Fromme, a member of the Charles Manson gang, tried to kill the president because he was a "polluter of water and air." Ford's life was saved when a Secret Service agent grabbed the woman's handgun away as she pulled the trigger. After the assassination attempt, Rockefeller's most pressing question was: "Who is Manson?" Just days later, a second woman, Sara Jane Moore, fired a shot at the president, missing him but hitting a bystander.

There is no evidence that Rockefeller was concerned that would-be assassins might target him, but he was worried that he might follow in the president's stumbling footsteps and trip and fall while out campaigning. With Ford's clumsiness getting daily coverage in the newspapers, Rockefeller knew that any trip by him would make the next day's headlines.

Rockefeller responded to the problem in typical fashion: He hired someone to help him walk. As he strolled through crowds at public appearances, Rockefeller would have an aide walk beside him and whisper instructions such as "Curb here" or "Up two steps."

As the 1976 election approached, Ford thought that he could get more votes with a running mate other than Nelson Rockefeller. Although Ford denied dumping Rocky, that was exactly what happened, and Rockefeller was miffed because of it.

After being shoved off the plank, Rocky tried to be a good Republican, and he even gave the nominating speech for his replacement on the Republican presidential ticket, Kansas senator Robert Dole. But eventually Rockefeller's frustrations came out. While campaigning with Dole in New York, Rockefeller faced heckling students as he began to speak. As he left the stage, the vice president gave the students an obscene hand gesture that didn't mean "we're number one."

Although many people were shocked by the vice president's vulgarity, others thought that for the first time in his life Rockefeller had acted like a regular Joe. Nelson was so thrilled with this view that for a time he sent out autographed photos of himself in his defiant posture, stopping only when it was pointed out to him that this wasn't the best way for a vice president to act.

Following the defeat of Ford and Dole, Rockefeller retired from politics, but the bird flying wasn't Rocky's last scandalous moment. Just two years after leaving the vice presidency, Rockefeller, married to a woman named Happy—though possibly not so happily married—and the father of six children, died of a heart attack in the company of a 25-year-old blond assistant, whom he had hired to help him write a book on his art holdings. They were supposedly having a business meeting, but the curious thing was that there were no papers or books to be found in the room where the meeting was being held, although there was wine and food on a table. Adding to the suspicion that the meeting may not have been all business was the fact that Rockefeller's assistant had been wearing a black evening gown at the time of his death, which might or might not have been appropriate business attire for a meeting being held after 10:00 P.M.

As reporters began investigating Rockefeller's death, they discovered that the call for help had not come from Rockefeller's assistant, as originally claimed, but from a friend of hers and that the call had come an hour after Rockefeller's death. There was little explanation of what may have transpired in that hour.

All told, because of his colossal wealth, everything Rocky did was bigger and better than what others might only hope to accomplish. Even of the missing minutes in the scandal, the *Washington Post* said, "Copious in all things, Nelson in the end produced a sixty-minute gap where Nixon could only manage eighteen and a half."

WALTER FREDERICK

MONDALE

Served with Jimmy Carter, 1977–81

Democrat from Minnesota

WALTER MONDALE WAS A MAN WITH THE SOUL OF A VICE PRESIDENT. During his long career in government, he never leapt without first giving things a hard look, and he never challenged when he could defer.

His own media director once said that Mondale "dares to be cautious," and Mondale himself once admitted that he had a reputation as a "kind of slug."

If he had been any duller, he would have been capable of photosynthesis.

Although he was able to climb the political ladder all the way to the next-to-highest rung, Mondale was appointed to every office (except the vice presidency) that he ever held, never winning (or entering) an election in which he didn't have the advantage of being the incumbent. When it came to being vice president, Walter Mondale was the closest thing to a natural the United States has ever seen.

☆ ☆ ☆

WALTER MONDALE WAS a preacher's kid, the middle son of Claribel and Theodore Mondale. Born Walter Frederick, the Mondales called him Fritz, which was Minnesotan for *Fred*. In 1946, while Fritz was a college student, he grabbed hold of the rising star of Minneapolis mayor Hubert Humphrey. In the years to come, Humphrey would develop a paternal political relationship with Mondale. Humphrey trusted the young Minnesotan enough to let him manage his Senate campaign in 1948, which Humphrey won.

After Mondale graduated from the University of Minnesota with honors in 1951, he joined the army, where he eventually rose to the rank of corporal. Mondale left the military after two years and returned to Minnesota to enter law school.

While in law school, Mondale made another beneficial political connection. He used his experience with the Humphrey campaign to assist Orville Freedman in winning the governorship of Minnesota in 1954, and he ran Orville's reelection campaign in 1956. In 1960, when the office of attorney general of Minnesota became vacant, Orville rewarded Mondale by appointing him to the position.

Mondale was able to hang on to his position in

the state election of 1962. Then came his big break. When Hubert Humphrey was picked by Lyndon Johnson as a vice-presidential candidate, Walter Mondale was appointed to Humphrey's vacant Senate seat.

In the Senate Mondale never introduced a major piece of legislation, and he was given a 100-percent approval rating by the liberal Americans for Democratic Action, or ADA (which Hubert Humphrey, who was also highly rated by the organization, sometimes tried to pass off on his rural constituents as the American Dairy Association). Despite his high marks for always backing the most liberal legislation, Mondale did delay in opposing the Vietnam War. Mondale was such a weak voice in the Senate that when he had to have an appendectomy, some of his Senate colleagues joked that they hoped the surgeon would "insert some guts before sewing him up."

Although Mondale did win reelection to the Senate twice, this was hardly a terrific endorsement of his efforts, since in modern times an incumbent virtually has to be caught in the midst of an illegal act to be turned out of office. With such a career to stand on, Mondale believed that the people were clamoring for him to run for president of the United States, and in 1974 he decided to answer that phantom call, hoping to win the Democratic presidential nomination in 1976.

Unfortunately, Mondale frequently ran behind "Undecided" in the polls. After a year of campaigning without success, he finally admitted that he lacked the fire to successfully run for president, saying that he didn't want to spend two years living "in Holiday Inns." Mondale's political ambitions were rekindled, however, when the winner of the Democratic presidential primaries, Jimmy Carter of Georgia, placed Fritz on his short list of possible running mates.

Jimmy Carter was always something of a micromanager—as president it was reported that he personally scheduled the court times for his staff who wished to play tennis at the White House—and he was no less fastidious in selecting a vice president. He had his staff prepare a list of more than four hundred potential candidates that was then winnowed down to just seven men, who were interviewed by Carter's staff and asked to fill out a seventeen-point questionnaire that asked about their finances, relatives, and "psychiatric or similar treatment."

Carter also invited the candidates to his home in Plains, Georgia, to interview them personally (which skeptics said was an audience at the "Court of St. James"). When he arrived in Plains, Mondale proved that he could think like a vice president. When reporters asked him how he had prepared for his job interview, Mondale said, "The first thing I did was to read the most remarkable book ever written, *Why Not the Best?*" which was Jimmy Carter's autobiography. Mondale added, "I found every word absolutely brilliant."

In one final check, Carter asked his 8-year-old daughter, Amy, whom she preferred as the vice-presidential nominee. Amy said she preferred John Glenn because he had been an astronaut, but despite Amy's counsel, Jimmy decided to pick Fritz as his running mate. When Carter called Mondale to tell him of his choice, Mondale joked that he had been up since early that morning "trying to fix my phone, which hadn't rung for three days."

Mondale then called his mentor Hubert Humphrey to tell him the news. Although Humphrey was near the end of his life, he gathered enough hyperbole to say that hearing that Mondale was the Democrats' vice-presidential nominee was like "Christmas, the Fourth of July, my birthday and Father's Day all rolled into one." When Mondale asked Humphrey what he should say in his acceptance speech, Humphrey told him, "Don't worry, they'll [Carter's aides] give you one."

Mondale joked that he was willing to return to the Holiday Inns on the campaign trail because "I've checked and found they've all been decorated. . . . I've thought it over and that's where I'd like to be."

Early in the 1976 campaign, Mondale was neither a liability nor an asset for Carter. Mondale was so unfamiliar to many voters that at campaign stops people asked reporters who he was and what he was running for. The Democratic vice-presidential nominee was even able to go to a Washington, D.C., supermarket and collect his family's groceries without having anyone recognize him.

On the stump Mondale was equally mediocre. He admitted that even he sometimes dozed off during his speeches, and he once asked the crowd to vote for "a people's president—Jimmy Ford!" (He quickly caught his own goof, and he pleaded to the heavens, "Jimmy, Jimmy, I didn't mean it, lemme try again.")

But Mondale did help Carter when he debated Republican vice-presidential candidate Robert Dole in the first vice-presidential debate, held in October of 1976. Dole amazingly tried to equate the Republicans' Watergate debacle with the wars that Americans had fought in the twentieth century. Dole said that Watergate was no more a campaign issue than "the Vietnam War would be, or World War I, or

World War II, or the Korean War—Democratic wars, all in this century.

"I figured up the other day," Dole continued, "that if we added up the killed and wounded in Democrat wars, it would be about a million Americans, enough to fill the city of Detroit."

"I think that Senator Dole has richly deserved his reputation as a hatchet man tonight," Mondale replied. "Does he really think there was a partisan difference over our involvement in the fight against Nazi Germany?"

Voters were dismayed at Dole's performance in the debate, and although the electorate almost never allows the vice-presidential candidate to influence its choice for president, the election that fall was so close that Carter needed all the help he could get.

☆ ☆ ☆

UNLIKE HIS PREDECESSOR, Mondale did not have a personal fortune tucked away; he was one of the most impecunious vice presidents, with total assets estimated at just seventy-seven thousand dollars. He sometimes joked that he had taken the vice presidency because he needed the money.

Mondale had an unusual vice presidency in that Carter, because of his inexperience in Washington, actually was interested in Fritz's input. Carter included Mondale in most of his discussions and asked that all memos sent to the Oval Office also be sent to Mondale. Despite such access, Mondale chose to remain in the shadows and seldom offered his advice to the president (which probably lengthened his political career by isolating him from the failures of the Carter administration).

Mondale always knew his place as vice president. After President Carter visited the site of the nuclear accident at Three Mile Island, Mondale liked to joke that experts said that that visit alone proved the area was safe—otherwise, "they would have sent the vice president."

In 1980 Carter and Mondale ran for reelection, but many people considered their administration a near failure because of the high inflation rate and the ongoing hostage crisis in Iran. Carter and Mondale were easily defeated in November of that year by the duo of Ronald Reagan and George Bush.

In 1984 Mondale decided to try for the presidency once again. With the war cry "Where's the Beef?" (which he stole from an inane commercial for a national hamburger chain) Mondale emerged from a pack of Democrats that included such party heavyweights as Teddy Kennedy, Gary Hart, and John Glenn to become the Democrats' presidential nominee. In winning the nomination, Mondale did his Democratic best to bow to every group. In selecting his own vice-presidential nominee, Mondale interviewed three women, two blacks, one Hispanic, and one white male who promised to be good. Even fellow Democrat Gary Hart said that Mondale appeared to be "pandering" to special interests. Mondale finally selected New York representative Geraldine Ferraro as his running mate.

In the race that fall against Reagan and Bush, Mondale won only a single state—his home state of Minnesota—losing the election in one of the largest landslides ever. The final tally in the electoral college was 525 votes for Reagan-Bush and only 13 votes for Mondale-Ferraro. Following this Super Bowl–strength blowout, Mondale retired from politics and returned home to Minnesota. At present, Mondale is hurrying to join most other former vice presidents in historical oblivion.

GEORGE HERBERT
WALKER BUSH

Served with Ronald Reagan, 1981–89

Republican from Texas

IN 1988, THE VAN BUREN CURSE WAS FI-
NALLY PUT TO REST. FOR MORE THAN 150
YEARS, SINCE 1837, no sitting vice president had
duplicated Matty Van Buren's feat of being elected
president while serving in the second office—until
George Bush.

For this accomplishment, George Bush might
have been heralded by future historians as the man

who restored respectability to the vice presidency. But after initial high grades from the public, George Bush suffered through much of his presidency with the lowest public support of any modern president who wasn't facing impeachment. He also managed to select as his vice president a man widely considered unqualified for the office.

Instead of restoring the vice presidency to a position of honor, Bush may have, because of his actions, caused many people to lose faith in the vice presidency. It may take the office another 150 years to gain back its luster.

☆ ☆ ☆

GEORGE HERBERT WALKER Bush was the son of a wealthy Wall Street banker and the namesake of his polo-playing grandfather, George Herbert Walker, the person for whom golf's Walker Cup was named in 1922. (Both Bush's grandfather and father served as president of the United States Golf Association—the ruling body of the sport. Bush's father, Prescott Bush, was known for eliminating the stymie rule from the game.)

From the beginning, little George, whom the family called Poppy, lived the life of affluence. When George and his friends went swimming, servants bearing towels and drinks greeted them when they got out of the water. In a profile of the president as a child, *Time* magazine noted that discipline in the Bush household meant not being allowed to order soft drinks at the tennis club.

George attended private schools from the time he was in elementary school, and he graduated from the Phillips Academy, a prep school that traced its beginnings to the revolutionary war (Paul Revere designed the school's seal). During his prep-school days, Bush was a star soccer player and the most popular fellow on campus. After graduation, Bush delayed his college career to join the navy during World War II. He became a navy pilot at age 18—the youngest aviator in that branch of the service during the war.

Unlike most of his vice-presidential predecessors, George Bush was a true veteran of heavy combat. He was known to be one of the best aircraft-carrier pilots in the South Pacific, despite losing four of his airplanes—each named *Barbie* for his wife—to mechanical glitches or enemy gunfire.

On one of those missions, Bush was shot down near a Japanese-occupied island. In jumping out of his burning plane, Bush was able to clear the canopy but struck his head on the plane's tail. Alone in the ocean, Bush managed to get a small life raft inflated and climb aboard. Although he was nauseous from the seawater and his head wound, Bush dog-paddled his tiny craft to avoid being carried to the Japanese-held island. He later recalled that while he was fighting against the ocean currents, he had thought about his parents, God and his faith, and "the separation of church and state." After four hours of bobbing in the ocean, Bush was rescued by a submarine, the USS *Finback*. Following the war, he was awarded four medals, including the Distinguished Flying Cross.

After the war Bush enrolled at Yale University. He was as popular in college as he had been in prep school, and despite a miserable batting average, he was named captain of the baseball team, which he twice helped lead to the College World Series finals. Bush graduated with honors from Yale in just two and a half years, but instead of following in his father's footsteps on Wall Street, George decided to make his fortune in the oil fields of Texas. (It must be pointed out that with his family's substantial wealth and connections, this choice of employment carried no more risk than a college student's summer job.)

Although other Easterners went west, made their fortunes, and returned to their country clubs, George Bush stayed behind and tried to make hisself a real Texan (although he did once try to convert a group of Texans from football fans to soccer players. The fact that George Bush is alive today is testament to his skill at diplomacy). By the time he was 41 years old, Bush was a millionaire.

☆ ☆ ☆

DESPITE HIS SUBSTANTIAL advantages of wealth and connections, George Bush's early life is impressive: prep standout, decorated war hero, collegiate BMOC, self-made millionaire. So how, one wonders, did he go from all of that to become, as one CNN commentator put it, "the national twit"?

His upper-crust background had furnished him a spinnaker to speed his progress, and his ambition provided plenty of wind. But something was wrong with this yacht: It appeared to lack a rudder. As a political animal, George Bush was the personification of bland ambition.

George Bush began his political life in 1964, when he challenged for a seat in the U.S. House of Representatives. He lost that race, but two years later when a new House seat was created in Texas, Bush ran for the office and won.

While in the House, George Bush was a supporter of President Richard Nixon, and in 1970 Nixon convinced Bush to run for a seat in the Senate against Democrat Lloyd Bentsen (who would run against the Bush-Quayle ticket as the Democratic vice-presidential nominee). Bush's father advised George to stay in the House, but Nixon made the

Senate race more attractive by promising George a job if he lost. Nixon even aided Bush by funneling to George's campaign some of his own questionable campaign funds. Bush lost to Bentsen, and he went to Nixon hoping to land a job in the State Department. But Nixon appointed Bush ambassador to the United Nations, and Bush thanked the president by reporting the names of people who were and weren't loyal to the Nixon administration. Following the 1972 election, Nixon prepared to offer Bush a new assignment. Storm clouds were forming already in the press over the Watergate scandal, and Barbara Bush warned her husband that the one job he shouldn't take was the chairmanship of the Republican National Committee. That was just the job Nixon offered him. "I'll do it," Bush told Nixon. "Not all that enthralled with RNC, but I'll do it." Bush later told his wife, "Boy, it's hard to turn down a president."

As Watergate unfolded, Bush remained a loyal apologist for Richard Nixon until it finally appeared that the House of Representatives would actually impeach the president. In August of 1974 Bush wrote a letter to Nixon asking him to resign as president, which Nixon did two days later.

Although Bush hoped to become Gerald Ford's vice president following Nixon's resignation, Bush's hearty defense of the disgraced Nixon made him a nearly impossible choice. Instead Ford offered Bush a choice of posts, and Bush passed over the more cushy assignments for a position as head of the liaison office in China. Bush served only a short time in China before Ford asked him to return to the United States to take over as head of the Central Intelligence Agency, a position Bush held until the presidency of Jimmy Carter in 1977.

☆ ☆ ☆

BY 1979 GEORGE Bush had one of the most impressive résumés in America. In the previous decade he had held five important and controversial positions, and although he had never held on to any of them long enough to leave a lasting legacy, as the 1980 election approached, Bush decided that the only job left for him to try was the presidency.

Bush began strong in a crowded Republican field, and after he won the early Iowa caucus, he crowed that he had Big Mo on his side. (Those who didn't follow football were puzzled by Bush's use of sports slang for *momentum*.) Soon, Big Mo turned to Big No as voters rejected Bush to support Ronald Reagan, with Ron winning the first primary in New Hampshire by a two-to-one margin over George.

As the primary battle traveled from state to state, the sniping between Bush and Reagan grew bitter and personal. Reagan reportedly said that George was "a preppy and a sissy," and Bush insisted that Reagan was a dangerous radical conservative who espoused "voodoo economics." (As vice president, Bush often protested that he had never used the phrase *voodoo economics*—until NBC News furnished him with a videotape so that he could read his own lips uttering the words.)

As the Republican National Convention approached, Reagan appeared to have the nomination locked up. Some Republican leaders and media pundits began suggesting that George would make a good pick as vice president. But although Bush had pined for the vice presidency in 1968 and 1974, he insisted that he wasn't currently interested. "Take Sherman and cube it" was how Bush expressed his displeasure with the idea. (He apparently meant that, like William Tecumseh Sherman, he would not accept the nomination and would not serve if elected, only more so—but this is a rough translation.)

Reagan, for his part, wasn't eager to give the vice presidency to Bush, whom he considered just another eastern lightweight in a Brooks Brothers suit. Reagan didn't believe, he confided to friends, that Bush was up to the job.

At the Republican National Convention, Reagan's aides explored the possibility of offering the vice presidency to former president Gerald Ford in what was being called a dream ticket. But while watching the convention activities on television, Reagan happened to watch an interview with Ford in which he said that such an arrangement would result in a "co-presidency." Reagan was not about to have a vice president—even one who had formerly propped his feet up in the Oval Office—share the marquee with him. Almost immediately Reagan called Bush, who forgot his previous Shermanesque mathematics and eagerly accepted the nomination.

☆ ☆ ☆

GEORGE BUSH CAME close to having a very brief vice presidency. Just six weeks after the inauguration, a disturbed young man named John Hinckley shot President Reagan and several others outside the Washington Hilton because he hoped that killing the president would impress a young actress.

In the moments following the assassination attempt, no one, including Reagan, realized that the president had been shot, but as the limousine headed back to the White House, Reagan began coughing up blood and his lungs filled with fluid. Although the president joked with doctors and reporters about the incident, he came much closer to dying than many realized. In the trauma room, as Reagan's lungs filled with blood and put pressure on his heart, the attending physicians yelled that they were losing the battle to save the president's life.

Outside of the hospital there was chaos. All three national television networks erroneously reported the death of presidential press spokesman James Brady. Vice President George Bush was in Texas making a speech, and while he hopped on an airplane to return to Washington, at the White House the cabinet officers and presidential aides were huddled trying to decide what to do next.

Al Haig, Reagan's secretary of state, met with the chief White House lawyer to examine the documents that would remove Reagan from the presidency. Their meeting was interrupted, however, by Jim Baker, Reagan's chief of staff, who ordered the documents locked in a safe. Later, Secretary of State Haig would announce to the world that despite the ordained order of succession—vice president, then Speaker of the House, then president pro tempore of the Senate—he was "in control," although he added that "if something came up, I would check with [Vice President Bush], of course." Soon, everything returned to normal as Reagan emerged from his surgery cracking jokes and telling stories cribbed from old B movies.

Past the early excitement, Bush settled into a normal vice-presidential routine. In November of 1982 he was called on to represent the United States at the funeral of Soviet premier Leonid Brezhnev. In February of 1984 Bush attended the funeral of Soviet premier Yuri Andropov.

"You die, I fly" was how Bush described his role in government.

☆ ☆ ☆

AS THE 1984 presidential election drew near, there was none of the usual talk of dumping the vice president for the second term. Bush had been a loyal and faithful servant to Reagan, and Ron bubbled that George was the best vice president in the nation's history. In the presidential race that year, the Republicans were challenged by former vice president Walter Mondale and Geraldine Ferraro, who made history by becoming the first woman to be nominated to an executive office of the United States by a major political party. Ferraro's candidacy placed George in a no-win situation. If Bush did well, people would say that it was because George was a man and had greater political strength. If Geraldine slam-dunked George, however, all the other politicians would point at George and laugh and say that he got beat by a girl.

Geraldine was well aware that she had something of an advantage over Bush. As they prepared to meet in a debate, she knew that she was free to take the low road and that a man, especially as polite a man as George Bush, would have to lay off the rough stuff to avoid looking like a pig. Instead of attacking Geraldine, however, Bush went after the presidential nominee, Walter Mondale. Bush tried to pin Jimmy Carter's malaise-ridden outlook on Mondale: "If somebody sees a silver lining, he sees a black cloud out there," the vice president said. "I mean, right on, whine on harvest moon!"

The tactic seemed to work, and in the next morning's newspapers most pundits gave the edge in the debate to Bush. Although he was concerned about appearing chivalrous during the debate, the next morning, speaking to a group of New Jersey longshoremen, he was less gracious. "We tried to kick a little ass last night," he bragged, adding "Whoops!

Oh, God, he heard me. Turn that thing off!" when he realized that the workers weren't the only ones listening to his postdebate summation.

The Republicans were put back on the defensive, however, after Walter Mondale displayed his honesty by saying that if elected president, he would raise taxes. (Mondale's attempt to portray himself as an honest politician was undermined by his insistence that he would give money to every special-interest group that asked and still cut the budget deficit. Nobody bought it in 1984 either.) After Mondale made his assertion, all the reporters rushed to President Reagan and asked if he planned to raise taxes. Reagan said that he would never raise taxes, "Period." But a reporter then ran to George Bush to see if the vice president saw any voodoo in this tax plan.

Bush wasn't as adamant as Reagan about not raising taxes. When it comes to taxes, Bush said, "any president would want to keep his options open." When reporters then asked Bush if this indicated a difference in policy between the president and his understudy, Bush insisted that there were no differences between him and Reagan, and that was that. "Zippity doo-dah," Bush babbled. "Now it's off to the races." (Whenever George Bush speaks, it is an idiomatic accident waiting to happen. Considering the price of his schooling, this would appear to be something of an endorsement of public education.)

As they neared the election, Bush continued to emphasize his allegiance to the Reagan revolution. "I'm for Mr. Reagan," he said, "blindly." Just a week later, Reagan and Bush were reelected by one of the widest margins in U.S. history.

☆ ☆ ☆

IN BUSH'S SECOND term as vice president, things picked up pretty much where they'd left off when, just two months after the inauguration, Bush represented the United States at the funeral of Soviet premier Konstantin Chernenko. Later that summer, however, George Bush temporarily became president for just under eight hours in an unusual and uncommon use of the Twenty-fifth Amendment to the Constitution.

President Reagan had been diagnosed as having cancerous colon polyps, and surgeons decided to remove a large section of the president's bowel (all of this was shown in full-color graphics on the evening news). Because Reagan would be under anesthesia and would be unable to perform the duties of his office, the White House decided to turn the presidency over to Bush for those few hours. In an amazing foreshadowing of his presidency, "President" Bush spent the day playing tennis with friends.

AS THE 1988 presidential campaign approached, Vice President Bush was the leading candidate to be Reagan's heir.

The first obstacle George Bush had to overcome was the well-known "wimp factor." Partially because of his station as vice president, and partially because of his innate prep-school genteelness, Bush was always having to prove that although he was a decorated war hero, he was no weakling. The same week Bush announced that he was running for president, *Newsweek* ran a cover story with a picture of Bush and the headline FIGHTING THE WIMP FACTOR. Vice President Bush was so upset by the article that he reportedly even noticed that the article called him a wimp nine times.

George might not have been the only one to see the article, because in the first test of the nomination process—a straw poll in Iowa—Bush stumbled, coming in third. Bush offered an incredibly lame excuse for his poor showing. "A lot of people . . . were at their daughters' coming-out parties," he said, obviously confusing the midwestern cornstalks for country-club flagsticks. Despite not finding enough Iowa Republicans willing to leave their debutante dances to vote for one of their own, Bush vowed to fight on. "They've unleashed a tiger now," he said.

Although Bush soon went on to win the first presidential primary in New Hampshire, many people still didn't consider the vice president ready for a promotion. For one thing, some people thought that the twit didth protest too much in his complaining about being called a wimp. But it was more than just his weak vertebrae that bothered voters. Bush had an irritating manner about him, whether it was his insistence that he was a normal guy—Look! I eat pork rinds! I don't eat vegetables! I listen to country music!—or his cheeky dismissal of legitimate concerns about his involvement in the missteps of the Reagan administration. When asked about his role in the Iran-contra scandal, for example, Bush had joked, "I didn't attend that meeting. . . . I was at the army-navy game."

Bush was never able to dissuade all his critics, but he did gain support when, in the defining moment of his presidential campaign, he flayed an unsteady network news anchor. While appearing live on the "CBS Evening News," Bush angrily said that since he didn't complain about the way Rather read the news, Dan had no right to bicker about the fact that he may have been involved with selling arms to a hostile foreign country. "Mr. Vice President. . . . How could you?" asked the hurt Rather.

After the interview, Bush was elated that he had yelled at someone in public, saying, "The bastard didn't lay a glove on me." The next day, Bush inflated his brief television confrontation to near heroic status. "I need combat pay for last night," he bragged. "You know, it's Tension City when you're in there."

Despite the dubious value of the victory, Bush seemed to gain confidence from the encounter. He went on to defeat fellow Republican Robert Dole in the primaries to become his party's choice for the fall race.

Bush's presidential nomination appeared to provide the Democratic party with an opportunity to win back the presidency. After all, even conservative newspaper columnist George Will said that by giving the presidential nomination to the vice president, "We are going to test the proposition of the Democrat who said of his party, 'If we can't beat Bush, we should pick another country.'"

But modern Democrats always seem to be surprised when a presidential election rolls around: "Ohmygosh!" they yell, "has it been four years already?" and they rush out a presidential candidate that no one in the country has thought of for the office. In 1988 Michael Dukakis, aka Zorba the Clerk, governor of Massachusetts, was selected as their next victim.

At their quadrennial revival meeting, the Democrats searched for a politician to attack Vice President Bush's integrity. They selected a person of dubious integrity himself, giving the assignment to Teddy Kennedy. Kennedy attempted to lead the Democrats in a critical review of the Reagan years, adding after each line "Where was George?" Most Americans hoo-hawed at the thought of Kennedy trying to lecture anyone on responsibility, and

Republican supporters soon began wearing T-shirts that bore the response "Dry, Sober, and Home with His Wife."

From that point it was smooth sailing for Bush. For one thing, he had a built-in advantage in the electoral-college vote because he was the favorite son of at least three states and one district: He was born in Connecticut, lived in Maine, listed his official residence as Texas, and spent most of his time in Washington, D.C.

The Democrats tried to embarrass Bush by holding a party in the Houston hotel suite that was Bush's legal residence. But Bush remained unfazed by the criticism. "I'm legally and every other way, emotionally, entitled to be what I want to be," he asserted, "and that's what I am."

Despite stumbling somewhat with his vice-presidential pick by selecting some golfer from Indiana to be his running mate, Bush was never really winded in that fall's race. He won the November election by a comfortable margin.

"A new breeze is blowing," Bush noted on the day of his inauguration. "The new breeze blows." As Dan Quayle would say, "How true that is."

☆ ☆ ☆

ALTHOUGH IN 1988 George Bush had overcome the Van Buren curse that had terrorized the vice presidency for more than 150 years, in 1992 Bush attempted an electoral trifecta that no person had accomplished since Thomas Jefferson: to be elected president while serving as vice president, and then go on to be elected to a second term. George Bush's success or failure in this attempt could help shape how people view the vice presidency in the decades to come.

JAMES DANFORTH
QUAYLE

Served with George Bush, 1989–

Republican from Indiana

J.DANFORTH QUAYLE MAY BE ONE OF
THE BEST VICE PRESIDENTS THE UNITED
STATES HAS EVER HAD—and that potentially li-
belous statement can be supported.

In America's history its people have survived a
vice president who committed murder, two vice presidents who would be charged with treason, two vice
presidents who were accused of accepting bribes,

and a vice president who was forced to resign when he was convicted of felonious tax evasion. Compared with this standard, the careful, loyal, and quiet vice presidency of Dan Quayle has been one of the most successful of all the nation's second officers'. Unfortunately for the nation, whether he is even close to being qualified to be president is an entirely different matter.

☆ ☆ ☆

LIKE BUSH, J. DANFORTH Quayle was born to a wealthy and powerful family. Eugene Pulliam, his grandfather, owned several newspapers in Quayle's home state of Indiana, including both newspapers in the state capital of Indianapolis. His fortune has been reported to be worth approximately one billion dollars.

Dan Quayle grew up in the picturesque small town of Huntington, Indiana, and, for a while, in Arizona. Although a much-publicized profile of Quayle by *Washington Post* reporters David Broder and Bob Woodward claimed that Quayle lived a typical "middle-class" life and breathlessly reported that Dan attended public schools (Bush's Phillips Academy does not have a branch school in Indiana), the series of articles also mentioned that when Dan was about 12 years old, he played golf with his billionaire grandfather and President Dwight Eisenhower. Billionaire grandfathers and golf with presidents—just another towheaded small-town boy leading a small-town life.

When it was time for Quayle to go off to college, he chose nearby DePauw University, a small school that had received extensive financial support from Dan's family. Since no one knows exactly what kind of student Quayle was—he steadfastly refuses to release any information about his undergraduate aca-

demic career—it can only be assumed that this description given by one of Quayle's professors has at least some validity: "Dan Quayle was one of the few people able to get from the Deke house to the golf course without passing through a classroom."
After graduating from DePauw—with some dif ficulty, since he flunked the comprehensive exam in his major, political science, the first time he took it—Quayle was eligible to be drafted. Through his family's influence, Quayle was able to avoid possible service in Vietnam by being admitted to a low-risk Indiana National Guard unit. Although he scored below average in fundamentals-of-writing section on a military test, Quayle was assigned to the 120th Public Information Detachment to help write a newspaper. It was a place, one former member of the unit recalled, "where they sent politicians' sons and troublemakers."

Since the guard duty only required one weekend a month of service, Quayle enrolled in law school at Indiana University. Despite his poor academic record, he was able to be admitted to the law school through a program designed to assist low-income or minority students.

While in law school, Quayle met the woman who would become his political adviser and wife. Marilyn Quayle, née Tucker, was a driven person who demanded much of herself and others (after finishing her law-school courses, the pregnant Mrs. Quayle had her labor induced so that she would not miss her bar exam). Marilyn and Dan fell in love immediately, and they were married just ten weeks after their first date.

After graduating from law school, Quayle decided to return to his hometown of Huntington to practice law and to serve as assistant publisher of his father's newspaper. Quayle's decision to return to the small town was a political one: The local state representative was a Democrat, and Dan thought that he might someday take a shot at a seat in the Indiana statehouse.

Instead, in 1976 local Republicans asked Quayle to run for the U.S. Congress against an eight-term incumbent Democratic representative. It was in this race that Dan (with the help of his wife, Marilyn) proved that he was a skillful politician. The Republican party was still suffering from the weight of the Watergate scandal, and in his campaign literature Quayle refused to mention his party affiliation, even going so far as to have his campaign signs and pamphlets printed in the same shade of green that was being used by Democratic presidential candidate Jimmy Carter. In that successful race—and in the others to follow—Quayle earned a reputation for running a fair and above-the-belt campaign.

In his two terms in the U.S. House of Representatives, Dan was better known for spending time in the House gymnasium and for playing golf than for his legislation. He was so often seen coming out of the gym's locker room that he earned the nickname "wethead." Not surprisingly, he had a dismal attendance record.

In 1980, Quayle decided to challenge Indiana's Democratic senator Birch Bayh in that fall's election. Bayh, a nationally known senator who had authored the Twenty-fifth Amendment to the Constitution (which dealt with presidential succession), refused to take Quayle's challenge seriously. "Come on, boys, don't bother me," one aide recalls Bayh saying. "I'm debating Danny Quayle." All Bayh thought he had to do to win the election was "not drool on himself."

But Quayle worked hard campaigning in Indiana, attacking Bayh as a big-spending Washington liberal who was out of touch with his Hoosier constituents. A majority of voters in Indiana agreed, and, riding the same wave that ensured Ronald Reagan's victory over Jimmy Carter, Quayle captured the Senate seat.

Quayle worked harder in the Senate than he had in the House of Representatives. Although he was known as an ardent supporter of Reagan's conservative policies, he teamed up with liberal Democrat Ted Kennedy to sponsor a bill that overhauled the federal government's troubled job-training programs, earning himself high marks for his performance in his freshman term. In 1986 Quayle was reelected to the Senate by a wide margin.

AFTER GEORGE BUSH locked up the Republican nomination for president in the spring of 1988, voters and members of the media began discussing what type of president Bush would make. Bush offered one hint: "Watch my vice-presidential decision," he said. "That will tell all."

Many Republicans were jockeying for the vice-presidential nomination, including Dan Quayle, but Bush remained tight-lipped about his thoughts on the matter, not telling even his aides who the top candidate was. When Bush asked Quayle's Republican peers in the Senate whom they thought he should choose as his running mate, not one listed Quayle among their top choices. On the airplane ride to the convention in New Orleans, four of his closest advisers wrote down on slips of paper whom they thought George would pick—none of them made the right choice.

Bush had planned to wait to announce his decision at the Republican convention in New Orleans, but he couldn't contain his secret that long. As soon as he arrived in New Orleans, Bush announced his choice for the man most qualified to be president of the United States if he was unable to serve out his term. People at the dock in New Orleans and around the world were shocked when they heard that that person was Dan Quayle. As Bush made the announcement, Quayle ran up onto the stage and began bouncing like a high-school student who was just picked as prom king. "Believe me, we will win because America cannot afford to lose!" Quayle shouted, and then, grabbing Bush by the shoulder, Quayle cheered: "Let's go get 'em! All right? You got it?"

At first, few people knew much about Dan Quayle. In its coverage of Bush's announcement, *Newsweek* magazine even got his name wrong, referring to Quayle as Daniel. But within hours of the announcement, Quayle's background was front-page news around the country.

Some reporters remembered that in 1981 Quayle had involved himself in a scandal by joining a group of congressmen for a weekend golf outing; tagging along for the weekend was a buxom female lobbyist who was looking to trade sex for votes. This minor scandal was dismissed, however, when Marilyn Quayle said that she knew that Dan had done nothing wrong that weekend because "anyone who knows Dan Quayle knows that he would rather play golf than have sex any day."

People also questioned if Quayle were smart enough to be the president's understudy, and the situation only worsened when Quayle refused to follow the example of the other candidates and release his school records.

Most damaging of all, though, were Quayle's own revelations that following college he had used his family's influence to get into the Indiana National Guard and avoid being drafted. "I did not know in

1969 that I would be in this room today," Quayle offered as an explanation (although Quayle's response was widely ridiculed, it was pretty much the same answer Lloyd Bentsen, Quayle's Democratic opponent, used to explain why he had charged lobbyists ten thousand dollars each to eat breakfast with him). Quayle added that although he had avoided the draft, his brother had been a marine.

People immediately began discussing the possibility of dumping Dan from the ticket, but Bush and his advisers knew that that would be a fatal mistake for their campaign. Bush called Quayle "the first choice and my only choice" (although he had reportedly first offered the vice presidency to Wyoming senator Alan Simpson) and insisted that Quayle would stay on the ticket. George Bush, the decorated war hero, even defended his running mate's efforts to avoid combat by saying, "He did not go to Canada, he did not burn his draft card, and he *damn sure* didn't burn the American flag."

The low point of Quayle's bid for the vice presidency came during his debate with Democratic vice-presidential candidate Lloyd Bentsen. It was bad enough that Quayle had trouble explaining what he would do if he suddenly became president—although many people sympathized with him when he said that one of the first things would be to say a prayer. But then Dan dropped his arms and gave his Democratic opponent a free shot to the jaw, and Bentsen hit him with a knockout punch.

For weeks Quayle had been comparing himself to Jack Kennedy in speeches around the country, saying that they were both approximately the same age when they ran for executive office (and leaving unsaid the obvious fact that they both had nice hair). Quayle's campaign handlers had warned him to lay off the Kennedy comparisons, but in the debate Dan

couldn't resist mentioning, "I have as much experience . . . as Jack Kennedy did when he sought the
presidency."

Bentsen was ready with a reply that he had probably been rehearsing for weeks. "Senator, I served
with Jack Kennedy," said Bentsen directly to Quayle.
"I knew Jack Kennedy. Jack Kennedy was a friend
of mine. Senator, you're no Jack Kennedy."

As the audience erupted in cheers, Quayle could
only manage to mutter, "That was really uncalled
for, senator."

As the election approached, the criticism of
Quayle continued. The *Philadelphia Daily News* said
they couldn't endorse Bush for president because of
his choice for vice president and called Quayle "a
callow moron." Even after the Bush-Quayle ticket
had won the popular election, the *New York Times*
suggested that the electoral voters consider voting
for someone else for vice president. A Washington
media-watchdog group found that on the basis of
jokes told by late-night comedians, Dan Quayle was
the most laughed-at person in the country.

Although polls showed that fewer than a quarter
of the voters thought that Dan Quayle was qualified
to be president, others polls showed that only 2 percent let that fact affect the way they marked their
ballots. That November, Dan Quayle was elected as
the forty-fourth vice president.

☆ ☆ ☆

AS VICE PRESIDENT, Quayle continued to be the
object of ridicule—one U.S. senator even joked,
"The Secret Service is under orders that if Bush is
shot, to shoot Quayle." But by keeping a low profile
and appearing only before the Republican faithful,
Vice President Quayle was able to improve his image,

moving up from "callow moron" to something more closely resembling a harmless party hack. During the Bush-Quayle administration there were times when Quayle was back in the news. In the summer of 1991 George Bush suffered a heart arrhythmia that was initially reported to be a heart attack, and many in the nation went into myocardial infarction themselves over the thought of a President Quayle. "A heart flutters, a nation shudders," said the *Chicago Tribune*. One CNN commentator estimated that the New York Stock Exchange would fall six hundred points the morning after a Quayle presidency became reality. But as quickly as Bush's heart rhythm returned to normal, people again forgot about Vice President Quayle.

☆ ☆ ☆

ALTHOUGH DURING HIS campaign for the vice presidency and his first couple of years in that office Dan Quayle became famous for his verbal gaffes, Quayle's president, George Bush, was no master of oration himself. "Poor George is hopelessly inarticulate," explained Bush's sister.

In picking a vice president, one of the fundamental rules is to not choose someone who will shine brighter than the presidential candidate in order to avoid being accused of having a kangaroo ticket (one that is stronger in the hindquarters). It looked as though it would be difficult to find someone who was worse on the stump than himself, but Bush succeeded in this mission by picking Quayle, who seems to combine Yogi Berra's mind with the body of a television-game-show host.

Quayle's most famous verbal stumble was his bumbling of the National Negro College Fund's motto—A Mind Is a Terrible Thing to Waste—at a speech in Nashville, Tennessee: "What a waste it is to lose one's mind—or not to have a mind. . . . How true that is," he stammered. This comment, which will, no doubt, cling to Dan throughout his career, became so famous that the editors of Bartlett's *Familiar Quotations* decided to include the quote in a revised edition of the famous reference book.

This was hardly the extent of Quayle's misuse of the English language. When he speaks in public, sometimes Dan's speeches seem hackneyed, at other times they become amusingly confused, and there are still other times when Dan seems to be reduced to a blathering idiot. Although a listing of Quayle's locutions could fill a small quote book, one needs only a sampling to get a feel for what's inside the head of the vice president. Here, then, is an incomplete look at the world according to Quayle:

On strategy: "*Bobby Knight told me, 'There is nothing that a good defense cannot beat a better offense.' In other words, a good offense wins.*"

On the Holocaust: "*It was an obscene period in our nation's history.*"

On the issues of the 1988 presidential election: "*This election is about who's going to be the next president of the United States!*"

On fall foliage: "*We have gold and yellow and some red and, believe me, those are Republican colors. Bold colors, bright colors, future colors.*"

On what to call his running mate: "*When I talked with him on the phone yesterday, I called him George rather than Mr. Vice President. But in public, it's Mr. Vice President, because that's who he is.*"

On the important importance of missile-guidance systems: "*Getting them more accurate so that we can have precise precision.*"

On the country's fiftieth state: *"Hawaii has always been a very pivotal role in the Pacific. It is in the Pacific. It is a part of the United States that is an island that is right there."* On life in the South Pacific: *"You all look like happy campers to me. Happy campers you are. . . . And as far as I'm concerned, happy campers you will always be."* On his campaign for vice president: *"I'm my own handler. Any questions, ask me. There's not going to be any more handler stories because I'm the handler. I'm Doctor Spin."* On the 1990 San Francisco earthquake: *"The loss of life will be irreplaceable."* On elocution: *"Verbosity leads to unclear, inarticulate things."* On his verbal gaffes: *"I stand by all my misstatements."*

☆ ☆ ☆

ONLY ONE QUESTION remains: If Dan Quayle is the Republican nominee for president in 1996, whom will he pick to be his vice-presidential running mate?

EPILOGUE

THE FACT IS, VOTERS GET THE VICE PRESIDENTS THEY DESERVE.

In the current lexicon, the American electorate has become dysfunctional. But no longer should voters hold their noses and pull the lever, praying for the president's health and hoping that everything works out. "Democracy, after all, must be a sound scheme at bottom, else it would not survive such cruel strains," H. L. Mencken observed, and although democracy will survive even the vice presidents, Americans may end up with a terrible shock one morning when someone never considered qualified for the presidency is sitting in the Oval Office with a wide grin.

Some say the vice presidency is unnecessary and should simply be done away with. They make some strong points. The vice presidency is the duck-billed platypus of our republic. The office itself violates the philosophy of the very Constitution it swears to protect. The United States has a democratic government, but the vice president is appointed, sometimes by a presidential candidate who isn't even an elected office holder at the time. (As the politicians well know, nobody really votes for the vice president in a presidential election.) And although every student learns the importance of a system of checks and balances, the vice presidency violates that principle: The vice president is an officer of the executive branch, but he presides over the Senate and can even vote there when there is a tie.

But the idea that the office will be dissolved is just an idle notion of political pundits. Citizens will never be able to eliminate, or even dramatically change, the office, because it is too convenient to the political parties.

But if the vice presidency can't be changed, at least it can be made useful. In the last quarter century, presidential nominees have been given free rein by the parties to pick their own running mates. This is the first major decision the candidates for president make in their proposed administrations, and it serves up a look at their presidency in microcosm.

If a presidential candidate picks someone for the vice presidency who is not qualified to immediately become president, it may be a sign that if that candidate is elected, his or her other decisions might be equally political, cynical, or just plain stupid. Voters should show such charlatans the back door of the electoral college.

And what should be done with those who possess a character of bland ambition—those politicians who possess ambition for ambition's sake, who have no vision, no place to lead? Whether they are running for president of the United States or president of the local school board, Americans should show them the contempt that the Chicago Bears' number fifty-one, Dick Butkus, used to show rookie wide receivers who loitered in the middle of the field. Voters should run at them, tackle them with both arms, drive them into the ground, and then step on them with their cleats.

Then again, that treatment may be too forgiving.

This wonderful and blessed nation produces many great women and men. In selecting a person for the democracy's second-highest office, Americans should not settle for someone who is second-rate.

Permission to reproduce the photographs included in this book was graciously granted by the following:

LIBRARY OF CONGRESS: John Adams, Elbridge Gerry, Daniel Tompkins, Richard Mentor Johnson, George Mifflin Dallsas, Millard Fillmore, William Rufus DeVane King, John Cabell Breckenridge, Schuyler Colfax, Henry Wilson, William Alman Wheeler, Chester Alan Arthur, Thomas Andrews Hendricks, Levi Parsons Morton, Adlai Ewing Stevenson, Garret Augustus Hobart, Charles Warren Fairbanks, James Schoolcraft Sherman, Thomas Riley Marshall, Hubert Horatio Humphrey, Gerald Rudolph Ford, Jr., Walter Frederick Mondale

THE BETTMANN ARCHIVE: Aaron Burr, Martin Van Buren, John Tyler, Hannibal Hamlin, Andrew Johnson, Theodore Roosevelt, Calvin Coolidge, Alben William Barkley

UPI/BETTMANN: John Nance Garner, Richard Milhous Nixon, George Herbert Walker Bush, J. Danforth Quayle; vice-presidenital seal

ARCHIVE PHOTOS: Henry Agard Wallace, Harry S. Truman, Lyndon Baines Johnson, Spiro Theodore Agnew

FREE LANCE PHOTOGRAPHERS GUILD: John Caldwell Calhoun, Charles Curtis, Nelson Aldrich Rockefeller

PACH/BETTMANN: Thomas Jefferson

KEYSTONE VIEW CO.: George Clinton

UNDERWOOD PHOTO ARCHIVES: Charles Gates Dawes